The Recognition of Emily Dickinson

Emily Dickinson

From a daguerreotype, in 1848

THE RECOGNITION OF EMILY DICKINSON

SELECTED CRITICISM SINCE 1890

EDITED BY

Caesar R. Blake

AND

Carlton F. Wells

Ann Arbor Paperbacks
The University of Michigan Press

First edition as an Ann Arbor Paperback 1968

Published in the United States of America by
The University of Michigan Press and simultaneously
in Rexdale, Canada, by Ambassador Books Limited
United Kingdom agent: The Cresset Press
Manufactured in the United States of America

PREFACE

Of the major nineteenth-century American writers, only Emerson and Mark Twain achieved in their lifetimes a recognition at all commensurate with what, in the slow accumulations of judgment, later generations have acknowledged to be their value as writers. Poe was largely ignored in his own country. Except by a few, Thoreau was thought to be a provocative writer but, more important, a troublingly singular man. Hawthorne fared well with fellow writers—Poe, Melville and, later, James—but not with any wide or enthusiastic public. Melville himself had a wide popular audience for his early books, but a like audience was not there for his major, most enduring works. Whitman created excitement for many, but it was not always clearly complimentary. And of course James long suffered the disappointments of a writer whose art only a small minority of his generation appreciated.

In time the French symbolists took Poe almost as their own, but in America he has only recently begun to be regarded widely with due seriousness. By the first decades of the twentieth century Emerson, Thoreau, Hawthorne, and Twain had gained substantially in critical favor, but a revival of Melville in the 1920's was virtually a first discovery of his genius, and Whitman's reputation was at last solidifying around his accomplishments as a poet rather than his interest as a personality. The decades after the 1920's saw also the critical triumph, still unabated, of the art of Henry James. We see these writers as representing the coming of age of American letters; their recognition, though, came slowly in this country's and the world's judgment.

The same was true of another great nineteenth-century American writer, Emily Dickinson, with the significant difference that, unlike her peers, she had no literary "career" to be judged—and shaped by judgment—in her lifetime. Barely a handful of her poems was published while she lived, and except for Colonel Thomas Wentworth

Higginson, few outside her family and close friends (usually correspondents) ever saw any of her verse until 1890. In that year, four years after her death, the world was given the first volume of poems by Emily Dickinson, edited by Mabel Loomis Todd, friend and neighbor of the Dickinson family, and Colonel Higginson.

The immediate critical response to these poems was mixed. Those, like William Dean Howells, who recognized a genuine and unusual poetical gift, were not always sure of the exact nature of its articulation. And those, like the Britisher Andrew Lang, who dismissed her as ignorant and incompetent, seemed even less certain of how in fact a Dickinson poem requires to be read. Admirers and detractors, both American and British, were clear enough in their critical sentiments, but to the present-day reader of their views, neither saw with clarity the full nature of her poetic gifts.

But Emily Dickinson sustained attention as more and more of her poems—and her letters—were published, though from 1897 to the early 1920's that attention was meager. Then interest in her poetry became broader in scope: to the problem of her unconventional form were added the problems of her biography, the significance of her major themes, and the reliability of the published texts. Especially in the 1920's and after, critics began to see the poems for what they are rather than for what they might have been. To some, Miss Dickinson was more easily a "modern" poet than a nineteenth-century one. To others she was of her own time and heritage but also clearly beyond it. And in 1921 Norman Foerster hesitantly said she would occupy an "inconspicuous but secure" place in American literary history. To be sure, there were British and American critics who maintained strong reservations about the poet's merits, but they were, by 1930, a steadily dwindling number.

From the 1930's to the present the reputation of Emily Dickinson has grown immensely, not in the sense of discovery or revival; rather, in the sense of clarification: what her poetry is and what, consequently, her stature must be. We are accustomed to think of the past several decades as an age of criticism with a very diverse and sophisticated range of beliefs and practices. That Emily Dickinson's poetry should find high favor in so many of these critical perspectives is itself a testament to her greatness. Furthermore, one sees in this criticism the frequent assumption that she *is* great, and then the careful exploration of her themes, her techniques, her method, the precise terms of her greatness. The facts and critical relevance of her biography and the definitive editions of her work have been accomplished. Her significance to American literature and culture is largely defined. The recognition of Emily Dickinson is now firm, and she joins Emerson, Hawthorne, Melville, and the other company of great nineteenth-century writers.

The essays collected here trace the growth of this recognition from 1890 to the present. Many of the earlier ones will be new to readers; some of the later ones will be justly familiar. Some are slight as criticism, and others are classics of their kind. Together, they show a reputation in the process of its own accomplishment through more than seven decades of criticism chosen to show the major trends in critical thought during the period as well as the major phases of a poet's fame.

ACKNOWLEDGMENTS

In the bringing together of this anthology of Emily Dickinson criticism the editors have had the encouragement and cooperation of many scholars, critics, librarians, and publishers.

First of all, our thanks go to those authors and publishers who uniformly responded affirmatively to the editors' requests for permission to reprint copyrighted material—from Professor Martha Hale Shackford and Miss Elizabeth Shepley Sergeant, whose essays of fifty years ago pioneered in advancing the recognition of Emily Dickinson in this century, to Charles R. Anderson and Archibald MacLeish writing in the 1960's.

The editors also wish to make the following specific acknowledgments. Mrs. Millicent Todd Bingham, author or editor of four important books on Emily Dickinson, not only gave valuable suggestions for this projected anthology but made available to one of the present editors the scrapbooks of reviews kept by her mother, Mabel Loomis Todd, editor both of Emily Dickinson's poems (1890, 1891, 1896) and of Emily Dickinson's letters (1894). Recently Mrs. Bingham has given her unique collection of Dickinson books and manuscripts to the Amherst College Library. Also at Amherst, in the Jones Library, is a fine collection of Emily Dickinson books and reviews, the work of its emeritus librarian, Charles R. Green. Some time ago, Mr. Green was the cordial and enlightening host to one of the editors. This visit, with Mr. Green, to Emily Dickinson's birthplace provided fresh insight into the totality of influences reflected in her poetry. Dr. Thomas H. Johnson, editor of the *Poems of Emily Dickinson* and of the *Letters of Emily Dickinson* (with Mrs. Theodora Ward), has on numerous occasions responded to inquiries with prompt and expert counsel. Among our colleagues at the University of Michigan we wish particularly to express our thanks to Warner G. Rice, chairman of the Department of English Language and Literature, for his interest, advice, and support.

Finally, the editors are happy to acknowledge the assistance provided by a grant for travel and preparation of the manuscript for publication made from the Research Fund of the Horace H. Rackham School of Graduate Studies, University of Michigan.

Caesar R. Blake
Carlton F. Wells

PERMISSIONS

The editors and publishers of *The Recognition of Emily Dickinson* gratefully acknowledge the cooperation of authors and publishers in granting permission to reprint the selections named below.

Conrad Aiken for "Introduction to Selected Poems of Emily Dickinson," from *Selected Poems of Emily Dickinson* (London: Jonathan Cape, 1924).

Gay Wilson Allen and the *American Book Company* for "Emily Dickinson's Versification," from Gay Wilson Allen's *American Prosody* (New York: American Book Company, 1935).

George Allen & Unwin Ltd. for "Emily Dickinson: Notes on Prejudice and Fact," from R. P. Blackmur's *Language as Gesture.*

Charles R. Anderson and *Holt, Rinehart and Winston* for "Center," from *Emily Dickinson's Poetry: Stairway of Surprise* by Charles R. Anderson (New York: Holt, Rinehart and Winston, 1960).

Martin Armstrong and the *Spectator* for "The Poetry of Emily Dickinson," *Spectator* (London), CXXX (January 6, 1923).

R. P. Blackmur and *Harcourt, Brace and Company* for "Emily Dickinson: Notes on Prejudice and Fact," from *Language and Gesture* (New York: Harcourt, Brace and Company, 1952).

Edmund Blunden and the *New Statesman and Nation* for "An Unguessed Poetry," *Nation and Athenaeum,* XLVI (March 22, 1930).

Harvard University Press and the Trustees of Amherst College for selections from Thomas H. Johnson, Editor, *The Poems of Emily Dickinson*. Cambridge, Mass.: The Belknap Press of Harvard University Press, copyright 1951, 1955 by The President and Fellows of Harvard College.

William Heinemann Ltd. for a portion of Charles Anderson's *Emily Dickinson's Poetry.*

Granville Hicks for "Emily Dickinson and the Gilded Age," from his *The Great Tradition* (The Macmillan Company, 1933).

Robert Hillyer for "Emily Dickinson," *The Freeman,* VI (October 18, 1922).

The Houghton Library, Harvard University, for the photograph for the frontispiece made from the Library's negative of the Emily Dickinson daguerreotype.

Houghton Mifflin Company for selections from Martha Dickinson Bianchi, *The Life and Letters of Emily Dickinson,* 1924.

Thomas H. Johnson and the *Saturday Review* for "The Prisms of a Poet," from *Saturday Review,* XXXIII (June 3, 1950).

Little, Brown and Company for selections from Thomas H. Johnson, Editor, *The Complete Poems of Emily Dickinson.* Copyright 1914, 1935, 1942, © 1963 by Martha Dickinson Bianchi; copyright 1929, © 1957 by Mary L. Hampson.

Liveright Publishing Company for Hart Crane's "To Emily Dickinson," from *Collected Poems of Hart Crane* (New York: Liveright, 1933).

Percy Lubbock and the *New Statesman and Nation* for "Determined Little Anchoress," *Nation and Athenaeum,* XXXVI (October 18, 1924).

Archibald MacLeish and the *Amherst College Press* for "The Private World," from *Emily Dickinson: Amherst College Anniversary Volume* (Amherst, Massachusetts: Amherst College Press, 1960).

The Macmillan Company for Norman Foerster's "Emily Dickinson," from W. P. Trent and others, *Cambridge History of American Literature,* Vol. IV (1921); and for Stanley T. Williams' "Experiments in Poetry: Emily Dickinson" from R. E. Spiller and others, *Literary History of the United States,* Vol. II (1948).

Alida Monro for Harold Monro's "Emily Dickinson—Overrated," *Criterion,* III (January, 1925).

New England Quarterly for Theodore Spencer's "Concentration and Intensity," *New England Quarterly,* II (July, 1929).

John Crowe Ransom, editor of *The Kenyon Review,* for F. O. Matthiessen's "The Private Poet: Emily Dickinson," *Kenyon Review,* II (Autumn, 1945).

Sir Herbert Read and the *Spectator* for "The Range of Emily Dickinson," *Spectator,* CLI (December 29, 1933).

Elizabeth Shepley Sergeant for "An Early Imagist," *New Republic,* IV (August 14, 1915).

Martha Hale Shackford for "The Poetry of Emily Dickinson," *Atlantic Monthly,* CXI (January, 1913).

Sir John Squire for Susan Miles's "The Irregularities of Emily Dickinson," *London Mercury,* XIII (December, 1925).

Allen Tate and *Alan Swallow* of *The Swallow Press* for "Emily Dickinson," from Allen Tate's *On the Limits of Poetry: Selected Essays.* Copyright 1936 by Charles Scribner's Sons; copyright 1948 by Allen Tate.

Mark Van Doren, William Sloane Associates, Inc., and Holt, Rinehart and Winston, Inc., for "Commentary on 'I Had Not Minded Walls,'" from *Introduction to Poetry* by Mark Van Doren (New York: William Sloane Associates, 1951); and from *Introduction to Poetry* (New York: Holt, Rinehart and Winston, Inc., 1951).

Alfred Charles Ward for "Emily Dickinson," from *American Literature: 1880–1930,* by Alfred Charles Ward (London: Methuen, 1932).

Austin Warren for "Emily Dickinson," from *Sewanee Review,* LXV (Autumn, 1957).

Mrs. George F. Whicher for "A Centennial Appraisal" by George F. Whicher, from *Emily Dickinson: A Bibliography* (Amherst, Massachusetts: The Jones Library, 1930); and for "Emily Dickinson among the Victorians," from *Poetry and Civilization* by George F. Whicher (Ithaca, New York: Cornell University Press, 1955).

Yvor Winters and *Alan Swallow* of *The Swallow Press* for "Emily Dickinson and the Limits of Judgment," from *In Defense of Reason* by Yvor Winters. Copyright 1938 by New Directions; copyright 1947 by Yvor Winters.

A Note on Emily Dickinson Bibliography

For the 1890's, a complete list of reviews and criticisms of Emily Dickinson's work is given in *Ancestors' Brocades: The Literary Debut of Emily Dickinson,* by Millicent Todd Bingham, New York, 1945, pp. 406–11.

For the twentieth century, in addition to the annual bibliographies of the Modern Humanities Research Association (since 1921), of the Modern Language Association (since 1922), and of *American Literature* (since 1929), the following bibliographies record with various degrees of completeness material published in English on Emily Dickinson:

Emily Dickinson: A Bibliography, The Jones Library, Amherst, Mass., 1930.

Robert E. Spiller and others, editors, *Literary History of the United States,* New York, 1948. Vol. III, Bibliography, pp. 467–70.

Lewis Gaston Leary, *Articles on American Literature, 1900–1950,* Durham, N.C., 1954, pp. 68–71.

Joseph M. Kuntz, *Poetry Explication, A Checklist of Interpretations since 1925 of British and American Poems Past and Present,* revised edition, Denver, 1962, pp. 71–79.

CONTENTS

I. 1890–1900

II. 1901–1930

III. 1931–to the Present

1

1890–1900

It is to THOMAS WENTWORTH HIGGINSON (1823–1911) that credit must be given for the first serious, if restrained, attention to Emily Dickinson's poetry in the 1890's. Teacher, preacher, champion of antislavery and of woman's suffrage, Higginson was also a critic of considerable reputation. Higginson "discovered" Emily Dickinson in 1862 when she wrote to ask his opinion of her verse. Subsequently, he became her correspondent, friend, and critic. In 1890 and 1891 he edited, with Mabel Loomis Todd, the first and second series of Emily Dickinson's poetry. Reprinted here are both Higginson's essay published two months before the appearance of the *Poems by Emily Dickinson* (1890) and his preface to that volume.

An Open Portfolio

THOMAS WENTWORTH HIGGINSON

Emerson said, many years since in the *Dial,* that the most interesting department of poetry would hereafter be found in what might be called "The Poetry of the Portfolio"; the work, that is, of persons who wrote for the relief of their own minds, and without thought of publication. Such poetry, when accumulated for years, will have at least the merit of perfect freedom; accompanied, of course, by whatever drawback follows from the habitual absence of criticism. Thought will have its full strength and uplifting, but without the proper control and chastening of literary expression; there will be wonderful strokes and felicities, and yet an incomplete and unsatisfactory whole. If we believe, with Ruskin, that "no beauty of execution can outweigh one grain or fragment of thought," then we may often gain by the seclusion of the portfolio, which rests content with a first stroke and does not over-refine and prune away afterwards. Such a sheaf of unpublished verse lies before me, the life-work of a woman so secluded that she lived literally indoors by choice for many years, and within the limits of her father's estate for many more—who shrank even from the tranquil society of a New England college town, and yet loved her few friends with profound devotedness, and divided her life between

From *The Christian Union,* XLII (September 25, 1890), 392–93.

them and her flowers. It absolutely startles one to find among the memorials of this secluded inland life a picture so vividly objective as this:

BY THE SEA

Glee! the great storm is over!
Four have recovered the land;
Forty gone down together
Into the boiling sand.

Ring! for the scant salvation!
Toll! for the bonnie souls,
Neighbor and friend and bridegroom,
Spinning upon the shoals.

How they will tell the shipwreck
When winter shakes the door,
Till the children ask, "But the forty?
Did they come back no more?"

Then a silence suffuses the story
And a softness the teller's eye,
And the children no further question;
And only the waves reply.

Celia Thaxter on her rocky island, Jean Ingelow by her English cliffs, never drew a sea picture in stronger lines than this secluded woman in her inland village, who writes elsewhere, as tersely:

I never saw a moor,
I never saw the sea,
Yet know I how the heather looks
And what the billows be.

I never spoke with God
Nor visited in heaven,
Yet certain am I of the spot,
As if the chart were given.

See now with what corresponding vigor she draws the mightier storms and shipwrecks of the soul; the title being here, as elsewhere, my own, for she herself never prefixes any:

ROUGE ET NOIR

Soul, wilt thou toss again?
By just such a hazard

Hundreds have lost, indeed,
But tens have won an all.

Angels' breathless ballot
Lingers to record thee;
Imps in eager caucus
Raffle for my soul!

Was ever the concentrated contest of a lifetime, the very issue between good and evil, put into fewer words? Then comes another, which might fairly be linked with it, and might be called

ROUGE GAGNE!

'Tis so much joy! 'Tis so much joy!
If I should fail, what poverty!
  And yet as poor as I
Have ventured all upon a throw;
Have gained! Yes! Hesitated so
  This side the victory.

Life is but life, and death but death!
Bliss is but bliss, and breath but breath!
  And if indeed I fail,
At least, to know the worst is sweet!
Defeat means nothing but defeat,
  No drearier can prevail.

And if I gain! O sun at sea!
O bells! that in the steeple be,
  At first, repeat it slow!
For heaven is a different thing
Conjectured and waked sudden in,
  And might o'erwhelm me so.

Many of these poems are, as might be expected, drawn from the aspects of Nature, but always with some insight or image of their own; as in the following, which might be called

THE SEA OF SUNSET

This is the land the sunset washes,
  These are the banks of the yellow sea;
Where it rose, or whither it rushes,
  These are the western mystery.

Night after night, her purple traffic
  Strews the landing with opal bales,
Merchantmen poise upon horizons,
  Dip and vanish with airy sails.

Or this:

THE WIND

Of all the sounds despatched abroad
  There's not a charge to me
Like that old measure in the boughs,
  That phraseless melody
The wind makes, working like a hand
  Whose fingers brush the sky,
Then quiver down, with tufts of tune,
  Permitted gods—and me.

I crave him grace of summer boughs
  If such an outcast be
Who never heard that fleshless chant
  Rise solemn in the tree;
As if some caravan of sound
  On deserts in the sky
Had broken rank, then knit, and passed
  In seamless company.

This last image needs no praise, and in dealing with Nature she often seems to possess—as was said of her fellow-townswoman, Helen Jackson ("H. H.")—a sixth sense. But most of her poems grapple at first hand—the more audaciously the better—with the very mysteries of life and death, as in the following:

TWO KINSMEN

I died for Beauty, but was scarce
Adjusted in the tomb
When one who died for Truth was lain
In an adjoining room.

He questioned softly, why I failed?
"For Beauty," I replied;
"And I for Truth—the two are one—
We brethren are," he said.

And so, as kinsmen, met a night,
We talked between the rooms

Until the moss had reached our lips
And covered up our names.

The conception is weird enough for William Blake, and one can no more criticise a faulty rhyme here and there than a defect of drawing in one of Blake's pictures. When a thought takes one's breath away, who cares to count the syllables? The same iron strength shows itself, merging into tenderness, in this brief dirge for one of the nameless Marthas, cumbered about many things:

REQUIESCAT

How many times these low feet staggered
  Only the soldered mouth can tell;
Try! can you stir the awful rivet?
  Try! can you lift the hasps of steel?

Stroke the cool forehead, hot so often;
  Lift, if you can, the listless hair;
Handle the adamantine fingers
  Never a thimble more shall wear.

Buzz the dull flies on the chamber window;
  Brave shines the sun through the freckled pane;
Fearless the cobweb swings from the ceiling;
  Indolent housewife! in daisies lain.

The unutterable dignity of death seems to have forced itself again and again upon this lonely woman, and she has several times touched it with her accustomed terse strength, as in these verses:

One dignity delays for all,
  One mitred afternoon.
None can avoid this purple;
  None can evade this crown.

Coach it insures, and footmen,
  Chamber and state and throng,
Bells also, in the village,
  As we ride grand along.

What dignified attendants!
  What service when we pause!
How loyally, at parting,
  Their hundred hats they raise!

What pomp surpassing ermine
When simple you and I
Present our meek escutcheon
And claim the rank to die!

Then, approaching the great change from time to eternity at a different angle, she gives two verses of superb concentration, like the following, which might be christened, after the mediaeval motto,

ASTRA CASTRA

Departed to the Judgment
A mighty afternoon;
Great clouds, like ushers, leaning,
Creation looking on.

The flesh surrendered, canceled,
The bodiless begun;
Two worlds, like audiences, disperse,
And leave the soul alone.

She shrinks from no concomitant of death; all is ennobled in her imagination:

Safe in their alabaster chambers,
Untouched by morning and untouched by noon,
Sleep the meek members of the resurrection;
Rafter of satin and roof of stone.

Light laughs the breeze in her castle above them;
Babbles the bee in a stolid ear;
Pipe the sweet birds in ignorant cadence—
Ah! what sagacity perished here!

This is the form in which she finally left these lines, but as she sent them to me, years ago, the following took the place of the second verse, and it seems to me that, with all its too daring condensation, it strikes a note too fine to be lost:

Grand go the years in the crescent above them,
Worlds scoop their arcs, and firmaments row;
Diadems drop, and Doges surrender,
Soundless as dots on a disk of snow.

But with these mighty visions of death and eternity, there are such touches of tender individual sympathy as we find in this, which may be called

TOO LATE

Delayed till she had ceased to know!
Delayed till in its vest of snow
  Her loving bosom lay.
An hour behind the fleeting breath!
Later by just an hour than Death!
  O! lagging yesterday!

Could she have guessed that it would be;
Could but a crier of the glee
  Have climbed the distant hill;
Had not the bliss so slow a pace,
Who knows but this surrendered face
  Were undefeated still?

O! if there may departing be
Any forgot by victory
  In her imperial sound,
Show them this meek-appareled thing,
That could not stop to be a king,
  Doubtful if it be crowned!

Almost all these poems are strangely impersonal, but here and there we have a glimpse of experiences too intense to be more plainly intimated, as in the following:

I shall know why, when time is over
  And I have ceased to wonder why;
Christ will explain each separate anguish
  In the fair schoolroom of the sky.

He will tell me what Peter promised,
  And I, for wonder at his woe,
I shall forget the drop of anguish
  That scalds me now—that scalds me now!

Surely this is as if woven out of the heart's own atoms, and will endear the name of Emily Dickinson, in some hour of trial, to those who never before encountered that name, and who will seek it vainly in the cyclopaedias. Her verses are in most cases like poetry plucked up by the roots; we have them with earth, stones, and dew adhering, and must accept them as they are. Wayward and unconventional in the last degree; defiant of form, measure, rhyme, and even grammar; she yet had an exacting standard of her own, and would wait many days for a word that satisfied. Asked again and again for verses to be published, she scarcely ever yielded, even to a friend so tried and dear as the late Mr. Bowles, of the Springfield *Republican;* but she sent her poems with gifts of flowers or—as in my own case—to correspondents whom she had never seen. It is with some misgiving, and almost with a sense of questionable publicity, that it has at last been decided by her surviving sister and her friends to print a small selection from these poems, which will be issued by Roberts Brothers, Boston. The only hint found among her papers of any possible contact with a wider public is found in these few lines, which—although probably the utterance of a passing mood only—have been selected as the prelude to the forthcoming volume:

This is my letter to the world
  That never wrote to me;
The simple news that nature told
  With tender majesty.

Her message is committed
  To hands I cannot see;
For love of her, sweet countrymen,
  Judge tenderly of me!

Preface to Poems by Emily Dickinson *(1890)*

THOMAS WENTWORTH HIGGINSON

The verses of Emily Dickinson belong emphatically to what Emerson long since called "the Poetry of the Portfolio,"—something produced absolutely without the thought of publication, and solely by way of expression of the writer's own mind. Such verse must inevitably forfeit whatever advantage lies in the discipline of public criticism and the enforced conformity to accepted ways. On the other hand, it may often gain something through the habit of freedom and the unconventional utterance of daring thoughts. In the case of the present author, there was absolutely no choice in the matter; she must write thus, or not at all. A recluse by temperament and habit, literally spending years without setting her foot beyond the doorstep, and many more years during which her walks were strictly limited to her father's grounds, she habitually concealed her mind, like her person, from all but a very few friends; and it was with great difficulty that she was persuaded to print, during her lifetime, three or four poems. Yet she wrote verses in great abundance; and though curiously indifferent to all conventional rules, had yet a rigorous literary standard of her own, and often altered a word many times to suit an ear which had its own tenacious fastidiousness.

Miss Dickinson was born in Amherst, Mass., Dec. 10, 1830, and died there May 15, 1886. Her father, Hon. Edward Dickinson, was the leading lawyer of Amherst, and was treasurer of the well-known college there situated. It was his custom once a year to hold a large reception at his house, attended by all the families connected with the institution and by the leading people of the town. On these occasions his daughter Emily emerged from her wonted retirement and did her part as gracious hostess; nor would any one have known from her manner, I have been told, that this was not a daily occurrence. The annual occasion once past, she withdrew again into her seclusion, and except for a very few friends was as invisible to the world as if she had dwelt in a nunnery. For myself, although I had corresponded with her for many years, I saw her but twice face to face, and brought away the impression of something as unique and remote as Undine or Mignon or Thekla.

This selection from her poems is published to meet the desire of her personal friends, and especially of her surviving sister. It is believed that the thoughtful reader will find in these pages a quality more suggestive of the poetry of William Blake than of anything to be elsewhere found,—flashes of wholly original and profound insight into nature and life; words and phrases exhibiting an extraordinary vividness of descriptive and imaginative power, yet often set in a seemingly whimsical or even rugged frame. They are here published as they were written, with very few and superficial changes; although it is fair to say that the titles have been assigned, almost invariably, by the editors. In many cases these verses will seem to the reader like poetry torn up by the roots, with rain and dew and earth still clinging to them, giving a freshness and a fragrance not otherwise to be conveyed. In other cases, as in the few poems of shipwreck or of mental conflict, we can only wonder at the gift of vivid imagination by which this recluse woman can delineate, by a few touches, the very crises of physical or mental struggle. And sometimes again we catch glimpses of a lyric strain, sustained perhaps but for a line or two at a time, and making the reader regret its sudden cessation. But the main quality of these poems is that of extraordinary grasp and insight, uttered with an uneven vigor sometimes exasperating, seemingly wayward, but really unsought and inevitable. After all, when a thought takes one's breath away, a lesson on grammar seems an impertinence. As Ruskin wrote in his earlier and better days, "No weight nor mass nor beauty of execution can outweigh one grain or fragment of thought."

ARLO BATES (1850–1918), before becoming a professor of English at Massachusetts Institute of Technology in 1893, had been both a novelist and editor of the Boston *Sunday Courier*. Prolific as a writer, Bates produced many volumes of fiction and verse, and several textbooks of English. It was to Bates that Thomas Niles of Roberts Brothers had sent the poems for appraisal before the Boston publisher agreed to bring them out in 1890.

Miss Dickinson's Poems

ARLO BATES

It is seldom that the reviewer is called upon to notice a book so remarkable as the "Poems" of Miss Emily Dickinson, which are published posthumously under the editorship of Mrs. Mabel Loomis Todd and Colonel Thomas Wentworth Higginson. The work which it contains has to be treated as so far outside of the ordinary groove, it is so wholly without the pale of conventional criticism, that it is necessary at the start to declare the grounds upon which it is to be judged as if it were a new species of art.

For, in the first place, there is hardly a line in the entire volume, and certainly not a stanza, which cannot be objected to upon the

From the *Boston Courier,* November 23, 1890.

score of technical imperfection. The author was as unlearned in the technical side of art as if she had written when the forms of verse had not yet been invented. She is not so much disdainful of conventions as she seems to be insensible to them. Her ear had certainly not been susceptible of training to the appreciation of form and melody, or it is inconceivable that she should have written as she did. There is on every page ground for the feeling that she was one of those strangely constituted creatures who experience a pleasure from metrical forms, yet who are so insensible to them as to be unable to understand that their own work lacks in that which moves them dimly in the poetry of others. There is evidence that Miss Dickinson was not without some vague feeling for metre and rhythm, yet she was apparently entirely unconscious that her own lines often had neither and constantly violated the canons of both.

There is hardly a line of her work, however, which fails to throw out some gleam of genuine original power, of imagination, and of real emotional thought. There is the real poetic motive here. The high muse has been with her in very truth, passing by to come to her many who have well and painfully learned the secrets of the technique of their art. That the muse was erratic in her choice may be allowed; but it is vain to attempt to deny that it was herself and no other who inspired Miss Dickinson's songs.

There is a certain rude and half barbaric naivete in many of the poems. They show the insight of the civilized adult combined with the simplicity of the savage child. There is a barbaric flavor often discernible, as if this gentle poet had the blood of some gentle and simple Indian ancestress in her veins still in an unadulterated current.

> Angels in the early morning
>   May be seen the dews among,
> Stooping, plucking, smiling, flying:
>   Do the buds to them belong?

Is not this the voice of a child?

> Some keep the Sabbath going to church;
>   I keep it staying at home,
> With a bobolink for a chorister,
>   And an orchard for a dome.
>
> . . . . . .

God preaches—a noted clergyman—
And the sermon is never long;
So instead of getting to heaven at last,
I'm going all along!

Could anything be more delightfully pagan, or worse in workmanship?

These two show how near she could come at times to a bit of good workmanship, and how inevitably she spoiled it.

AUTUMN

The morns are meeker than they were,
The nuts are getting brown;
The berry's cheek is plumper,
The rose is out of town.

The maple wears a gayer scarf,
The field a scarlet gown.
Lest I should be old-fashioned,
I'll put a trinket on.

BECLOUDED

The sky is low, the clouds are mean,
A traveling flake of snow
Across a barn or through a rut
Debates if it will go.

A narrow wind complains all day
How some one treated him;
Nature, like us, is sometimes caught
Without her diadem.

The touch of humor at the end of the former of these is in a way delightful, but it is not enough to justify the place it holds. The first four verses of the second give a picture with a vividness and grace that could hardly be bettered, but the rest does not please us.

Of the poems dealing with nature this seems to us one of the best.

THE SEA OF SUNSET

This is the land the sunset washes,
These are the banks of the Yellow Sea;
Where it rose, or whither it rushes,
These are the Western mystery.

Night after night her purple traffic
  Strews the landing with purple bales;
Merchantmen poise upon horizons,
  Dip and vanish with fairy sails.

It is not in her poems dealing with nature, however, that Miss Dickinson seems to us most interesting. These are often marked with much felicity of phrase, and they are apt to be less irregular in form than some of the rest, but there is in her poems upon life and ethical themes far more depth and originality. Take, for example, these two:

The heart asks pleasure first,
  And then, excuse from pain;
And then, those little anodynes
  That deaden suffering;

And then to go to sleep;
  And then, if it should be
The will of its Inquisitor,
  The liberty to die.

THE MYSTERY OF PAIN

Pain has an element of blank;
  It cannot recollect
When it began, or if there were
  A day when it was not.

It has no future but itself,
  Its infinite realms contain
Its past, enlightened to perceive
  New periods of pain.

Here is genuine, emotional insight into life, united with no small power of feeling, and, too of expressing. What, too, need be more charming and touching than the spirit of these love songs?

WITH A FLOWER

I hide myself within my flower,
  That wearing on your breast,
You, unsuspecting, wear me too—
  And angels know the rest.

I hide myself within my flower,
  That fading from your vase,

You, unsuspecting, feel for me
Almost a loneliness.

THE OUTLET

My river runs to thee;
Blue sea, wilt welcome me?

My river waits reply.
Oh, sea, look graciously!

I'll fetch thee brooks
From spotted nooks,—

Say, sea, take me!

A little rhyme which is eminently characteristic in its breaks and technical faults.

TRANSPLANTED

As if some little Arctic flower,
Upon the polar hem,
Went wandering down the latitudes,
Until it puzzled came
To continents of summer,
To firmaments of sun,
To strange bright crowds of flowers,
And birds of foreign tongue!
I say, as if this little flower
To Eden wandered in—
What then? Why, nothing, only
Your inference therefrom!

The religious poems are distinguished by a singularly frank fearlessness which is most easily described in Mrs. Browning's phrase as an

—infantine,
Familiar clasp of things divine.

Her spiritual life was evidently so much a part of her existence that it never occurred to her that there was a difference made in the manner of treating one serious feeling because it is a fashion of the conventional world so to treat it. She was always reverent because she could not have been irreverent, but she was reverent toward nature, man and God in the same way. Her theology is of a sort to puzzle metaphysicians, and yet one finds it often most suggestive and stimulating. The strangeness of some of the mixtures which she offers may be seen from this bit:

I reason that in Heaven
Somehow it will be even,
Some new equation given;
  But what of that?

Perhaps there is nothing in the volume which is better than the poem which the editors have called "Apotheosis," and which they have placed among the love poems instead of the religious, perhaps rightly, since Miss Dickinson is more fervid in her expressions concerning love than concerning religion.

APOTHEOSIS

Come slowly, Eden!
  Lips unused to thee,
Bashful, sip thy jasmines,
  As the fainting bee,
Reaching late his flower,
  'Round her chamber hums,
Counts his nectars—enters,
  And is lost in balms!

There is little of the imitative in the book. Such a suggestion of Browning as one may find in this last poem or of Emerson in some of the poems to nature there is now and then, but it is not enough to interfere with the feeling of untrammeled freshness with which one reads. We have quoted thus largely because of the charm of this work for us, and because, the poems having never been published before, are sure to be fresh to the reader. It is necessary to lay aside all fondness for technical perfection, and to give one's self up to the spirit, but this being done, the lover of the poetical will find the book a rare delight. There will be those, indeed, who will contend that the book is better for having disregarded technical form, or at least no worse. It is not wholly impossible that in the Editor's Study something looking in this direction will some day see the light. The truth, however, is not so. Had Miss Dickinson possessed the aptitude and the will to learn technical skill, she would have enriched the language with lyrics which would have endured to the end of time, it well might be. As it is, she has put upon paper things which will delight the few, but which will hold their place on suffrance, and as showing what she might have been rather than for what she was. The book gives us keen delight, but it is delight mingled with regret equally keen for what it fails to be.

As a man of letters WILLIAM DEAN HOWELLS (1837–1920) achieved a wide reputation and influence. The "new realism" of his novels alone would have earned him a place in American literary history; but in addition, he published a vast body of poetry, criticism, travel, biography, and plays—over one hundred titles in all. Howells also distinguished himself in literary journalism as contributor or editor for the *Atlantic Monthly, Century, North American Review,* and *Harper's.* It was a signal recognition for Emily Dickinson that in 1891 a critic of Howells' reputation and influence should have a high regard for her poetry.

The Strange Poems of Emily Dickinson

WILLIAM DEAN HOWELLS

The strange *Poems of Emily Dickinson* we think will form something like an intrinsic experience with the understanding reader of them. They have been edited by Mrs. Mabel Loomis Todd, who was a personal friend of the poet, and by Colonel T. W. Higginson, who was long her epistolary and literary acquaintance, but only met her twice. Few people met her so often, as the reader will learn from Colonel Higginson's interesting preface, for her life was mainly spent in her father's house at Amherst, Massachusetts; she seldom passed its doors, and never, for many years, passed the gates of its grounds. There is no hint of what turned her life in upon itself, and probably this was its natural evolution, or involution, from tendencies inherent in the New England, or the Puritan, spirit. We are told that once a year she

From *Harper's New Monthly Magazine,* LXXXII (January, 1891), 318–20.

met the local world at a reception in her father's house; we do not know that there is any harm in adding, that she did not always literally meet it, but sometimes sat with her face averted from the company in another room. One of her few friends was Helen Hunt Jackson, whom she suffered to send one of her poems to be included in the volume of anonymous pieces which Messrs. Roberts Brothers once published with the title of *A Masque of Poets*. Whether the anonymity flattered her love of obscurity or not, it is certain that her darkling presence in this book was the occasion of her holding for many years a correspondence with its publishers. She wrote them, as the fancy took her, comments on their new books, and always enclosed a scrap of her verse, though without making any reference to it. She never intended or allowed anything more from her pen to be printed in her lifetime; but it was evident that she wished her poetry finally to meet the eyes of that world which she had herself always shrunk from. She could not have made such poetry without knowing its rarity, its singular worth; and no doubt it was a radiant happiness in the twilight of her hidden, silent life.

The editors have discharged their delicate duty toward it with unimpeachable discretion, and Colonel Higginson has said so many apt things of her work in his introduction, that one who cannot differ with him must be vexed a little to be left so little to say. He speaks of her "curious indifference to all conventional rules of verse," but he adds that "when a thought takes one's breath away, a lesson on grammar seems an impertinence." He notes "the quality suggestive of the poetry of William Blake" in her, but he leaves us the chance to say that it is a Blake who had read Emerson who had read Blake. The fantasy is as often Blakian as the philosophy is Emersonian; but after feeling this again and again, one is ready to declare that the utterance of this most singular and authentic spirit would have been the same if there had never been an Emerson or a Blake in the world. She sometimes suggests Heine as much as either of these; all three in fact are spiritually present in some of the pieces; yet it is hardly probable that she read Heine, or if she had, would not have abhorred him.

Here is something that seems compact of both Emerson and Blake, with a touch of Heine too:

> I taste a liquor never brewed,
> From tankards scooped in pearl;

Not all the vats upon the Rhine
Yield such an alcohol!

Inebriate of air am I,
And debauchee of dew,
Reeling, through endless summer days,
From inns of molten blue.

When landlords turn the drunken bee
Out of the foxglove's door,
When butterflies renounce their drams,
I shall but drink the more!

Till seraphs swing their snowy hats,
And saints to windows run,
To see the little tippler
Leaning against the sun!

But we believe it is only seeming; we believe these things are as wholly her own as this:

The bustle in a house
The morning after death
Is solemnest of industries
Enacted upon earth,—

The sweeping up the heart,
And putting love away
We shall not want to use again
Until eternity.

Such things could have come only from a woman's heart to which the experiences in a New England town have brought more knowledge of death than of life. Terribly unsparing many of these strange poems are, but true as the grave and certain as mortality. The associations of house-keeping in the following poem have a force that drags us almost into the presence of the poor, cold quiet thing:

TROUBLED ABOUT MANY THINGS

How many times these low feet staggered,
Only the soldered mouth can tell:
Try! Can you stir the awful rivet?
Try! Can you lift the hasps of steel?

Stroke the cool forehead, hot so often,
Lift, if you can, the listless hair;

Handle the adamantine fingers
Never a thimble more shall wear.

Buzz the dull flies on the chamber window;
Brave shines the sun through the freckled pane;
Fearless the cobweb swings from the ceiling—
Indolent housewife, in daisies lain!

Then in this, which has no name—how could any phrase nominate its weird witchery aright?—there is the flight of an eerie fancy that leaves all experience behind:

I died for beauty, but was scarce
Adjusted in the tomb,
When one who died for truth was lain
In an adjoining room.

He questioned softly why I failed.
"For beauty," I replied.
"And I for truth,—the two are one;
We brethren are," he said.

And so, as kinsmen met a night,
We talked between the rooms,
Until the moss had reached our lips,
And covered up our names.

All the Puritan longing for sincerity, for veracious conduct, which in some good New England women's natures is almost a hysterical shriek, makes its exultant grim assertion in these lines:

REAL

I like a look of agony,
Because I know it's true;
Men do not sham convulsion,
Nor simulate a throe.

The eyes glaze once, and that is death.
Impossible to feign
The beads upon the forehead
By homely anguish strung.

These mortuary pieces have a fascination above any others in the book; but in the stanzas below there is a still, solemn, rapt movement of the thought and music together that is of exquisite charm:

New feet within my garden go,
New fingers stir the sod;
A troubadour upon the elm
Betrays the solitude.

New children play upon the green,
New weary sleep below;
And still the pensive spring returns,
And still the punctual snow!

This is a song that sings itself; and this is another such, but thrilling with the music of a different passion:

SUSPENSE

Elysium is as far as to
The very nearest room,
If in that room a friend await
Felicity or doom.

What fortitude the soul contains,
That it can so endure
The accent of a coming foot,
The opening of a door!

The last poem is from the group which the editors have named "Love"; the other groups from which we have been quoting are "Nature," and "Time and Eternity"; but the love poems are of the same piercingly introspective cast as those differently named. The same force of imagination is in them; in them, as in the rest, touch often becomes clutch. In them love walks on heights he seldom treads, and it is the heart of full womanhood that speaks in the words of this nun-like New England life.

Few of the poems in the book are long, but none of the short, quick impulses of intense feeling or poignant thought can be called fragments. They are each a compassed whole, a sharply finished point, and there is evidence, circumstantial and direct, that the author spared no pains in the perfect expression of her ideals. Nothing, for example, could be added that would say more than she has said in four lines:

Presentiment is that long shadow on the lawn
Indicative that suns go down;

The notice to the startled grass
That darkness is about to pass.

Occasionally, the outside of the poem, so to speak, is left so rough, so rude, that the art seems to have faltered. But there is apparent to reflection the fact that the artist meant just this harsh exterior to remain, and that no grace of smoothness could have imparted her intention as it does. It is the soul of an abrupt, exalted New England woman that speaks in such brokenness. The range of all the poems is of the loftiest; and sometimes there is a kind of swelling lift, an almost boastful rise of feeling, which is really the spring of faith in them:

I never saw a moor,
I never saw the sea;
Yet know I how the heather looks,
And what a wave must be.

I never spoke with God,
Nor visited in heaven;
Yet certain am I of the spot
As if the chart were given.

There is a noble tenderness, too, in some of the pieces; a quaintness that does not discord with the highest solemnity:

I shall know why, when time is over,
And I have ceased to wonder why;
Christ will explain each separate anguish
In the fair school-room of the sky.

He will tell me what Peter promised,
And I, for wonder at his woe,
I shall forget the drop of anguish
That scalds me now, that scalds me now.

The companionship of human nature with inanimate nature is very close in certain of the poems; and we have never known the invisible and intangible ties binding all creation in one, so nearly touched as in them.

If nothing else had come out of our life but this strange poetry we should feel that in the work of Emily Dickinson, America, or New

England rather, had made a distinctive addition to the literature of the world, and could not be left out of any record of it; and the interesting and important thing is that this poetry is as characteristic of our life as our business enterprise, our political turmoil, our demagogism, our millionairism. "Listen!" says Mr. James McNeill Whistler in that "Ten o'Clock" lecture of his which must have made his hearers feel very much lectured indeed, not to say browbeaten,—"Listen! There never was an artistic period. There never was an art-loving nation." But there were moments and there were persons to whom art was dear, and Emily Dickinson was one of these persons, one of these moments in a national life, and she could as well happen in Amherst, Mass., as in Athens, Att.

This anonymous British reviewer of the first published collection of Emily Dickinson's poetry developed a point of view that many early readers of the poems held. For them, her "ignorance" of grammar and of the accepted conventions of poetry were both embarrassing and irreparable. Howells had viewed her irregularities perceptively and sympathetically, but this London reviewer, like Thomas Bailey Aldrich in Boston, saw only "bad poetry . . . divorced from meaning, from music, from grammar, from rhyme."

The Newest Poet

ANONYMOUS

"If nothing else had come out of our life but this strange poetry," says Mr. W. D. Howells in *Harper's Magazine,* "we should feel that in the work of Emily Dickinson, America, or New England rather, had made a distinctive addition to the literature of the world." Much more Mr. Howells has to say in favour of the newest poetry and the newest poet. Mr. Howells is a critic not always easy to please, and the world cannot but be interested in hearing what the strains of the Tenth Muse

From the *London Daily News,* January 2, 1891.

are like. As Mr. Howells justly says, "They will form something like an intrinsic experience with the understanding reader of them." This is exactly right. No experience in literature can be more intrinsic than this. The verses remind Mr. Howells of what might be written by "a Blake who had read Emerson who had read Blake," a statement so intrinsic that it quite takes the breath away. What is a Blake who had read Emerson who had read Blake? Is it at all like a Howells who had read Dickinson who had read Howells? Miss Dickinson "sometimes suggests Heine" as much as either Blake or Emerson. To other critics Miss Dickinson's numbers "suggest" a Walt Whitman who had read the Poet Close and attempted to blend with the German Hebrew. For example, here is a piece which Mr. Howells regards as a compound of Emerson, Heine, and Blake. Here it is:

I taste a liquor never brewed
   From tankards scooped in pearl;
Not all the vats upon the Rhine
   Yield such an alcohol.

"Alcohol" does not rhyme to pearl, but Miss Dickinson is not to be regarded as responsible for mere rhymes. Nor for grammar! It is literally impossible to understand whether she means that she tastes a liquor never brewed at all, or a liquor never brewed "from" tankards scooped in pearl. By "from" she may mean "in." Let us give her the benefit of the doubt, and she still writes utter nonsense. It is clearly impossible to scoop a tankard from pearl. The material is inadequate. Now, neither Blake, nor Mr. Emerson, nor Heine was an idiot. Miss Dickinson must bear her own poetic sins; she reminds us of no sane nor educated writer. Indeed, Mr. Howells himself repents and says, "These things are as wholly her own" as another masterpiece which follows. They are, indeed, and we apologize to the Poet Close.

Here is another example of the Newest Poetry from New England:

How many times those low feet staggered
Only the soldered mouth can tell.
Try! can you stir the awful rivet?
Try! can you lift the hasps of steel?

We could perhaps if we tried, but we cannot make sense out of balderdash. What are "low feet?" The words are meaningless. This remarkable composition ends thus:

Indolent housewife in daisies lain!

This is no more English than it is Coptic. "In Daisy's lane" might have a meaning. There might be a lane called after a lady whose *petit nom* was Daisy. But the conjectural emendation rests on a belief that the poet was as ignorant of spelling as of sense and grammar. If the poet meant "in daisies laid"—buried in daisies or under daisies—why not say so? "Laid" rhymes to "pane" (and a rhyme was wanted) quite as well as "pearl" rhymes to "alcohol." But Mr. Howells has been captivated by a minstrel who subdues grammar to rhyme, and puts even grammar before sense. "In the stanzas below," says Mr. Howells, "there is a still, solemn, rapt movement of the thought and music together that is of exquisite charm." Here are "the verses below," or a few of them; they are assuredly below contempt:

New feet within my garden go,
New fingers stir the sod,
A troubadour upon an elm
Betrays the solitude.

What in the world has a troubadour to do in New England? And why did he climb a tree? Or was he a bird? And how can solitude be betrayed by a troubadour, somewhere near Boston, in the foliage of an elm? "Touch often becomes clutch" in these poems, exclaims the admiring critic. Touch would be very welcome to become, not only "clutch," but sense, rhyme, and grammar, if it could. Mr. Howells admires

The notice to the startled grass,
That darkness is about to pass.

This is mere maundering. The grass would not be startled in the least, even if it was informed that darkness was not only "about to pass," but about to take high honours. According to the poet, a sacred Person whom we cannot name here

will explain each separate anguish
In the fair school room of the sky.

It were enough if Mr. Howells would explain each separate stanza.

Of course the idea occurs that Mr. Howells is only bantering; that he cannot really mean to praise this farrago of illiterate and uneducated sentiment. It is as far below the level of the Poet's Corner in a country newspaper as that is usually below Shakespeare. There are no words that can say how bad poetry may be when it is divorced from meaning, from music, from grammar, from rhyme; in brief, from articulate and intelligible speech. And Mr. Howells solemnly avers that this drivel is characteristic of American life!

The unlucky lady who produced these lines only once printed a poem while she was alive. "She never intended or allowed anything more from her pen to be printed in her lifetime." She did well, and far from regretting her resolution every person of sense will admire it. Many uneducated and incompetent persons get pleasure out of scribbling incoherences. These vaguely correspond to vague sentiments and vague emotions. There is no harm in the exercise, but there is a good deal of harm in publicly praising as excellent and typical poetry, the trash which every editor of a magazine receives in bales. If poetry exists it is by virtue of original, or at least of agreeable thought, musically and magically expressed. Poetry has been defined as "the best thought in the best words." The verses adored by Mr. Howells are conspicuously in the worst possible words, and the thought, as far as any thought can be detected, is usually either commonplace or absurd. The thoughts "take Colonel Higginson's breath away," Colonel Higginson being the editor of the poems. But where is the novelty of thought in

> Stroke the cool forehead, hot so often,
> Lift, if you can, the listless hair,
> Handle the adamantine fingers
> Never a thimble more shall wear.

Any reader of Byron's "He who hath bent him o'er the dead" will be familiar enough with such thought as this piece contains, and will be familiar with it in grammar. The pathos of the absence of thimble in mortality is perfectly legitimate, but not so novel as to warrant raptures. It is, in itself, a touching thing that a lady of extremely solitary habits should have solaced herself by writing a kind of verses; but to proclaim that such verses as we have quoted are poetry, and good poetry, is to be guilty of "the pathetic fallacy" in an original manner, and is to encourage many impossible poets.

MAURICE THOMPSON (1844–1901) served in the Confederate army and subsequently followed a career in civil engineering and law. In the 1880's he turned to writing and criticism, and in time exerted an important literary influence in the Midwest, especially as a stern opponent of the rising realism. For twelve years before his death he was literary editor of the *Independent*. Like others of his generation, Thompson regarded Emily Dickinson's poetry as, in a sense, partly successful in spite of itself, its shortcomings due to her neglect of the orthodoxies of prosody.

Miss Dickinson's Poems

MAURICE THOMPSON

In the "Poems of Miss Emily Dickinson" just published under the editorial care of Mabel Loomis Todd and T. W. Higginson, there is a strange mixture of rare individuality and originality; moreover, the touch of surprise here and there excites a novel reaction and sends a tingle through the imagination. Perhaps it ought to satisfy the critic when frequent draughts of genuine refreshment are to be had from a small volume of verses. Certainly there comes a dewy fragrant drop, if not a draught, at short intervals, while we read Miss Dickinson's curiously fragmental poetry. Here is song that has a classic suggestiveness, as of a strange fortunate deposit wherein precious jewels, gold and crystals water-clear, are jumbled with worthless clay and fragments of coarse rock. I am aware that the comparison may appear strained, but it will be found strikingly apt. Something primitive and rude set over against the subtlest refinement of culture makes Miss Dickinson's verses still more forcibly remind us of the haphazard arrangement of nature's mines. We might change the view so that we could compare these curious flowers of poesy with the fossils of ancient plants pressed in the grip of cold stone, save that the flowers live and wane and exhale delicate perfume and flaunt a whole rainbow of colors.

Colonel Higginson has written a most appreciative preface to the

From *America,* V (January 8, 1891), 425.

volume. He classes the poems with "The Poetry of the Portfolio"—the verse written for the satisfaction of the poet's own desire to write. This is another way of avoiding outright criticism, or it is a lack of insight. Miss Dickinson was a highly educated and exceptionally studious woman, the daughter of a "leading lawyer of Amherst," who was also the treasurer of Amherst College. Her limitations show plainly in her work and much study of Emerson has colored and shaped her vision; it has also cramped her methods of expression. It will not do to say that the "discipline of public criticism and the enforced conformity to accepted ways" could have broadened Miss Dickinson to the stature of a first-class poetical genius. Her lack was intrinsic and constitutional. Mere functional derangement of the organ of expression is curable; but here was organic lesion of the most unmistakable type. Her vision was clear and surprisingly accurate, but her touch was erratic and at frequent intervals nerveless, while her sense of completeness was singularly dull. She exaggerated the faults of Emerson's verse-style into absurdity. She rhymes *tell* and *still, book* and *think, own* and *young, denied* and *smiled, gate* and *mat, care* and *hour,* and so on into hundreds of the like, perhaps, with the singular misfortune of failing often just at the point where a perfect rhyme is absolutely necessary to complete the turn of grace or the point of lyrical surprise. Here are two examples of the former:

I taste a liquor never brewed
From tankards scooped in pearl;
Not all the vats upon the Rhine
Yield such an alcohol!

What fortitude the soul contains,
That it can so endure
The accent of a coming foot,
The opening of a door!

The rhyming of *pearl* with *alcohol* is ludicrous; but the syllable *dure* when set to match *door* cannot be received by any ear that is not hopelessly defective. The identical rhyme in the following stanza is preferable:

And nobody knows, so still it flows,
That any brook is there;

And yet your daily draught of life
Is daily drunken there.

Here is a striking example of a beautiful conceit marred almost to destruction by slip-shod rhyme:

As if some little Arctic flower,
Upon the polar hem,
Went wandering down the latitudes,
Until it puzzled came
To continents of summer,
To firmaments of sun,
To strange, bright crowds of flowers,
And birds of foreign tongue!

It gives one a thrill of vexation to be trifled with just on the horizon of what appears about to turn out a fine lyrical discovery. Look over the stanza last quoted and observe what a glimpse of paleontology it flashes and what a promise it makes of a memorable lyric setting for the migration of the flowers during the coming on of the great ice age. Not that the poet had this foremost in mind; but the suggestion had come out of geological reading and had been modernized and narrowed to suit the sudden flash of poetic vision. We see the conceit struggling for expression until it is almost strangled amidst such rhymes as *hem* with *came* and *sun* with *tongue*. The poet's sight is perfect; she sees a lyric limpid as a brook and prismatic as a bubble, but her modeling is almost fatally defective. What a heavy ear for accord! She seems to wander through the wilderness of phrase-possibilities only to choose with droll indiscretion at the critical moment. But even this faltering and halting expression has its fascination arising out of its utter freedom from affectation. Whatever else may be said of Miss Dickinson's verse there is no room for doubting the sincerity of its origin. Let me quote three stanzas of the poem "Renunciation"; they will show the extremes of blunder and felicity:

The sun, as common, went abroad.
The flowers, accustomed, blew,
As if no soul the solstice passed
That maketh all things new.

The time was scarce profaned by speech;
The symbol of a word

Was needless, as at sacrament
The wardrobe of our Lord.

Each was to each the sealed church,
Permitted to commune this time,
Lest we too awkward show
At supper of the Lamb.

The first and second of these stanzas are very near the line of absolute expression; the third has nothing in it to make it worthy of print. The surprise that the former led us to expect proves to be a sort of absurdity such as some person utterly without imagination or a feeling for music might treat us to. In a certain way these unaccountable discords serve to accentuate the beautiful snatches of melody with which they are so often associated. Occasionally the happy strokes follow the unhappy ones so as to give the effect of art. Thus:

New feet within my garden go,
  New fingers stir the sod;
A troubadour upon the elm
  Betrays the solitude.

New children play upon the green,
  New weary sleep below;
And still the pensive spring returns,
  And still the punctual snow!

How suggestive the two closing verses of each stanza! I have heard New England folk pronounce *Emma* as if it were written *Emmar* and *saw* like *sor;* can this account for the matching of *door* with *draw* in the following:

  Until the daffodil
Unties her yellow bonnet
  Beneath the village door,
Until the bees, from clover rows,
  Their hock and sherry draw.

I have called attention to these defects, and the book teems with them, for the purpose of showing that it was not mere lack of public criticism that caused Miss Dickinson to write such curious stuff as this, for example—

One dignity delays for all,
One mitred afternoon;
None can avoid this purple,
None evade this crown....

Departed to the judgment,
A mighty afternoon;
Great clouds like ushers leaning,
Creation looking on....

On this long storm the rainbow rose,
On this late morn the sun;
The clouds, like listless elephants,
Horizons straggled down....

Why could she not feel the inaptitude that forced her to murder art thus:

I lost a world the other day,
Has anybody found?
You'll know it by the row of stars
Around its forehead bound.

A rich man might not notice it;
Yet to my frugal eye
Of more esteem than ducats.
Oh, find it, sir, for me!

Here the first four lines are notably strong in the qualities of terseness, vigor and originality of thought and expression; and if the others had kept up the momentum the culmination must have been a strong shock of true poetic energy. Instead of doing this they drop below the commonplace. It is so all through the book; and yet no lover of poetry can read it without frequent starts of glad surprise and many lingerings over lines, phrases, stanzas, of the richest and most exquisitely original overflow from a nature incomparably individual and independent. To me it is like nothing else so much as it is like a crude translation of some freshly discovered Greek lyrical fragments, the spirit of which, not the art, has been perfectly caught by the translator. Miss Dickinson was a poet who (as Baudelaire described one), like an albatross, could not walk because her wings tripped her feet. If she held up the wing of thought, the wing of expression was sure to drag. Look at this curious conceit:

I asked no other thing,
No other was denied.
I offered being for it;
The mighty merchant smiled.

Brazil? He twirled a button,
Without a glance my way;
"But, madam, is there nothing else
That we can show to-day?"

A large part of the fascination of verse like this is generated by the friction of disappointment on delight. You are charmed with the thought and fretted by the lapses from intelligible expression. The following eight lines, with which the first part of the book closes, are suggestive of the limitation of a genius like Miss Dickinson's:

The brain within its groove
Runs evenly and true;
But let a splinter swerve,
'T were easier for you

To put the water back
When floods have slit the hills,
And scooped a turnpike for themselves,
And blotted out the mills.

In all my reading I have not found a more interesting book of verse; one with so many beauties almost buried in so many blemishes. The good things in it are like incomparable crystals set in ugly fragments of worthless stone.

The particular interest of this anonymous review is its effort to define more precisely than many of Emily Dickinson's detractors had, the problem of her "formlessness," the theoretical relation of form and substance. In alluding to Whitman, he shows his awareness—and distrust—of the growing tendency in the 1890's to acknowledge the possibility of various kinds of poetic form rather than to assume a single, absolute law for poetry.

Form and Substance

ANONYMOUS

"When a thought takes your breath away a lesson in grammar is an impertinence," remarks Mr. T. W. Higginson in his sympathetic introduction to the remarkable "Poems" of the late Miss Emily Dickinson, recently published. This is a happy if rhetorical way of restating the familiar contention that in all departments of art substance is more important than form. By this time anything that may be said *ex parte* on either side of this time-honored discussion is sure to seem a platitude. One thinks of Mill's felicitous tabling of the classics *vs.* the sciences question in education by the query: "Should a tailor make coats or trousers?" Or of the settlement, by a recent authority upon etiquette, of the great problem whether, passing each other in the street, the lady or the gentleman should bow first: "They should bow together," he decides. In irresponsible moments, however—that is to say in most moments—one is apt to have a preference due to the domination of his reflective powers by his temperament. And in the presence of these poems of Miss Dickinson I think a temperament of any sensitiveness must feel even an alternation of preferences—being inclined now to deem them, in virtue of their substance, superior to the ordinary restrictions of form, and now to lament the loss involved in a disregard of the advantages of form. Having one's breath taken away is a very agreeable sensation, but it is not the finest sensation of which we are susceptible; and instead of being grateful for it one is very apt to suffer annoyance at the perversity which is implied in a poet who, though capable of taking one's breath away, nevertheless

From *Scribner's Magazine,* IX (March, 1891), 395–96.

prefers to do so in arbitrary rather than in artistic fashion. Such a poet, one feels instinctively, should rise above wilfulness, whimsicality, the disposition to challenge and defy.

After all, what do we mean by "importance?" Would it not be fair to say that the term is a relative one to this extent, that as to the importance of any specific thing the contemporary judgment, and that of posterity, are almost sure to be at variance. And is it not true that from the nature of things the contemporary judgment lays most stress on substance, and that the "final" judgment is favorable to form? How many historic things of immense contemporary vogue seem insipid to us, whereas scarcely anything of great formal merit has been allowed to perish. Is there not an element of universality about perfection of form which significance of thought does not possess; or is not perfection more nearly attainable in form than it is in substance? And nothing is so preservative as perfection or any approach to it.

One thing is very certain—neglect of form involves the sacrifice of an element of positive attractiveness as well as offending positively by perverseness and eccentricity. Whether rhyme and rhythm, cadence, purity, flawlessness, melody are essential or not to poetry, the abandonment of the artistic quality which they imply is obviously a loss. "The first indispensable faculty of a singer is ability to sing," exclaims Mr. Swinburne with his usual peremptoriness in his essay on Collins. And all poetry—it may be conceded to him, in spite of the notorious overweighting of his own thought by his musical quality—has at least a lyric element, though, of course, it does not all demand the "lyric cry." Formlessness is the antithesis of art, and so far as poetry is formless it loses that immensely attractive interest which is purely aesthetic. It not merely offends by perversely ignoring the conventionally established though rationally evolved and soundly based rules of the game it purports to play, but in announcing thus, boldly, its independence of any aesthetic, any sensuous, interest, it puts a severe strain on the quality of its own substance—handicaps it in most dangerous fashion instead of giving it that aid and furtherance which the best substance is sure to need. If, as in Miss Dickinson's case, there be occasionally a subtle but essential order in what, superficially, seems chaotic, it may legitimately be maintained that to lay any stress on this is merely to argue against conventionality and not at all in favor of amorphousness. It is simply to assert the elasticity of orchestration and emphasize its range—to exalt the value of new forms over the old. And it is curious to note how prone are all apologists for formlessness, including Mr. Higginson in the present instance, and the admirers of Walt Whitman, *passim,* for example, to insist that what to the convention-steeped sense appears amorphous is in reality the very acme of form. Singularly enough, Mr. Higginson concludes his introduction to these poems by citing a sentence of Mr. Ruskin in favor of "thought" as opposed to "workmanship." Was there ever so striking an example as Mr. Ruskin of what "workmanship" has done even for the most *saugrenu* thought?

Scholar, poet, historian, journalist, and novelist, ANDREW LANG (1844–1912) valued himself most as an anthropologist. His *Custom and Myth* (1884), *Myth, Ritual, and Religion* (1887; 1894), and *The Making of Religion* (1898) involved him in much controversy, but his contribution to modern learning in this field was substantial. He translated Homer's *Odyssey* (1879), with S. H. Butcher, and the *Iliad* (1883), with W. Leaf and E. Myers. His training in classical literary scholarship and his dislike of Howells' advocacy of the "new realism" probably help to account for his uncompromising dismissal of Emily Dickinson's poetry.

Some American Poets

ANDREW LANG

I read somewhere, lately, that the Americans possess, at present, more minor poets, and better minor poets, than we can boast in England. The phrase "minor poet" is disliked by minstrels, and here let it be taken to denote merely poets who have not yet a recognized national fame, like Lord Tennyson with us and Mr. Whittier in America. Whether, in the larger and less recognized class, we have not at least as many poets to show as the States is a question of statistics. But it is very probable that the Western singers, whether better than ours or not, are, at all events, different from ours, and therefore, so far, interesting.

The works of four new Transatlantic poets lie beside me.* *Place aux*

* The four poets reviewed were Emily Dickinson, *Poems* (Boston: Roberts, 1890); Thomas Bailey Aldrich, *The Sister's Tragedy* (New York: Macmillan, 1890); *Poems of Sidney Lanier,* edited by his wife; Eugene Field, *Little Book of Western Verse* (New York: Scribner's Sons). Of Aldrich, Lang concludes: "... Almost everyone who cares

dames. Let us take, first, "Poems" by the late Miss Emily Dickinson. This is certainly a very curious little book. It has already reached its fourth edition, partly, no doubt, because Mr. Howells praised it very highly. I cannot go nearly so far as Mr. Howells, because, if poetry is to exist at all, it really must have form and grammar, and must rhyme when it professes to rhyme. The wisdom of the ages and the nature of man insist on so much. We may be told that Democracy does not care, any more than the Emperor did, for grammar. But even if Democracy overleaps itself and lands in savagery again, I believe that our savage successors will, though unconsciously, make their poems grammatical. Savages do not use bad grammar in their own conversation or in their artless compositions. That is a fault of defective civilizations. Miss Dickinson, who died lately at the age of fifty-six, was a recluse, dwelling in Amherst, a town of Massachusetts. She did not write for publication. Her friends have produced her work. Sometimes it is as bad as this—

Angels' breathless ballot
Lingers to record thee;
Imps in eager caucus
Raffle for my soul.

This, of course, is mere nonsense. What is a "breathless ballot"? How can a ballot record anything, and how can it "linger" in recording, especially if it is in such a hurry as to be breathless? Indeed, one turns over Miss Dickinson's book with a puzzled feeling that there was poetry in her subconscious, but that it never became explicit. One might as well seek for an air in the notes of a bird as for articulate and sustained poetry here. One piece begins—

This is the land the sunset washes
These are the banks of the Yellow Sea.

And here is rhythm and the large sense of evening air—

Where it rose, or whither it rushes,
These are the Western mystery.

Night after night her purple traffic
Strews the landing with opal bales;

for modern verse will take pleasure in that of Mr. Aldrich"; of Lanier, he also thinks rather favorably—"his poems, to people who buy poetry still, are worth buying"; and Field he praises as "... more of a poet than he cares to acknowledge."

From the *Illustrated London News,* XCVIII (March 7, 1891), 307.

Merchantmen poise upon horizons,
Dip and vanish with fairy sails.

The second verse is not very easy to construe, but there was poetry in the writer. This, again, has the true lyrical note—

I never saw a moor,
I never saw the sea,
Yet know I how the heather looks,
And what a wave must be.

There is not much else that can be quoted without bringing in the fantastic, irresponsible note of a poet who has her own audience, and had constructed her own individual "Ars Poetica." The words of Mr. Aldrich in "The Sister's Tragedy" (Macmillan) might have been written about Miss Dickinson—

A twilight poet groping quite alone,
Belated in a sphere where every nest
Is emptied of its music and its wings.

Much less harsh than Andrew Lang, this British reviewer, like many in America, sensed Miss Dickinson's unmistakable originality and flashes of genius. Though he regretted "the uneducated and illiterate character" of some of her verses, his final judgment is sympathetic: the "fair-minded reader" will see in her no mere mechanical versifier.

A Poet

ANONYMOUS

The poems of Miss Emily Dickinson (who has hitherto been known to Englishmen chiefly if not only by some very injudicious praise of the kind usual with Mr. Howells) are posthumously published, and

From the *Saturday Review,* LXXII (September 5, 1891), 279. A review of *Poems* by Emily Dickinson (London: Osgood, McIlvaine, & Co.).

from the short preface written by her sympathetic and friendly editor we learn some interesting facts of her life. She appears never to have travelled, or, indeed, left the house of her father in Amherst, Mass., where she led the life of an absolute recluse, and only appeared in society at a yearly reception given by her father to his friends. We are told that she wrote verses abundantly, but "absolutely without the thought of publication, and solely by way of expression of the writer's own mind." The editor prepares us for the want of form and polish in her poems, but expects us to regard them as "poetry torn up from the roots, with rain and dew and earth still clinging to them, giving a freshness and a fragrance not otherwise to be conveyed." A merit is here implied in their very imperfections as producing the effect of poetry drawn from an absolutely natural unconventional source. We very much doubt, however, whether this conclusion may be fairly adduced from the uneducated and illiterate character of some of these verses, although we fully recognize in them the unmistakable touch of a true poet. In these days considerable mastery over form in poetry is not uncommon, but in our minor poets it is rare indeed to find much original thought, or a strongly marked individuality. For this reason it is, perhaps, difficult not to overvalue these qualities, when we find them, as in Miss Dickinson, separated from any merits of form. We continually see the thoughts of prose put into verse, but, while some of the poems in the present volume can scarcely be described as in verse at all, they almost all contain a genuinely poetical thought, or image, or feeling. Miss Dickinson's chief characteristics are, first, a faculty for seizing the impression or feelings of the moment, and fixing them with rare force and accuracy; secondly, a vividness of imagery, which impresses the reader as thoroughly unconventional, and shows considerable imaginative power. The following quotation is a fair specimen of some of the most striking poems in the book:—

Exultation is the going
Of an inland soul to sea—
Past the houses, past the headlands,
Into deep eternity!

Bred as we, among the mountains,
Can the sailor understand
The divine intoxication
Of the first league out from land?

The editor suggests a comparison between the poems of this writer and those of William Blake; but, beyond the fact that they are both quite indifferent to the technical rules of art, the comparison is not very far-reaching. Miss Dickinson possesses little of that lyrical faculty to which Blake owes his reputation; but, on the other hand, she is gifted with a far saner mind. Her poems, however, may be said to be distinctively American in their peculiarities, and occasionally call to mind the verses of Emerson. The editor with his unfailing sympathy tells us that, "though curiously indifferent to all conventional rules," she yet had "a rigorous literary standard of her own, and often altered a word many times to suit an ear which had its own tenacious fastidiousness." Some of the poems, however, seem destitute of any metre whatever, the lines do not scan, the rhymes are arbitrarily thrown in or left out, in accordance with no fixed system, and grammar and even good taste are sometimes only conspicuous by their absence. But in some of her roughest poems there is still an idea which forces the reader to attend to its meaning, and impresses him, in spite of the irritation he may feel at the form. Take, for instance, the little poem on "The Mystery of Pain":—

Pain has an element of blank;
  It cannot recollect
When it began, or if there were
  A day when it was not.

It has no future but itself,
  Its infinite realms contain
Its past, enlightened to perceive
  New periods of pain.

These poems for the most part are of a purely reflective character; but a few, such as the two on shipwreck, show considerable descriptive and emotional power. Moreover, though never perfectly finished or satisfactory in form, some of them are conceived in a lyrical way, and are not without music. Take this verse, for instance:—

Night after night her purple traffic
  Strews the landing with opal bales;
Merchantmen poise upon horizons,
  Dip, and vanish with fairy sails.

In many of the poems there is a deep underlying sense of the mystery of existence, a yearning to set the soul free, and to know the "why" of things. Death is a subject constantly harped upon, either from the point of view of the dying, or of those who watch the departure of others to that "undiscovered country, from whose bourn no traveller returns." The writer dwells on the final pomp and ceremony which attends the poor as well as the rich when they leave this world; the equality of death; the sense that the finite ended is the infinite begun; the agonizing and absorbing watchfulness over life that is ebbing, and then the sudden stillness, the "awful leisure," that succeeds when the end has come and the watchers can do no more. There is much that is very striking in these poems, they reveal great depth of feeling, and the tone of them, though melancholy, is not morbid. In some there is a kind of exultation and a concentrated force of expression which is really remarkable:—

> At last to be identified!
> At last, the lamps upon thy side,
> The rest of life to see!
> Past midnight, past the morning star!
> Past sunrise! Ah! what leagues there are
> Between our feet and day!

The little volume contains much to exercise the satire and scorn of critics. The sublime in Miss Dickinson's poems comes sometimes dangerously near to the ridiculous; but any fair-minded reader will, nevertheless, acknowledge that there is something in her poems which cannot be found in the mechanical productions of mere verse-writers, and that the editor is not far wrong when he says that her poetry contains "flashes of wholly original and profound insight into nature and life, words and phrases exhibiting an extraordinary vividness of descriptive and imaginative power, yet often set in a seemingly whimsical, or even rugged, frame."

After the death of Emily Dickinson in 1886, her sister Lavinia appealed to MABEL LOOMIS TODD (1857–1932), neighbor of the Dickinson family and wife of a young professor of astronomy at Amherst, to help prepare the poet's manuscripts for publication. Collaborating with Thomas Wentworth Higginson, Mrs. Todd worked with great patience and devotion to transcribe and arrange the two series of poems published in 1890 and 1891. Working independently, Mrs. Todd edited two volumes of Miss Dickinson's letters (1894) and a third volume of poems (1896). But her claim that no changes "not absolutely inevitable" were made in the original manuscripts of the poems has been disproved by the publication of Millicent Todd Bingham's *Ancestors' Brocades: The Literary Debut of Emily Dickinson* (1945) and *The Poems of Emily Dickinson,* edited by Thomas H. Johnson (1955).

Preface to Poems: Second Series *(1891)*

MABEL LOOMIS TODD

The eagerness with which the first volume of Emily Dickinson's poems has been read shows very clearly that all our alleged modern artificiality does not prevent a prompt appreciation of the qualities of directness and simplicity in approaching the greatest themes,—life and love and death. That "irresistible needle-touch," as one of her best critics has called it, piercing at once the very core of a thought, has found a response as wide and sympathetic as it has been unexpected even to those who knew best her compelling power. This second volume, while open to the same criticism as to form with its predecessor, shows also the same shining beauties.

Although Emily Dickinson had been in the habit of sending occasional poems to friends and correspondents, the full extent of her writing was by no means imagined by them. Her friend "H. H." must at least have suspected, for in a letter dated 5th September, 1884, she wrote:—

My Dear Friend,—What portfolios full of verses you must have! It is a cruel wrong to your "day and generation" that you will not give them light.

If such a thing should happen as that I should outlive you, I wish you would make me your literary legatee and executor. Surely after you are what is called "dead" you will be willing that the poor ghosts you have left behind should be cheered and pleased by your verses, will you not? You ought to be. I do not think we have a right to withhold from the world a word or a thought any more than a *deed* which might help a single soul....

Truly yours,
Helen Jackson

The "portfolios" were found, shortly after Emily Dickinson's death, by her sister and only surviving housemate. Most of the poems had been carefully copied on sheets of notepaper, and tied in little fascicules, each of six or eight sheets. While many of them bear evidence of having been thrown off at white heat, still more had received thoughtful revision. There is the frequent addition of rather perplexing footnotes, affording large choice of words and phrases. And in the copies which she sent to friends, sometimes one form, sometimes another, is found to have been used. Without important exception, her friends have generously placed at the disposal of the Editors any poems they had received from her; and these have given the obvious advantage of comparison among several renderings of the same verse.

To what further rigorous pruning her verses would have been subjected had she published them herself, we cannot know. They should be regarded in many cases as merely the first strong and suggestive sketches of an artist, intended to be embodied at some time in the finished picture.

Emily Dickinson appears to have written her first poems in the winter of 1862. In a letter to one of the present Editors the April following, she says, "I made no verse, but one or two, until this winter."

The handwriting was at first somewhat like the delicate, running Italian hand of our elder gentlewomen; but as she advanced in breadth of thought, it grew bolder and more abrupt, until in her latest years each letter stood distinct and separate from its fellows. In most of her poems, particularly the later ones, everything by way of punctuation was discarded, except numerous dashes; and all important words began with capitals. The effect of a page of her more recent manuscript is exceedingly quaint and strong. The facsimile given in the present volume is from one of the earlier transition periods. Although there is nowhere a date, the handwriting makes it possible to arrange the poems with general chronologic accuracy.

As a rule, the verses were without titles; but "A Country Burial," "A Thunder-Storm," "The Humming-Bird," and a few others were named by their author, frequently at the end,—sometimes only in the accompanying note, if sent to a friend.

The variation of readings, with the fact that she often wrote in pencil and not always clearly, have at times thrown a good deal of responsibility upon her Editors. But all interference not absolutely inevitable has been avoided. The very roughness of her own rendering is part of herself, and not lightly to be touched; for it seems in many cases that she intentionally avoided the smoother and more usual rhymes.

Like impressionist pictures, or Wagner's rugged music, the very absence of conventional form challenges attention. In Emily Dickinson's exacting hands, the especial, intrinsic fitness of a particular order of words might not be sacrificed to anything virtually extrinsic; and her verses all show a strange cadence of inner rhythmical music. Lines are always daringly constructed, and the "thought-rhyme" appears frequently,—appealing, indeed, to an unrecognized sense more elusive than hearing.

Emily Dickinson scrutinized everything with clear-eyed frankness. Every subject was proper ground for legitimate study, even the sombre facts of death and burial, and the unknown life beyond. She touches these themes sometimes lightly, sometimes almost humorously, more often with weird and peculiar power; but she is never by any chance frivolous or trivial. And while, as one critic has said, she may exhibit toward God "an Emersonian self-possession," it was because she looked upon all life with a candor as unprejudiced as it is rare.

She had tried society and the world, and found them lacking. She was not an invalid, and she lived in seclusion from no love-disappointment. Her life was the normal blossoming of a nature introspective to a high degree, whose best thought could not exist in pretence.

Storm, wind, the wild March sky, sunsets and dawns; the birds and bees, butterflies and flowers of her garden, with a few trusted human friends, were sufficient companionship. The coming of the first robin was a jubilee beyond crowning of monarch or birthday of pope; the first red leaf hurrying through "the altered air," an epoch. Immortality was close about her; and while never morbid or melancholy, she lived in its presence.

The enthusiasm for Emily Dickinson reflected in most parts of this Chicago review is, again, tempered by the writer's sense of the poet's imperfections of form. The final sentence here—"Artless, imperfect as they are, these verses have a freshness that is only too rare in our self-conscious age"—recalls another Midwesterner, Maurice Thompson, on Emily Dickinson.

Second Series of the Poems by Emily Dickinson

ANONYMOUS

This second series of the poems of Emily Dickinson, compiled by her literary administrators, Mr. Thomas Wentworth Higginson and Mrs. Mabel Loomis Todd, will revive public interest in the personality of that remarkable woman. Of her appearance, habits, and tastes, of the few events in her pure and sequestered life, we already knew the little there was to be told. In one of her letters to Mr. Higginson—those quaint, shy effusions, of which the unconventionality is tempered by a certain primness—she says of herself: "I am small, like the wren, and my hair is bold, like the chestnut bur, and my eyes like the sherry in the glass that the guest leaves." Her own language, again, can best describe the timidity and love of solitude that impelled her to a life of almost conventual seclusion. "You ask of my companions. Hills, sir, and the sundown, and a dog large as myself that my father bought me. They are better than [human] beings because they know, but do not tell; and the noise in the pool at noon excels my piano." "[You speak] of shunning men and women. They talk of hallowed things aloud and embarrass my dog. He and I don't object to them if they'll exist their side." "I sing, as the boy does of the burying-ground, because I am afraid." In contrast with these qualities she revealed an arch and playful humor, together with a critical insight of the most thorough-going frankness. To a shyness that shrank at times from the gaze of a flower she united an audacity that assumed to treat with deity on equal terms. A childlike simplicity and directness added a final charm to this most unworldly of souls.

From the *Chicago Tribune*, December 12, 1891.

It is this childlike element, we think, that appeals most strongly to the reader of her poems. One occasionally finds the same difficulty in following the irregular hop-step-and-jump of her thought as in attempting to keep pace with the skipping mental gait of an intelligent child. Her wayward and irresponsible fancy describes every sort of abrupt angle and eccentric curve, but naturally and without effort. This naturalness distinguishes her work from that of Quarles and his fellows, whose far-fetched conceits are so lacking in spontaneity. Of the coquetry and self-consciousness that mar the work of so many poets one never sees a trace; she composes with her eye upon her object and seeks to please herself alone. Her wonderful acuteness and her uncompromising naturalism are not the effect of culture, but a part of her childhood's unforfeited inheritance. She has a child's ignorance of the world, a child's imagination and love of color. One smiles at the significance with which she invests the idea of an Earl; to be "Duke of Exeter"—ah, that is a too, too daring flight! How like a child's fancy is this, which describes the "clear shining after rain":

> The boldest stole out of his covert,
> To see if time was there;
> Nature was in her beryl apron,
> Mixing fresher air.

One compares her with Emerson, with Scott's "Pet Marjorie," and with Blake, the English painter-poet; but, after all, she is just herself, the solitary example of a floral species as yet unclassified.

Of these characteristics the effect is intensified by the eccentricities of her style. Her verse is often grammatically obscure; she does not hesitate to employ a word in a sense which is foreign to it; the metaphysical quips and fetches in which she indulges are sometimes too fine-spun to be intelligible. Her rhythm, too, is frequently irregular, though never devoid of a certain music; and her numerous false rhymes are unpardonable. Rhymed, unrhymed, and imperfectly rhymed stanzas occur in the same poem, conforming to no rule but that of the writer's caprice. Mrs. Todd speaks of the "thought-rhymes" which appear in her friend's work, "appealing to an unrecognized sense more elusive than hearing." If we understand the term aright, the "thought-rhyme" is as often absent as present in these irregular stanzas; at any rate, one cannot go jumping from word-rhymes to thought-rhymes and back again, all in the same piece. Mrs. Todd should have taken stronger ground. We are willing to condone these technical offenses because the offender is Emily Dickinson. An Emily who was willing to conform to rules, to suppress her individuality, and to follow the beaten track, would not have been the Emily Dickinson of our admiration. Her faults were merely the defects of her qualities: her originality and her eccentricity were fostered by the same conditions. "When I try to organize," she says of herself, "my little force explodes and leaves me bare and charred." Her imperfections, then, are the price of her charm, and a price we are only too ready to pay.

Of the quality of these poems it is difficult to give an idea by the aid of selections. Their effect is cumulative; then, too, the emotional element is less conspicuous than the esthetic, the esthetic less than the intellectual. Her landscape studies are, perhaps, the most pictorially effective, especially the storm scenes. Here is a pretty sketch.

APRIL

An altered look about the hills;
A Tyrian light the village fills;
A wider sunrise in the dawn;
A deeper twilight on the lawn;
A print of a vermillion foot;
A purple finger on the slope;
A flippant fly upon the pane;
A spider at his trade again;
An added strut in chanticleer;
An ax shrill ringing in the woods;
Fern odors on untraveled roads—
All this, and more I cannot tell,
A furtive look you know as well,
And Nicodemus' mystery
Receives its annual reply.

With all the fine sympathy with nature and its teeming life which her poems of this class display, we do not regard them as thoroughly characteristic of the writer's genius. The great mysteries of existence touch her with a keener thrill. What plaintiveness in a cry like this:

Let down the bars, O Death!
The tired flocks come in
Whose bleating ceases to repeat,
Whose wandering is done.

Thine is the stillest night,
Thine the securest fold;
Too near thou art for seeking thee,
Too tender to be told.

Or in this other:

At least to pray is left, is left,
O Jesus! in the air
I know not which thy chamber is—
I'm knocking everywhere.

Thou stirrest earthquake in the South,
And maelstrom in the sea;
Say, Jesus Christ of Nazareth,
Hast thou no arm for me?

The low key of the ensuing poem is characteristic:

Their height in heaven comforts not,
Their glory naught to me;
'Twas best imperfect, as it was;
I'm finite, I can't see.

The house of Supposition,
The glimmering frontier
That skirts the acres of Perhaps,
To me shows insecure.

The wealth I had contented me;
If 'twas a meaner size,
Then I had counted it until
It pleased my narrow eyes

Better than larger values,
However true their show;
This timid life of evidence
Keeps pleading, "I don't know."

The next is the child of a brighter mood:

Pompless no life can pass away;
The lowliest career
To the same pageant wends its way
As that exalted here.

How cordial is the mystery!
The hospitable pall

A "this way!" beckons spaciously,
A miracle for all!

And this has a sweet, sympathetic note:

To learn the transport by the pain,
As blind men learn the sun;
To die of thirst suspecting
That brooks in meadows run;

To stay the homesick, homesick feet
Upon a foreign shore
Haunted by native lands the while
And blue, beloved air—

This is the sovereign anguish,
This, the signal woe!
These are the patient laureates
Whose voices, trained below,

Ascend in ceaseless carol,
Inaudible, indeed,
To us, the duller scholars
Of the mysterious bard.

One more quotation, and we have done:

The nearest dream recedes, unrealized.
The heaven we chase
Like the June bee
Before the school boy
Invites the race;
Stoops to an easy clover—
Dips—evades—teases—deploys;
Then to the royal clouds
Lifts his light pinnace
Heedless of the boy
Staring, bewildered, at the mocking sky.

Homesick for steadfast honey;
Ah! the bee flies not
That brews that rare variety.

Artless, imperfect as they are, these verses have a freshness that is only too rare in our self-conscious age.

This review of the second volume of Emily Dickinson's poems said nothing substantially new about Miss Dickinson's qualities or defects, but it was the occasion for Francis Stoddard's specific answer to the recurring charge that the poems lacked form.

Recent Poetry: Emily Dickinson

ANONYMOUS

One year ago a volume of curiously formless poems, revealing an unusual quality of grasp and insight and written by a woman who had spent her life in seclusion, was edited by Col. T. W. Higginson and Mrs. Mabel Loomis Todd, two of the author's friends. It was well received by the reviewers, who recognized the writer's unusualness and originality of thought, and it has since gone through several editions, proving that a great many persons care comparatively little for the form of expression in poetry so long as the thoughts expressed are startling, eccentric and new. The success of that volume has led the editors to prepare another one containing a quantity of the same sort of strange verse in which are to be found the same beauties and same faults as were noticed in its predecessor. There are many things in *Poems: Second Series,* which, as somebody has said of the former verses, "take away one's breath." But one does not wish to have one's breath taken away entirely. A thought may be striking, but the stroke should not be fatal. After reading two volumes of Miss Dickinson's poems one gets exhausted, and a healthy mind begins to fear paralysis. There is too much of the same thing in them—morbid feeling, jerky and disjointed writing, and occasional faults of grammar. We do not agree with Colonel Higginson that in considering these poems, "a lesson on grammar seems an impertinence"; it is their lack of grammatical correctness and their absolute formlessness which keeps them almost outside the pale of poetry. Nevertheless, to those who liked

From *The Critic,* XVI (December 19, 1891), 346.

the first book we commend the second, even though it does contain a stanza like this:—

> A few incisive mornings
> A few ascetic eves,—
> Gone Mr. Bryant's golden-rod,
> And Mr. Thomson's sheaves.

It is Mrs. Todd who writes the preface. In it we are told of the author that "she had tried society and the world, and found them lacking. ... Her life was the normal blossoming of a nature introspective to a high degree, whose best thought could not exist in pretence."

FRANCIS H. STODDARD (1847–1936) was a professor of English at New York University. His letter to *The Critic* answers the reviewer who had made the usual complaints about Emily Dickinson's flawed technique. His defense of her poetic form employs a method of analysis unusual in 1892, but suggesting the critical approach of the "New Criticism" of the 1940's. It is ironic, perhaps, that Stoddard looks backward for his justification, calling the form he sees in her "mediaeval."

Technique in Emily Dickinson's Poems

To the Editors of *The Critic*:—

In your issue of Dec. 19 an evidently competent reviewer refers to the first volume of Miss Dickinson's poems, issued a year ago, as a "volume of curiously formless poems," and suggests that the fact of the issuance of several editions proves "that a great many persons care little for the form of expression in poetry so long as the thoughts expressed are startling, eccentric and new." In the same review the critic says of the two volumes taken together that "their absolute formlessness keeps them almost outside the pale of poetry." The thought here seems to be that real poetry must have perfection of technique, must have metrical and grammatical finish: the poems of Emily Dickinson do

From *The Critic,* XX (January 9, 1892), 24–25.

not have such finish; hence these verses are almost out of the pale of poetry. The major premise here set down has not been attacked of late. The minor one is not so easily disposed of. For Miss Dickinson's poems may be formless, or they may be worded to so fine and subtle a device that they seem formless, just as the spectrum of a far-off star may seem blankness until examined with a lens of especial power. I wish to examine one poem of Miss Dickinson's, taken almost at random, and search for the fine lines of the spectrum. For such example I take this poem:—

I died for beauty, but was scarce
Adjusted in the tomb,
When one who died for truth was lain
In an adjoining room.

He questioned, softly, why I failed?
"For beauty," I replied.
"And I for truth,—the two are one;
We brethren are," he said.

And so as kinsmen met a night,
We talked between the rooms,
Until the moss had reached our lips,
And covered up our names.

Now the notion here is the notion of the unity of truth and beauty. If harmony with the thought is to prevail in the verse we should expect a closely parallel structure with a figure in dual accent—i.e., based upon two factors. Such a figure we get:—

I díed for beautý, but was scarce
Adjústed in the tómb,
When one who díed for trúth was lain
In an adjóining róom.

Two pairs of lines, each with two accents, the similar words being matched in pairs—*justed* : *joining, died* : *died, tomb* : *room. Beauty* and *truth* do not perfectly match, of course, because not yet proved to be one in nature. These exact correspondences would produce mechanical regularity, overprove the proposition by overemphasizing the innate notion of harmony, if care were not taken. So care is taken to contrast the positions of the members of the separate pairs.

That is, in the first line, the slurred words *but was scarce* are at the end, while in the corresponding line the slurred words *when one who* are at the beginning. Similarly, the slurred words *in the* in the second line are contrasted with the slurred words *in an* in the fourth line.

In the second stanza we have a more perfectly parallel figure, in accord with the development of the notion of harmony between truth and beauty.

> He questionéd, softlý, whý I failéd?
> "For beautý," I repliéd.
> "And Í—for trúth—the twó are óne,
> We brethrén are," he saíd.

Almost a formal balancing, but with a suggestion of relief; as, for example, in the harmonic echo of *he questioned,* in the opening line, with *We brethren,* in the closing line, suggesting a recurrence of the first verse motive.

In the last verse comes the deeper verity that though truth and beauty are one spiritually, they can never be at one in this world. So at the close the pattern changes and together with the hint of the attainment of perfect harmony we have a reversion both in form and tone. It is a suggestion of the death reversion which springs the thought to a harmony more subtle and remote.

> And so as kinsmén met a níght,
> We talkéd betwéen the rooms,
> Until the móss had reached our lipś
> And coveréd up our namés.

The rhyme changes to alliteration which is beginning-rhyme instead of end-rhyme—*night* : *names*. Our earthly names are lost in the endless night of death; ourselves, at one with each other, at one with truth and beauty, entered into the endless day of beauty and of truth.

I submit that such art as this may be subtle and mediaeval, but it is not formlessness.

FRANCIS H. STODDARD.

University of the City of New York.

THOMAS BAILEY ALDRICH (1836–1907), poet and novelist in the genteel tradition, succeeded Howells as editor of the *Atlantic Monthly* in 1881. While his interests extended to many concerns besides literature, Aldrich's major vocation was belles lettres. The reasons for his rejection of Miss Dickinson's poetry were standard at the time, but coming as they did from the *Atlantic Monthly,* they were specially influential. The divergence of opinion between the sympathetic Howells and the derisive Aldrich, both recognized arbiters of literary taste, emphasizes the mixed reception of Emily Dickinson in the 1890's.

In Re Emily Dickinson

THOMAS BAILEY ALDRICH

The English critic who said of Miss Emily Dickinson that she might have become a fifth-rate poet "if she had only mastered the rudiments of grammar and gone into metrical training for about fifteen years,"—the rather candid English critic who said this somewhat overstated his case. If Miss Dickinson had undergone the austere curriculum indicated, she would, I am sure, have become an admirable lyric poet of the second magnitude. In the first volume of her poetical chaos is a little poem which needs only slight revision in the initial stanza in order to make it worthy of ranking with some of the odd swallow flights in Heine's lyrical *intermezzo.* I have ventured to desecrate this stanza by tossing a rhyme into it, as the other stanzas happened to rhyme, and here print the lyric, hoping the reader will not accuse me of overvaluing it:

I taste a liquor never brewed
In vats upon the Rhine;
No tankard ever held a draught
Of alcohol like mine.

Inebriate of air am I,
And debauchee of dew,

From the *Atlantic Monthly,* LXIX (January, 1892), 143–44. Reprinted, with minor revisions, as "Un Poète Manqué" in *Ponkapog Papers* (1903).

Reeling, through endless summer days,
From inns of molten blue.

When landlords turn the drunken bee
Out of the Foxglove's door,
When butterflies renounce their drams,
I shall but drink the more!

Till seraphs swing their snowy caps
And saints to windows run,
To see the little tippler
Leaning against the sun!

Certainly those inns of molten blue, and that disreputable honey-gatherer who got himself turned out-of-doors at the sign of the Foxglove, are very taking matters. I know of more important things that interest me less. There are three or four bits of this kind in Miss Dickinson's book; but for the most part the ideas totter and toddle, not having learned to walk. In spite of this, several of the quatrains are curiously touching, they have such a pathetic air of yearning to be poems.

It is plain that Miss Dickinson possessed an extremely unconventional and grotesque fancy. She was deeply tinged by the mysticism of Blake, and strongly influenced by the mannerism of Emerson. The very way she tied her bonnetstrings, preparatory to one of her nunlike walks in her claustral garden, must have been Emersonian. She had much fancy of a queer sort, but only, as it appears to me, intermittent flashes of imagination. I fail to detect in her work any of that profound thought which her editor professes to discover in it. The phenomenal insight, I am inclined to believe, exists only in his partiality; for whenever a woman poet is in question Mr. Higginson always puts on his rose-colored spectacles. This is being chivalrous; but the invariable result is not clear vision. That Miss Dickinson's whimsical memoranda have a certain something which, for want of a more precise name, we term *quality* is not to be denied except by the unconvertible heathen who are not worth conversion. But the incoherence and formlessness of her—I don't know how to designate them—versicles are fatal. Sydney Smith, or some other humorist, mentions a person whose bump of veneration was so inadequately developed as to permit him to damn the equator if he wanted to. This certainly established a precedent for independence; but an eccentric, dreamy, half-educated recluse in an out-of-the-way New England village (or anywhere else) cannot with impunity set at defiance the laws of gravitation and grammar. In his charming preface to Miss Dickinson's collection, Mr. Higginson insidiously remarks: "After all, when a thought takes one's breath away, a lesson on grammar seems an impertinence." But an ungrammatical thought does not, as a general thing, take one's breath away, except in a sense the reverse of flattering. Touching this matter of mere technique Mr. Ruskin has a word to say (it appears that he said it "In his earlier and better days"), and Mr. Higginson quotes it: "No weight, nor mass, nor beauty of execution can outweigh one grain or fragment of thought." This is a proposition to which one would cordially subscribe, if it were not so intemperately stated. A suggestive commentary on Mr. Ruskin's impressive dictum is furnished by the fact that Mr. Ruskin has lately published a volume of the most tedious verse that has been printed in this century. The substance of it is weighty enough, but the workmanship lacks just that touch which distinguishes the artist from the bungler,—the touch which Mr. Ruskin seems not to have much regarded either in his later or "in his earlier and better days."

If Miss Dickinson's *disjecta membra* are poems, then Shakespeare's prolonged imposition should be exposed without further loss of time, and Lord Tennyson ought to be advised of the error of his ways before it is too late. But I do not hold the situation to be so desperate. Miss Dickinson's versicles have a queerness and a quaintness that have stirred a momentary curiosity in emotional bosoms. Oblivion lingers in the immediate neighborhood.

Born in Ironton, Connecticut, and educated at Vassar, MARY AUGUSTA JORDAN (1855–1941) taught English at Smith College from 1884 until her retirement in 1921. Miss Jordan's review of the two-volume collection of Emily Dickinson's letters (1894) is remarkably free of the apologies and condemnations to be found in much criticism of Emily Dickinson's poems in the 1890's. Emphasizing the creative integrity of Emily Dickinson's life, her poems, and her letters, Miss Jordan anticipates some twentieth-century views of the poet.

Emily Dickinson's Letters

MARY AUGUSTA JORDAN

These letters begin in reasonable conformity to the principles of the polite letter-writer. By degrees date, address, formal structure drop off or are developed away. At all events, the last of the periods into which the editor divides the letters holds only notes, whose structure reminds the reader of sheet-lightning when they are most connected, of nothing in literature when they are disconnected. These letters cannot fail to arouse sharp differences of opinion, but also they cannot fail to arouse interest. They are an important contribution to our collection of human documents. Valued at their lowest as literature, they are suggestive studies in applied Lombroso. At their best, they are brilliant expressions of an unusual and original personality.

They extend from 1845 to the author's death in 1886, and the labor involved in arranging them, mainly from internal evidence, has been simply enormous. It has been a task, too, calling for exceptional powers of interpretation and sympathy. Mrs. Todd's preface suggests the two lines of interest likely to be felt in the letters: they deepen the impression made by Miss Dickinson's poems, and they afford material for the study of an extraordinary style. The style of a recluse is as definite and legitimate an object of investigation as the conditions that make the writer seclude herself; and these letters, in their early stage, show the usual human tendency to commonplaceness. Miss Dickinson defines genius as the ignition of the affections, and it seems likely in her case to have been true. The preternatural compression and point of her

From the *Nation*, LIX (December 13, 1894), 446–47.

expression appears to be the revenge exacted by an over-sensitive temperament for its failure to maintain the ordinary social relations.

The contents of the letters show the writer a less sprite-like, more human, being than she seemed in the poems. There is less of the daemonic love in her affections, more of the familiar attachment to horse and house, kith and kin. Her enjoyments, too, sometimes fall short of the elevated ecstasy of a metaphysical sunset or of the consolations of death. But her easy acceptance of the terms of life becomes more and more impossible as the letters go on. The pathos of her recurring, short-lived revivals of the effort to live life whole instead of by spasms is extreme. One cannot help wishing that the writer's sense of humor had been more persistently indulged, or, perhaps, less persistently translated into paradox. The epigram and paradox of the later periods are excellent of their kind, and were doubtless a relief to the writer; but we cannot help profanely wondering what would have been the effect on the author's genius if she had reduced the nervous tension now and then by indulging in a genuine bout of gossip. Her attitude is depressingly superior. She does not abuse her neighbors enough to love them temperately. Her life grows more and more interior, until it reminds the reader of Plato's cave dweller who saw life only as it shadowed itself in the mouth of the den. Her family affections and her friendships are passionately strong, her hold on life slight and shifting. The contemporary life of her country, for example, does not interest her except as a source of disturbance to her own emotional condition, or to the wider self that she found in certain aspects of family, neighborhood, and town. The civil war was apparently unthinkable, and so unspeakable to her. Its record is the slightest possible in her pages, but the reserve is formidable. Things had a tendency to become unthinkable to her. She had little practical skill in what a clever writer calls "the art of taking hold by the small end."

What name will be given to experience of this sort, what estimate made of its expression, is an interesting question. A still more interesting question is what ought to be the name and estimate. Opinion will probably swing between the conviction that these letters are a precious legacy of genius for which we have to thank the scrupulous industry of Mrs. Todd and the generosity of Miss Lavinia Dickinson, and the equally strong feeling that they are the abnormal expression of a woman abnormal to the point of disease, and that their publication by a friend and a sister is not the least abnormal thing about them. But this difference of opinion involves an endless controversy about standards of taste and the legitimate in art. There have been great geniuses who have not been admired by other great geniuses, and whose genius even was denied. There have been numberless little men who could not impress their talent on men as little as themselves. But whatever the total judgment on Emily Dickinson's letters may be, a judicious selection from them must impress any reader; and if some who persevere to the end complain of a monotonous redundancy, others who have been irresistibly drawn along will rejoice that they are not more select and expurgated. The most Philistine of them will enjoy Miss Dickinson's account of herself written to Colonel Higginson in 1862. Her story of her education compares favorably in its way with St. Augustine's, John Stuart Mill's, Mark Pattison's, and J. H. Newman's. Here is a part of it, beginning (p. 301) with the paragraph introduced by "You asked how old I was?" Evading an answer to this question, Miss Dickinson proceeds without a pause:

I made no verse, but one or two, until this winter, sir.

I had a terror since September I could tell to none; and so I sing as the boy does of the burying ground, because I am afraid.

You inquire my books. For poets, I have Keats and Mr. and Mrs. Browning. For prose, Mr. Ruskin, Sir Thomas Browne, and the *Revelations*. I went to school, but, in your manner of the phrase, had no education. When a little girl, I had a friend who taught me Immortality; but venturing too near, himself, he never returned. Soon after, my tutor died, and for several years my lexicon was my only companion. Then I found one more, but he was not contented I be his scholar, so he left the land.

You ask of my companions. Hills, sir, and the sundown, and a dog large as myself that my father bought me. They are better than beings, because they know but do not tell; and the noise in the pool at noon excels my piano.

I have a brother and sister; my mother does not care for thought, and father, too busy with his briefs to notice what we do. He buys me many books, but begs me not to read them, because he fears they joggle the mind. They are religious, except me, and address an eclipse, every morning, whom they call their "Father."

Every one will be conscious of refreshment on opening the second volume, which introduces the letters to her cousins, by far the most spontaneous of all. Elsewhere, in the longer efforts at least, there is a sense of strain and consciousness, not to call it affectation, as if the solitary instance of a rough draft adduced by Mrs. Todd (p. 424) were not the only one. The tendency, however, of Miss Dickinson's prose to fall into the favorite rhythm of her poems is, whenever observable (and it occurs constantly), the best evidence of the naturalness of her orphic outpourings. It was often pure chance whether she wrote continuously the full width of the line, or chopped up her measures into verse lengths. For example:

Travel why to Nature, when she dwells with us? Those who lift their hats shall see her, as devout do God (p. 180).

Not that he goes—we love him more who led us while he stayed. Beyond earth's trafficking frontier, for what he moved he made (p. 224). (Should not this, by the way, read: "Who led us—while he stayed—beyond earth's trafficking frontier?")

Be but the maid you are to me, and they will love you more (p. 256).

A word is dead when it is said, some say. I say it just begins to live that day (p. 269).

The competitions of the sky corrodeless ply (p. 285).

I work to drive the awe away, yet awe impels the work (p. 296).

The new bits of poetry presented in these volumes in connection with the letters are mostly of little worth, but there are one or two striking exceptions. Too original and individual, we fear, for Dr. Murray's use are some neologisms and colloquial phraseology of a curious kind; and how so ingrained a New Englander could confound *shall* and *will* passes understanding. There is no lack of bright and witty touches throughout; and on occasion, as in the letter relating the death in battle and burial of young Stearns (p. 242), there is a fine and effective coherency. It would be easy to multiply instances of a style whose early promise was considerable, but hardly maintained. These two are from the girl of twenty and twenty-one (pp. 48, 102):

Oh, I struggled with great temptation, and it cost me much of denial; but I think in the end I conquered—not a glorious victory, where you hear the rolling drum, but a kind of a helpless victory, where triumph would come of itself: faintest music, weary soldiers, not a waving flag, nor a long, loud shout.

Of Professor Park's preaching:

The students and chapel people all came to our church, and it was very full and still—so still the buzzing of a fly would have boomed like a cannon.

And when it was all over, and that wonderful man sat down, people stared at each other, and looked as wan and wild as if they had seen a spirit, and wondered they had not died.

Mrs. Todd's arrangement of the letters by correspondents rather than chronologically was perhaps the best for readability, but the biographical impression is necessarily weakened thereby, especially as so many of these notes relate to the death of friends and kindred. For example, to ascertain that they give no clue to the nature of the "terror since September," 1861, one has to search the whole of volume i. and part of volume ii. By way of compensation there is a good index. As the volumes are consecutively paged, there is a prospect, we suppose, some day of a one-volume edition.

For *Poems of Emily Dickinson: Third Series* (1896), Thomas Wentworth Higginson wrote a very favorable review.* Little else appeared about this third volume, but WILLIAM BLISS CARMAN (1861–1929), Canadian poet and journalist, founder of the magazine *The Chap-Book* and author of the very popular *Songs from Vagabondia* series (1894; 1896; 1900), wrote an essay which considered all the Dickinson poems so far published. Carman developed rather fully the sympathetic view of the poetry, defining its peculiarly American character, its claim to genius and originality, and—most important, perhaps, in the 1890's—offering a rather far-sighted justification for its irregularities.

A Note on Emily Dickinson

BLISS CARMAN

Pending the coming in of [Kipling's] "The Seven Seas," it is safe to say that the publication of a new volume of poems by Emily Dickinson is the literary event of the season. Six years ago when her first book was given to the public, it ran through several editions, achieving a

* "The Instantaneous Line," *Nation,* LXIII (October 8, 1896), 275.

From the *Boston Evening Transcript,* November 21, 1896.

larger sale, I believe, than any other first volume ever printed at the University Press, and that is saying a good deal, when one recalls the distinguished works that have issued from that excellent printing shop. Its author's name was entirely unknown, and she herself already passed beyond the confusion of renown; yet so distinctive was her note, so spiritual and intense and absolutely sincere, that she sprang at once into a posthumous fame, unadulterated and almost splendid. It was one more tribute to the New England ideal, the American interest in morality, the bent for transcendentalism inherited from Emerson; and, by the way, it was at the same time another evidence of the alertness of the American reading public, and its sensitiveness to excellent originality. For while there was novelty in the verse of Emily Dickinson, there was nothing sensational, hardly anything strange; no peculiarity on which a cult could batten. Those who admired her verse must admire it for its poetry alone.

I have just said that there is nothing sensational in Emily Dickinson's poetry; and yet there was, in a small way, a genuine sensation in the editorial rooms of one of the oldest journals in New York when our chief, with that tireless and impetuous enthusiasm of his, came rushing in with his bright discovery—like a whirl of October leaves. He is one of the two American editors who have the superfluous faculty of knowing poetry when they see it; he had fallen upon the immortal maid's first book, and the slumbering poet in him was awake. Nothing would suffice but we must share his youthful elation, listen to the strains of this original and accredited singer. The heat of New York, the routine of an office, the jaded mind of a reviewer, the vitiated habit of the professional manuscript-taster—it was not easy to shake off these at once; we were somewhat cold, perhaps, and a little sceptical of the chief's discovery. Still, we must listen. Hear this—

Belshazzar had a letter—
He never had but one;
Belshazzar's correspondent
Concluded and begun
In that immortal copy
The conscience of us all
Can read without its glasses
On revelation's wall.

Why, yes, certainly that is original enough. But can your wonderful prodigy turn off another verse like it?

"Can she? To be sure! Listen again!"

I taste a liquor never brewed.
  From tankards scooped in pearl;
Not all the vats upon the Rhine
  Yield such an alcohol!

Inebriate of air am I,
  And debauchee of dew,
Reeling, through endless summer days,
  From inns of molten blue.

When landlords turn the drunken bee
  Out of the foxglove's door,
When butterflies renounce their drams,
  I shall but drink the more!

Till seraphs swing their snowy hats,
  And saints to windows run,
To see the little tippler
  Leaning against the sun.

Well, we are convinced, indeed. There can be no doubt of the genuineness of this writer. Such work is fresh from the mint; not immediately current without some scrutiny; yet stamped plainly enough with the hall-mark of genius. We could but give unqualified assent; put the new book on the old shelf at once, with its peers, the acknowledged classics of American literature.

Following this first venture, there has been a second collection of poems, two volumes of letters and now this third book of verse. And allowing one's judgment time to cool, I must say the conviction remains that Emily Dickinson's contribution to English poetry (or American poetry, if you prefer to say so) is by far the most important made by any woman west of the Atlantic. It is so by reason of its thought, its piquancy, its untarnished expression. She borrowed from no one; she was never commonplace; always imaginative and stimulating; and finally, the region of her brooding was that sequestered domain where our profoundest convictions have origin, and whence we trace the Puritan strain within us.

For this New England woman was a type of her race. A life-long recluse, musing on the mysteries of life and death, she yet had that stability of character, that strong sanity of mind, which could hold out against the perils of seclusion, unshaken by solitude, undethroned by doubt. The very fibre of New England must have been there, founded of granite, nourished by an exhilarating air. We are permitted, through Colonel Higginson's introduction to the first series of poems, the merest glimpse into the story of her life in that beautiful college town in the lovely valley of the Connecticut. We imagine her in the old-fashioned house with its stately decency, its air of breeding and reserve, set a little back from the street, ambushed behind a generous hedge, and flanked by an ample garden on the side—a garden full of roses and tall elms and the scent of new-mown hay. There among her own, she chose an unaustere and voluntary monasticism for her daily course, far indeed removed from the average life of our towns, yet not so untypical of that strain of Puritan blood which besets us all. It would never, I feel sure, occur to anyone with the least insight into the New England character, or the remotest inheritance of the New England conscience (with its capacity for abstemiousness, its instinct for being always aloof and restrained, rather than social and blithe), to think of Emily Dickinson as peculiar, or her mode of life as queer. Somewhat strange as the record of it may show to foreign eyes, it was natural enough in its own time and place, though sufficiently unusual to claim something of distinction even of itself. Illumined and revealed in her poems, the life and character of this original nature make a fit study for the subtlest criticism—such a criticism, indeed, as I know not where they will receive. And all the while, as we speak of Emily Dickinson's secluded life, and her individual habit of isolation, her parsimony in friendship and human intercourse, I have a conviction that we should guard against the fancy that she was tinged with any shadow of sadness, or any touch of misanthropy or gloom. It seems rather that she must have had the sunniest of dispositions, as she certainly had the most sensitive and exquisite organization. It was not that the persons or fellows seemed to her superfluous or harsh or unnecessary, but rather that in one so finely organized as she must have been, the event of meeting another was too exquisite and portentous to be borne. For there are some natures so shy and quick, so undulled by the life of the senses, that they never quite acquire the easy part of the world. You will hear of them shunning the most delightful acquaintance, turning a corner sharply to avoid an encounter, hesitating at the very threshold of welcome, out of some dim inherited, instinctive dread of casual intercourse. They are like timorous elusive spirits, gone astray, perhaps, and landed on the rough planet Earth by a slight mischance; and when they are compelled by circumstance to share in the world's work, their part in it is likely to be an unhappy one. Theirs is the bent for solitude, the custom of silence. And once that fleeing sense of self-protection arises within them, the chances are they will indulge it to the end. And fortunate, indeed, it is, if that end be not disaster. But in Emily Dickinson's case, the stray health of genius came to the support of this hermit's instinct, and preserved her to the end of life sweet and blithe and contented in that innocent nun-like existence in which she chose to be immured. Her own room served her for native land, and in the painted garden beyond her window-sill was foreign travel enough for her. For that frugal soul, the universe of experience was bounded by the blue hills of a New England valley.

It was, of course, part of the inheritance of such a woman to have the religious sense strongly marked. She came of a race that never was at ease in Zion, yet never was content out of sight of the promised land. It best suited their strenuous and warlike nature always to be looking down on the delectable Canaan from the Pisgah of their own unworthiness. Yet, however severe a face life wore to them, and unlovely as their asperity often was, they were still making, though unwittingly, for the liberation of humanity. They were laying a substructure of honesty and seriousness, on which their intellectual inheritors might build, whether in art or politics. And their occupation with religion, with the affairs of the inward life and all its needs, has left an impress on ourselves, given us a trend from which we swerve in vain. And on every page of Emily Dickinson's poetry this ethical tendency, this awful environment of spirituality, is evident. Meditations of Psyche in the House of Clay; epigrams of an immortal guest, left behind on the chamber wall on the eve of silent departure, these brief lyrics seem:

This world is not conclusion;
A sequel stands beyond,

Invisible as music,
But positive as sound.

It beckons and it baffles;
Philosophies don't know,
And through a riddle, at the last,
Sagacity must go.

To guess it puzzles scholars;
To gain it, men have shown
Contempt of generations,
And crucifixion known.

That is an orphic utterance, no doubt; and such is all of this poet's work. She is, like Emerson, a companion for solitude, a stimulating comrade in the arduous intellectual ways. A symbolist of the symbolists, she is with them a reviver and establisher of the religious sentiment. Full of scepticism and the gentle irony of formal unbelief, putting aside the accepted and narrowing creed, she brings us, as Emerson did, face to face with new objects of worship. In their guidance we come a step nearer the great veil. For it is quite true that he who was hailed as a sceptic and destroyer in his early career, was in reality a prophet and a founder.

And it was inevitable, too, that one so much at home in spiritual matters should be deeply versed in nature—should be on intimate terms of friendship with all Nature's creatures.

Not that her knowledge of them was wide; it could hardly be that. But her sympathy with them was deep. She had ever a word of interpretation for the humblest of the mute dwellers in her garden world, clover or bee or blade. Often in these verses on the natural world there is a touch of whimsical humor that shows her character in very delightful color; as, for instance, in the lines on cobwebs:

The spider as an artist
Has never been employed,
Though his surpassing merit
Is freely certified

By every broom and Bridget
Throughout a Christian land.
Neglected son of genius,
I take thee by the hand.

There is the touch of intimacy, of fellowship, of kinship with all creation, which is so characteristic of modern poetry, and which is to become characteristic of modern religion. It is the tolerant, gay, debonair note of blameless joy which has been banished so long from the world, coming back to claim its own again.

Did I say that Emily Dickinson's contribution to poetry was more important than that of any other woman in America? Perhaps it is. Yet it has its faults, so hard a thing is perfection in any art, and so perfect the balance of fine qualities necessary to attain it. For while this poet was so eminent in wit, so keen in epigram, so rare and startling in phrase, the extended laborious architecture of an impressive poetic creation was beyond her. So that one has to keep her at hand as a stimulus and refreshment rather than as a solace. She must not be read long at a sitting. She will not bear that sort of treatment any more than Mr. Swinburne will; and for the very opposite reason. In Swinburne there is such a richness of sound, and often such a paucity of thought that one's even mental poise is sadly strained in trying to keep an equilibrium. He is like those garrulous persons, enamored of their own voice, who talk one to death so pleasingly. While in Emily Dickinson there is a lack of sensuousness, just as there was in Emerson. So that, like him, she never could have risen into the first rank of poets. And it was a sure critical instinct that led her never to venture beyond the range where her success was sure.

There is one thing to be remembered in considering her poetry, if we are to allow ourselves the full enjoyment of it; and that is her peculiar rhymes. As Colonel Higginson well remarks, "Though curiously indifferent to all conventional rules, she had a rigorous literary standard of her own, and often altered a word many times to suit an ear which had its own tenacious fastidiousness."

It is usual in verse to call those sounds perfect rhymes in which the final consonants (if there be any) and the final vowels are identical, but the consonants preceding these final vowels, different. So that we call "hand" and "land" perfect rhymes. But this is only a conventional custom among poets. It is consonant with laws of poetry, of course; but it is not in itself a law. It is merely one means at the writer's disposal for marking off his lines for the reader's ear. And when Emily Dickinson chose to use in her own work another slightly different convention, she was at perfect liberty to do so. She violated no law of poetry. The laws of art are as inviolable as the laws of nature.

Who never wanted—maddest joy
Remains to him unknown;
The banquet of abstemiousness
Surpasses that of wine.

"Wine" and "unknown" are not perfect rhymes. No more are "ground" and "mind," "done" and "man"; yet they serve to mark her lines for her reader quite well. Why? Because she has made a new rule for herself, and has followed it carefully. It is simply this—that the final vowels need not be identical; only the final consonants need be identical. The vowels may vary. It is wrong to say that she disregarded any law here. The question is rather: Did her new usage tend to beautiful results? For my part I confess that I like that falling rhyme very much. There is a haunting gypsy accent about it, quite in keeping with the tenor of that wilding music. What a strange and gnomelike presence lurks in all her lines!

2

1901–1930

ELLA GILBERT IVES (d. 1913), an 1867 alumna of Mt. Holyoke College, was a teacher with cultivated literary interests. From 1867 to 1871 she taught in New Haven, Conn., and then moved to Chicago as associate principal of the Dearborn Seminary (1871–85). In 1885 she returned to the East, and later established a private school for girls. A volume of her poetry was published in 1908, and in 1915 a posthumous autobiography. In 1907 she published this essay on Emily Dickinson in the *Boston Transcript,* the first extended essay on Miss Dickinson in the twentieth century.

Emily Dickinson: Her Poetry, Prose and Personality

ELLA GILBERT IVES

"If fame belonged to me, I could not escape her." [E.D.]

Emily Dickinson long eluded her pursuer; but no sooner had she left her chrysalis than Fame, also a winged elf, flew by her side, became her unescapable companion. In life she was arrogantly shy of a public that now shares her innermost confidence, and touches with rude or hallowed finger the flesh of her sensitive poetry; the soul of it, happily only the sympathetic can reach.

Many obvious, many contradictory things, have been said about this profound thinker and virile writer on a few great themes. Those who cling to the old order and regard perfect form essential to greatness, have had their fling at her eccentricities, her blemishes, her crudities; they place her with the purveyors of raw material to the artistic producers of the race. They deny her rank with the creators of permanent beauty and value. Others such as hail a Wagner, a Whitman, or a Turner, as an originator of new types and a contributor of fresh streams of life blood to art or literature, accept Emily Dickinson as another proof of Nature's fecundity, versatility and daring. All acknowledge in her elements of power and originality; but especially a certain probing quality that penetrates and discloses like an X-ray.

By long-accepted standards, doubtless, she does not measure up to greatness. The first bullet was an innovation to one who drew the long

From the *Boston Evening Transcript,* October 5, 1907.

bow. He did not know what to make of hot shot without the whiz and the grace of the arrow—least of all when it struck home and shattered his pet notions. Emily Dickinson's power of condensation, the rhythmic hammer of her thoughts, whether in prose or verse, is so phenomenal that it calls for a new system of weights and measures. Perhaps there is nothing essentially new here. Franklin merely identified an acquaintance of Noah's when he flew his kite; Newton, had he talked the apple over with Eve, might have found her intelligent on the fall; but both philosophers drew as near to originality as mortal is ever permitted to draw by the jealous gods. Emily Dickinson, whatever her size, is of nobody's kind but her own. The nearest approach to a family resemblance in her intellectual physiognomy is a feminine idiosyncracy, the counterpart of Thoreau's masculine one; but it begins and ends in mere suggestion. I make bold to attach "Dickinsonian" to such verse as this:

We play at paste,
Till qualified for pearl.

The truth never flaunted a sign.

The vane a little to the east
Scares muslin souls away.

No squirrel went abroad;
  A dog's belated feet
Like intermittent plush were heard
  Adown the empty street.

Also to this prose: "Enough is so vast a sweetness, I suppose it never occurs, only pathetic counterfeits." . . . " 'Tis not what well conferred it, the dying soldier asks, it is only the water." . . . "We dignify our faith when we can cross the ocean with it, though most prefer ships." . . . "The golden rule is so lovely it needs no police to enforce it." . . . "Thomas's faith in anatomy was stronger than his faith." . . . "How vast is the chastisement of beauty, given us by our maker!" . . . "Was he not an aborigine of the sky?" . . . "Memory's fog is rising." . . . "A morning call from Gabriel is always a surprise. Were we more fresh from Eden we were expecting him—but Genesis is a 'far journey.' "

... "It is true that the unknown is the largest need of the intellect, though for it, no one thinks to thank God."... "We must be careful what we say. No bird resumes its egg."... "Truth, like ancestors' brocades, can stand alone."... "To multiply the harbors does not reduce the sea."... "Not what the stars have done, but what they are to do, detains the sky."

Many of Emily Dickinson's letters are caskets of jewels. Not a shell, but contains its pearl. There are phrases that are poems in epitome; others are sufficiently expanded to take on rhyme and rhythm. Her thought clothed itself in the essential graces of poetry, simplicity and music. These for specimen: "A word is dead when it is said, some say. I say it just begins to live that day."... "Could we see all we hope, or hear the whole we fear, told tranquil, like another tale, there would be madness near."... "How strange that nature does not knock and yet does not intrude!"

Her poems must be seen whole in their sky, and must be touched to yield their lightning. Some of them are ragged-edged clouds, but hanging in an atmosphere and drifting one way—toward God and eternity. Touch them and you get an electric shock. The recurrent themes are life, love, death, immortality; but especially the veiled majesty of death. Did any other peer so curiously, so insistently, into the unseen, with such a baffling sense of impotence and folly?

At least to pray is left, is left,
  O Jesus! in the air
I know not which thy chamber is—
  I'm knocking everywhere.

Thou stirrest earthquake in the south,
  And maelstrom in the sea;
Say, Jesus Christ of Nazareth,
  Hast thou no arm for me?

Death is a dialogue between
  The spirit and the dust,
"Dissolve," says Death. The Spirit, "Sir,
  I have another trust."

Death doubts it, argues from the ground.
  The Spirit turns away,
Just laying off, for evidence,
  An overcoat of clay.

I would that this writer on the mysteries had possessed a more joyous temper and greater certitude; but she could rise no higher than her faith, being first of all, sincere. On the sweet, safe level of the grass, the plane of the low-flying robin and bluebird, she is serene and poised. Of all

> The simple news that Nature told,
> With tender majesty

she is a delightful bearer; a voice that has tones of pure gladness. What abandon of joy in what an Englishman calls "A Woman's Drinking Song!"—"I taste a liquor never brewed." If language could intoxicate, the second stanza were such a draught:

> Inebriate of air am I,
> And debauchee of dew,
> Reeling, through endless summer days,
> From inns of molten blue.

And how her mind plays holiday in these lines:

> He ate and drank the precious words,
> His spirit grew robust;
> He knew no more that he was poor,
> Nor that his frame was dust.
> He danced along the dingy days,
> And this bequest of wings
> Was but a book. What liberty
> A loosened spirit brings!

And her heart—she fails herself to find a plummet for sounding its depths, though she tries in such lines as these:

> Alter? When the hills do.
> Falter? When the sun
> Question if his glory
> Be the perfect one.
> Surfeit? When the daffodil
> Doth of the dew;
> Even as herself, O friend!
> I will of you.

As to her philosophy—and one can suck wisdom from her writings —I know no space so small more packed with nutriment than this quatrain:

The pedigree of honey
   Does not concern the bee;
A clover, any time, to him
   Is aristocracy;

Or these stanzas:

I'm nobody! Who are you?
   Are you nobody, too?
Then there's a pair of us—don't tell!
   They'd banish us, you know.

How dreary to be somebody!
   How public, like a frog,
To tell your name the livelong day
   To an admiring bog!

Critical acumen usually accompanies the poetic gift. The very travail of the mind—and how sore it was with Emily Dickinson!—to give birth to an organic thought, renders one sensitive to the throes of others, and joyous over any man child born into the world. There are passing comments in her letters that flash light upon the bearer of the torch. Desiring to send the *Life of George Eliot* to Colonel Higginson, she made this pregnant comment: "Emblem is immeasurable—that is why it is better than fulfillment, which can be drained." Ten years before she had written, "What do I think of *Middlemarch?* What do I think of glory—except that in a few instances this mortal has already put on immortality? George Eliot is one." Of the same novel, sent to Mrs. Higginson, she said, "I am bringing you a little granite book for you to lean upon." At the time of the great novelist's death, she wrote with the prescience of love: "Now, my George Eliot. The gift of belief which her greatness denied her, I trust she receives in the childhood of the kingdom of heaven. As childhood is earth's confiding time, perhaps, having no childhood, she lost her way to the early trust, and no later came." To a favorite poet she made this allusion, as delicately fragrant as a violet in the grass: "Love, you know, is God, who certainly 'gave the love to reward the love,' even were there no Browning." Of the greatest she wrote: "While Shakespeare remains, literature is firm. An insect cannot run away with Achilles's head."

No art can be adequately understood apart from the artist. Emily Dickinson is the best commentary upon her verse. I have recently visited "the house behind the hedge," where she was born and died. I have stood in the old-fashioned garden where she strolled, and grew intimate with bird and bee, butterfly and flower. I have listened to her bluebird, who

> Shouts for joy to nobody
> But his seraphic self,

and seen her robin brood its young. I have looked across her landscape on a June day at the Pelham range and repeated:

> The skies can't keep their secret,
> They tell it to the hills.

And letting thought and feeling slip in her accustomed grooves, I have ceased to wonder that Emily Dickinson shut herself in behind that austere but tonic hemlock hedge, and made her house a nunnery. I seemed to hear her voice saying:

> The soul selects her own society,
> Then shuts the door;
> On her divine majority
> Obtrude no more.

The events of Emily Dickinson's life are singularly few, but she invests each with significance. Her perception is at times as vivid as if, called to die, she were taking a last look. Deep and powerful are the strokes with which she limns an emotion, as if she were standing at a judgment bar. If the adjective "intense" were not so overworked, I should employ it. Had Emily Dickinson written novels they would have had the Brontëan quality—flame. A friend tells me that during the later years of her life the poet was accustomed to keep a candle burning in her window at night for the belated traveller. It is symbolic of her genius.

It is the brevity and searching quality (in inverse ratio) of Emily Dickinson's poetry that render it unique, and augur permanence, not so much that it lights the pathway, as that it explores the heart and touches the quick of experience. Her verse is never didactic, yet always earnest; too serious for wit, yet having the very kernel of wit—surprise —to an extraordinary degree. This dressing up of the primal emotions in strange, often outlandish garb, or exhibiting them naked yet not ashamed, has a singular effect, and throws the mind back with questioning upon the writer herself, and the influences that made her what she was—the loneliest figure in the world of letters.

They are not far to seek. There was the mother, whom "Noah would have liked," and the father, who stepped "like Cromwell, when he gets the kindlings." She sketches both saliently: "Mother drives with Tim to carry pears to settlers. Sugar pears with hips like hams, and the flesh of bonbons.... Father is growing better, though physically reluctant.... You know he never played, and the straightest engine has its leaning hour." To Colonel Higginson she wrote: "My mother does not care for thought, and father, too busy with his briefs to notice what we do. He buys me many books, and begs me not to read them, because he fears they joggle the mind." To another friend she wrote: "Mother is very fond of flowers and of recollection, that sweetest flower."

To Colonel Higginson she talked much about her father—a man who "read on Sunday lonely and rigorous books"; and so inspired her with awe that she did not learn to tell time until fifteen years old, because he had tried to explain it to her when a little child, and she was afraid to tell him she did not understand; also afraid to ask anyone else lest he should hear of it. He did not wish his children when young to read anything but the Bible. But at least two books early ran the blockade: *Kavanagh,* brought home by her brother, was hidden under the piano cover; and Lydia Maria Child's *Letters from New York,* sent by a friend, found refuge in a box beside the doorstep.

After the first book, "Emily," says Higginson, "thought in ecstasy, 'This then is a book and there are more of them!'" "When I lost the use of my eyes," she said, "it was a comfort to think that there were so few real books, that I could easily find one to read me all of them." Afterward, when sufficiently restored to read Shakespeare, she thought to herself, "Why is any other book needed?" She had earlier written to Colonel Higginson: "You inquire my books? For poets, I have Keats and Mr. and Mrs. Browning. For prose, Mr. Ruskin, Sir Thomas

Browne, and the *Revelations*. I went to school, but in your manner of the phrase had no education. When a little girl, I had a friend who taught me Immortality; but venturing too near, himself, he never returned.... My companions: hills, sir, and the sundown, and a dog as large as myself that my father bought me. They are better than beings, because they know, but do not tell."

With this birthright, with this nature, thrust back upon itself—recoil inevitable—life to Emily Dickinson was fraught with peril. But she saw the danger signal in her solitary way. Providentially the road forked, and one stood ready to meet her necessity. For the unique service rendered this woman of genius by a man of genius, all who love and admire Emily Dickinson thank Thomas Wentworth Higginson.

It is not difficult to see from what he saved her. Mr. Higginson has noted her touch of likeness to William Blake. It seems to me to lie deeper than in any quality of her verse—to reach down to that delicate mainspring of the mind, the more exquisite whose mechanism the more easily jarred. A certain correspondence in their verse is symptomatic of a common peril. In her second letter to Mr. Higginson Miss Dickinson wrote: "I had a terror since September I could tell to none; and, so I sing, as the boy does in [by] the burying ground, because I am afraid." Six years later, when her nature was flowering under the sunshine of his appreciation, and the pruning of his criticism, she wrote to him—her "master": "Of our greatest acts we are ignorant. You were not aware that you saved my life. To thank you in person has been since then one of my few requests."

This was granted, and in 1870 occurred Higginson's first interview with the poet. She met her own description: "Small like the wren; and my hair is bold, like the chestnut burr; and my eyes like the sherry in the glass that the guest leaves." Another friend has said of her: "She was not beautiful, yet had many beauties"—a word that suits, too, her intellect.

I have not dwelt upon Emily Dickinson's faults; they speak for themselves, and sometimes with such a din that the virtues cannot be heard. Granted that her poetry is uneven, so rugged of rhyme and rhythm that it jolts the mind like a corduroy road—I prefer it to a flowery bed of ease. Many can lull, but few can awake.

MARTHA HALE SHACKFORD (1875–1963), educated at Wellesley College and Yale (Ph.D., 1901) and professor of English at Wellesley, was a distinguished teacher and scholar, publishing an extensive list of studies in medieval, Renaissance, and nineteenth-century literature. This article in the *Atlantic* in 1913 encouraged Martha Dickinson Bianchi to go forward with the publication, one year later, of a new volume of Emily Dickinson's poetry, *The Single Hound*.

The Poetry of Emily Dickinson

MARTHA HALE SHACKFORD

Not long ago a distinguished critic, reviewing Father Tabb's poetry, remarked, 'At his most obvious affinity, Emily Dickinson, I can only glance. It seems to me that he contains in far finer form pretty much everything that is valuable in her thought.' Are we thus to lose the fine significance of poetic individuality? A poet is unique, incomparable, and to make these comparisons between poets is to ignore the primary laws of criticism, which seeks to discover the essential individuality of writers, not their chance resemblances. It is as futile as it is unjust to parallel Father Tabb's work with Emily Dickinson's: his is full of quiet reverie, hers has a sharp stabbing quality which disturbs and overthrows the spiritual ease of the reader. Emily Dickinson is one of our most original writers, a force destined to endure in American letters.

There is no doubt that critics are justified in complaining that her work is often cryptic in thought and unmelodious in expression. Almost all her poems are written in short measures, in which the effect of curt brevity is increased by her verbal penuriousness. Compression and epigrammatical ambush are her aids; she proceeds, without preparation or apology, by sudden, sharp zigzags. What intelligence a reader has must be exercised in the poetic game of hare-and-hounds, where ellipses, inversions, and unexpected climaxes mislead those who pursue sweet reasonableness. Nothing, for instance, could seem less poetical than this masterpiece of unspeakable sounds and chaotic rhymes:—

From *Atlantic Monthly,* CXI (January, 1913), 93–97.

COCOON

Drab habitation of whom?
Tabernacle or tomb,
Or dome of worm,
Or porch of gnome,
Or some elf's catacomb.

If all her poems were of this sort there would be nothing more to say; but such poems are exceptions. Because we happen to possess full records of her varying poetic moods, published, not with the purpose of selecting her most artistic work, but with the intention of revealing very significant human documents, we are not justified in singling out a few bizarre poems and subjecting these to skeptical scrutiny. The poems taken in their entirety are a surprising and impressive revelation of poetic attitude and of poetic method in registering spiritual experiences. To the general reader many of the poems seem uninspired, imperfect, crude, while to the student of the psychology of literary art they offer most stimulating material for examination, because they enable one to penetrate into poetic origins, into radical, creative energy. However, it is not with the body of her collected poems but with the selected, representative work that the general reader is concerned. Assuredly we do not judge an artist by his worst, but by his best, productions; we endeavor to find the highest level of his power and thus to discover the typical significance of his work.

To gratify the aesthetic sense was never Emily Dickinson's desire; she despised the poppy and mandragora of felicitous phrases which lull the spirit to apathy and emphasize art for art's sake. Poetry to her was the expression of vital meanings, the transfer of passionate feeling and of deep conviction. Her work is essentially lyric; it lacks the slow, retreating harmonies of epic measures, it does not seek to present leisurely details of any sort; its purpose is to objectify the swiftly-passing moments and to give them poignant expression.

Lyric melody finds many forms in her work. Her repressed and austere verses, inexpansive as they are, have persistent appeal. Slow, serene movement gives enduring beauty to these elegiac stanzas:

Let down the bars, O Death!
The tired flocks come in

Whose bleating ceases to repeat,
Whose wandering is done.

Thine is the stillest night,
Thine the securest fold;
Too near thou art for seeking thee,
Too tender to be told.

The opposite trait of buoyant alertness is illustrated in the cadences of the often-quoted lines on the humming-bird:

A route of evanescence
With a revolving wheel;
A resonance of emerald,
A rush of cochineal.

Between these two margins come many wistful, pleading, or triumphant notes. The essential qualities of her music are simplicity and quivering responsiveness to emotional moods. Idea and expression are so indissolubly fused in her work that no analysis of her style and manner can be attempted without realizing that every one of her phrases, her changing rhythms, is a direct reflection of her personality. The objective medium is entirely conformable to the inner life, a life of peculiarly dynamic force which agitates, arouses, spurs the reader.

The secret of Emily Dickinson's wayward power seems to lie in three special characteristics, the first of which is her intensity of spiritual experience. Hers is the record of a soul endowed with unceasing activity in a world not material, but one where concrete facts are the cherished revelation of divine significances. Inquisitive always, alert to the inner truths of life, impatient of the brief destinies of convention, she isolated herself from the petty demands of social amenity. A sort of tireless, probing energy of mental action absorbed her, yet there is little speculation of a purely philosophical sort in her poetry. Her stubborn beliefs, learned in childhood, persisted to the end,—her conviction that life is beauty, that love explains grief, and that immortality endures. The quality of her writing is profoundly stirring, because it betrays, not the intellectual pioneer, but the acutely observant woman, whose capacity for feeling was profound. The still, small voice of tragic revelation one hears in these compressed lines:

PARTING

My life closed twice before its close;
  It yet remains to see
If Immortality unveil
  A third event to me.

So huge, so hopeless to conceive,
  As these that twice befell.
Parting is all we know of heaven,
  And all we need of hell.

For sheer, grim, unrelieved expression of emotional truth there are few passages which can surpass the personal experience revealed in the following poem:

Pain has an element of blank;
It cannot recollect
When it began, or if there were
A day when it was not.

It has no future but itself,
Its infinite realms contain
Its past, enlightened to perceive
New periods of pain.

Her absorption in the world of feeling found some relief in associations with nature; yet although she loved nature and wrote many nature lyrics, her interpretations are always more or less swayed by her own state of being. The colors, the fragrances, the forms of the material world, meant to her a divine symbolism; but the spectacle of nature had in her eyes a more fugitive glory, a lesser consolation, than it had for Wordsworth and other true lovers of the earth.

Brilliant and beautiful transcripts of bird-life and of flower-life appear among her poems, although there is in some cases a childish fancifulness that disappoints the reader. Among the touches of unforgettable vividness there are:

These are the days when skies put on
The old, old sophistries of June,—
A blue and gold mistake;

and

Nature rarer uses yellow
  Than another hue;
Leaves she all of that for sunsets,—
  Prodigal of blue,

Spending scarlet like a woman,
  Yellow she affords
Only scantly and selectly,
  Like a lover's words.

Never has any poet described the haunting magic of autumnal days with such fine perception of beauty as marks the opening stanzas of 'My Cricket':

Farther in summer than the birds,
Pathetic from the grass,
A minor nation celebrates
Its unobtrusive mass.

No ordinance is seen,
So gradual the grace,
A pensive custom it becomes,
Enlarging loneliness.

Most effective, however, are those poems where she describes not mere external beauty, but, rather, the effect of nature upon a sensitive observer:

There's a certain slant of light,
On winter afternoons,
That oppresses, like the weight
Of cathedral tunes.

Heavenly hurt it gives us;
We can find no scar,
But eternal difference
Where the meanings are.

None may teach it anything,
'Tis the seal, despair,—
An imperial affliction
Sent us of the air.

When it comes, the landscape listens,
Shadows hold their breath;

When it goes, 't is like the distance
On the look of death.

It is essentially in the world of spiritual forces that her depth of poetic originality is shown. Others may describe nature, but few can describe life as she does. Human nature, the experiences of the world of souls, was her special study, to which she brought, in addition to that quality of intensity, a second characteristic,—keen sensitiveness to irony and paradox. Nearly all her perceptions are tinged with penetrating sense of the contrasts in human vicissitude. Controlled, alert, expectant, aware of the perpetual compromise between clay and spirit, she accepted the inscrutable truths of life in a fashion which reveals how humor and pathos contend in her. It is this which gives her style those sudden turns and that startling imagery. Humor is not, perhaps, a characteristic associated with pure lyric poetry, and yet Emily Dickinson's transcendental humor is one of the deep sources of her supremacy. Both in thought and in expression she gains her piercing quality, her undeniable spiritual thrust, by this gift, stimulating, mystifying, but forever inspiring her readers to a profound conception of high destinies.

The most apparent instances of this keen, shrewd delight in challenging convention, in the effort to establish, through contrast, reconcilement of the earthly and the eternal, are to be found in her imagery. Although her similes and metaphors may be devoid of languid aesthetic elegance, they are quivering to express living ideas, and so they come surprisingly close to what we are fond of calling the commonplace. She reverses the usual, she hitches her star to a wagon, transfixing homely daily phrases for poetic purposes. Such an audacity has seldom invaded poetry with a desire to tell immortal truths through the medium of a deep sentiment for old habitual things. It is true that we permit this liberty to the greatest poets, Shakespeare, Keats, Wordsworth, and some others; but in America our poets have been sharply charged not to offend in this respect. Here tradition still animates many critics in the belief that real poetry must have exalted phraseology.

The poem already quoted, 'Let down the bars, O Death!' has its own rustic vividness of association. Even more homely is the domestic suggestion wherewith the poet sets forth an eternally, profoundly significant fact:

> The trying on the utmost,
>   The morning it is new,
> Is terribler than wearing it
>   A whole existence through.

Surely such a commonplace comparison gives startling vividness to the innate idea. Many are the poetic uses she makes of practical everyday life:

> The soul should always stand ajar;

and

> The only secret people keep
> Is Immortality;

and

> Such dimity convictions,
>   A horror so refined,
> Of freckled human nature,
>   Of Deity ashamed;

and

> And kingdoms, like the orchard,
> Flit russetly away;

and

> If I couldn't thank you,
>   Being just asleep,
> You will know I'm trying
>   With my granite lip.

More significantly, however, than in these epithets and figures, irony and paradox appear in those analyses of truth where she reveals the deep note of tragic idealism:

Not one of all the purple host
Who took the flag to-day
Can tell the definition,
So clear, of victory,

As he, defeated, dying
On whose forbidden ear
The distant strains of triumph
Break, agonized and clear;

and

Essential oils are wrung;
The attar from the rose
Is not expressed by suns alone,
It is the gift of screws.

She took delight in piquing the curiosity, and often her love of mysterious challenging symbolism led her to the borderland of obscurity. No other of her poems has, perhaps, such a union of playfulness and of terrible comment upon the thwarted aspirations of a suffering soul as has this:

I asked no other thing,
No other was denied.
I offered Being for it;
The mighty merchant smiled.

Brazil? He twirled a button,
Without a glance my way;
'But, madam, is there nothing else
That we can show to-day?'

Since life seemed, to her, seldom to move along wholly simple and direct ways, she delighted to accentuate the fact that out of apparent contradictions and discords are wrought the subtlest harmonies:

To learn the transport by the pain,
As blind men learn the sun;

and

Sufficient troth that we shall rise—
Deposed, at length, the grave—

To that new marriage, justified
Through Calvaries of Love;

and

The lightning that preceded it
Struck no one but myself,
But I would not exchange the bolt
For all the rest of life.

The expectation of finding in her work some quick, perverse, illuminating comment upon eternal truths certainly keeps a reader's interest from flagging, but passionate intensity and fine irony do not fully explain Emily Dickinson's significance. There is a third characteristic trait, a dauntless courage in accepting life. Existence, to her, was a momentous experience, and she let no promises of a future life deter her from feeling the throbs of this one. No false comfort released her from dismay at present anguish. An energy of pain and joy swept her soul, but did not leave any residue of bitterness or of sharp innuendo against the ways of the Almighty. Grief was a faith, not a disaster. She made no effort to smother the recollections of old companionship by that species of spiritual death to which so many people consent. Her creed was expressed in these stanzas:

They say that 'time assuages,'—
  Time never did assuage;
An actual suffering strengthens,
  As sinews do, with age.

Time is a test of trouble,
  But not a remedy.
If such it prove, it proves too
  There was no malady.

The willingness to look with clear directness at the spectacle of life is observable everywhere in her work. Passionate fortitude was hers, and this is the greatest contribution her poetry makes to the reading world. It is not expressed precisely in single poems, but rather is present in all, as key and interpretation of her meditative scrutiny. Without elaborate philosophy, yet with irresistible ways of expression, Emily Dickinson's poems have true lyric appeal, because they make abstractions, such as love, hope, loneliness, death, and immortality, seem near and intimate and faithful. She looked at existence with a vision so exalted and secure that the reader is long dominated by that very excess of spiritual conviction. A poet in the deeper mystic qualities of feeling rather than in the external merit of precise rhymes and flawless art, Emily Dickinson's place is among those whose gifts are

Too intrinsic for renown.

After graduation from Bryn Mawr (1903), ELIZABETH SHEPLEY SERGEANT **lived in France for a number of years. In 1916 she published** ***French Perspectives,*** **and in 1917–18 she was a correspondent in France for the** ***New Republic.*** **She has been a frequent contributor to magazines, has written several books—among them** ***Fire Under the Andes*** **(1927),** ***Willa Cather—A Memoir*** **(1953), and** ***Robert Frost: The Trial by Existence*** **(1960). This 1915 essay on Emily Dickinson is an early example of the tendency to regard her as essentially modern.**

An Early Imagist

ELIZABETH SHEPLEY SERGEANT

"Criticism is timid," writes Emerson. "When shall we dare to say only that is poetry which cleanses and mans me?" "The Single Hound" is poetry of this tonic sort, and—though the lifetime it records ended nearly thirty years ago—throws a searching light on the revolutionary volumes of 1915. For starkness of vision, "quintessentialness" of expression, boldness and solidity of thought, and freedom of form, a New England spinster who flourished between 1830 and 1886 in an elm-shaded college town above the Connecticut valley, might give the imagists "pointers": here is a discovery to quicken the modern New England heart. To this day in western Massachusetts Sundays are al-

From the *New Republic,* IV (August 14, 1915). A review of *The Single Hound* by Emily Dickinson (Boston: Little, Brown and Co.).

most Sabbaths, "ministers" almost men of awe, and Longfellow is almost a great poet. Where, then, in the golden age of "Evangeline" and the Congregational Church, did Emily Dickinson get her daring inspiration?

Certainly she did not go abroad for it, but dug it out of her native granite. To me she is one of the rarest flowers the sterner New England ever bore, and justifies, as Carlyle justified his narrow Scotch inheritance—there is a curious analogy between his prose and her nubbly, elliptical verse—the stiff-necked Puritan elders from whom we all sprang. For without those elders and their family Bibles, and the mystical marriage of the absolute and the homely which was the very essence of their minds and hours, Emily Dickinson could never have been on such friendly, not to say familiar terms with God, or sported so whimsically and so stupendously with the mysteries of living and dying. The peculiar quality of her short concentrated poems is that they bring infinity and eternity within a village hedge; and to her, as to the early Puritan, the great earthly experience was poignantly individual:

> Adventure most unto itself
>   The Soul condemned to be;
> Attended by a Single Hound—
>   Its own Identity.

For Emily Dickinson—of how few, even among "strong-minded" women, can it be said—was a genuine solitary.

> There is a solitude of space,
>   A solitude of sea,
> A solitude of death, but these
>   Society shall be,
> Compared with that profounder site,
>   That polar privacy,
> A Soul admitted to Itself:
>   Finite Infinity.

The theme finds many variations in "The Single Hound":

> The Soul that hath a Guest
> Doth seldom go abroad.

Diviner Crowd at home
Obliterate the need, . . .

and it was probably this "other loneliness," not occasioned by "want, or friend, or circumstances, or lot," in which she felt herself so richly companioned by her own spirit, that led her to keep her verse out of print during her life.

The poems collected in the present volume—the fourth to be published since her death—were all addressed, "on any chance slip of paper," during many years of "romantic friendship," to a sister-in-law who lived the width of a green lawn away. Yet "days, and even weeks, slipped by sometimes without their actual meeting." Mrs. Martha Dickinson Bianchi, deciding at last to publish her mother's treasury, adds a suggestive preface of anecdote and reminiscence to prove how little the aunt she loved resembled the poetess as she is "taught in colleges"—"a weird recluse eating her heart out in morbid or unhappy longing, or a victim of unsatisfied passion."

Emily Dickinson, to her nieces and nephews, was "of fairy lineage"—"the confederate in every contraband desire," ready to start with horse and buggy for the moon at a moment's notice. "Fascination was her element." She was "lightning and fragrance in one." Mrs. Bianchi's delicate phrases give one hints of it: "her way of flitting, like a shadow upon the hillside, a motion known to no other mortal"; the way "her spirit seemed merely playing through her body as the aurora borealis through darkness"; her revelling "in the wings of her mind—I had almost said the fins, too—so universal was her identification with every form of life and element of being." We read of her wiles and ruses for escaping dull society: "He has the facts, but not the phosphorescence of learning"; of her respect for her father, the august leading lawyer of Amherst: "If Father is asleep on the sofa the house is full, though it were empty otherwise."

We learn, too, of the many lovers who attended her elusive and skittish path, and who were on the whole—though men were more stimulating to her than the gentlewomen of her day, whom she once set down in verse as "soft cherubic creatures" of "dimity convictions"—well lost as husbands. For "she was not daily bread. She was stardust." As Emily Dickinson herself puts it:

The missing All prevented me
From missing minor things—

The colleges must be losing their sense of humor. For what thwarted old maid could write:

To this apartment deep
No ribaldry may creep.
Untroubled this abode
By any man but God.

Or say so perfectly:

That Love is all there is,
Is all we know of Love.
It is enough: the freight should be
Proportioned to the groove.

There is, I think, less of human passion in this collection than in the earlier ones; and somewhat less, perhaps, of that so exquisite and intense identification with nature which Mrs. Bianchi mentions. Yet what a skipping sense—one feels it in one's very heels—of the life of bee, bird, flower, hill, cloud, wind and sun is here.

Beauty crowds me till I die,

she cries. There are also nature poems, as the one that begins:

The winds drew off
Like hungry dogs
Defeated of a bone—

which for sheer "decorative" quality might go into an imagist anthology. The following is typical of the more resonant and abstruse Dickinsonian manner:

The long sigh of the Frog
Upon a Summer's day,
Enacts intoxication
Upon the revery.
But his receding swell

Substantiates a peace,
That makes the ear inordinate
For corporal release.

For the "phosphorescence" of poetry, however, give me:

A little madness in the Spring
Is wholesome even for the King,
But God be with the Clown,
Who ponders this tremendous scene—
This whole experiment of green,
As if it were his own!

"Pondering" kept Emily Dickinson face to face with the other side of the visible world. Half her impatience with her kind was that they prated of "charming April Day"; mistook "the outside for the in"; talked, as she says in a letter, "of sacred things aloud and embarrass my dog." Her own curious imagination sought the "area superior" beyond each day and life. Death was her constant preoccupation; the "overtakelessness" of those who had accomplished it was more majestic than the majesties of earth. Sometimes she wrote of it with utter simplicity:

To-day or this noon,
She dwelt so close,
I almost touched her;
To-night she lies
Past neighborhood—
And bough and steeple—
Now past surmise.

Again, inquisitively sybilline:

How went the agile kernel out—
Contusion of the husk,
Nor rip nor wrinkle indicate,—
But just an Asterisk.

There are poems, too, where lovers of literary "influence" might find echoes of Donne's rhetoric and abstract vocabulary:

Eternity will be
  Velocity, or pause,
At fundamental signals
  From fundamental laws.

To die, is not to go—
  On doom's consummate chart
No territory new is staked,
  Remain thou as thou art.

Donne may well have been in the Hon. Mr. Dickinson's library. But provincial New England kept, well through the nineteenth century, much of the seventeenth century tradition; and transcendentalism was, of course, in Emily Dickinson's air—the academic-minded should take these facts to heart before assuming that either her ideas or her quaint expression were borrowed. They should read Emerson's Journals and compare Emily with his "Cousin Margaret." Her letters show that she thought obliquely, yet unflinchingly, as Meredith did; if ever his "Comic Spirit" found personification, it was in this woman, with her wit, her glancing mind, her range from the sublime to the ridiculous. The difficulties of syntax, the obscurities and abstractions which mark her verse were no more derived than her Amherst realisms, but a very part of her. So were her impertinencies towards her Creator and his prophets.

Papa above!
  Regard a Mouse
O'erpowered by the Cat—

"To live," she once wrote, "is so startling it leaves but little room for other occupations"; and I believe it is her deeply "startled" sense of man and the universe that keeps her terse and pregnant yet thistledown verse from archaism, though it sometimes has a jingle, sometimes no rhyme at all. "The Single Hound" is as surprising as a cold douche, as acute as the edge of a precipice, as lambent as a meteor cleaving the night. "If I feel physically as if the top of my head were taken off," she said, "I know that is poetry." To those who like to find their brains exposed to the illimitable I recommend this white and fearless New England spinster.

Except the smaller size, no Lives are round.
These hurry to a sphere, and show, and end.
The larger, slower grow, and later hang—
The Summers of Hesperides are long.

NORMAN FOERSTER (1887–), one of the chief spokesmen in America for the New Humanism, has had a notable career as teacher, scholar, and critic. Central to the development of his critical beliefs are *American Criticism* (1928), *The American Scholar* (1929), and *Towards Standards: a Study of the Present Critical Movement in American Letters* (1930). In the *Cambridge History of American Literature* (1921), Foerster's essay on later nineteenth-century poets grants Emily Dickinson the distinction of gaining more with time than any of her contemporaries, then cautiously predicts for her a "place in American letters . . . inconspicuous but secure."

Emily Dickinson

NORMAN FOERSTER

In the expanding, heterogeneous America of the second half of the nineteenth century, poetry lost its clearly defined tendencies and became various and experimental. It did not cease to be provincial; for although no one region dominated as New England had dominated in the first half of the century, the provincial accent was as unmistakable, and the purely national accent as rare, as before. The East, rapidly becoming the so-called "effete East," produced a poetry to which the West was indifferent; the West, still the West of "carnivorous animals of a superior rank," produced a poetry that the cultivated classes of the East regarded as vulgar. In a broad way it may perhaps be said that the poetry of this period was dedicated either to beauty or to "life"; to a revered past, or to the present and the future; to the civilization of Asia and Europe, or to the ideals and manners of America, at least the West of America. The virtue of the poetry of beauty was its fidelity to a noble tradition, its repetition, with a difference, of familiar and justly approved types of beauty; its defect was mechanical repetition, petty embellishment. The virtue of the poetry of "life" was fidelity to experience, vitality of utterance; its defect, crudity, meanness, insensitiveness to fineness of feeling and beauty of

From the *Cambridge History of American Literature* (New York: Macmillan Co., 1921), III, 52–54.

expression. Where the poets are many and all are minor it is difficult to make a choice, but on the whole it seems that the outstanding poets of the East were Emily Dickinson, Aldrich, Bayard Taylor, R. H. Stoddard, Stedman, Gilder, and Hovey; and of the West, Bret Harte, Joaquin Miller, Sill, Riley, and Moody.

None of these has gained more with time than has Emily Dickinson. Despite her defective sense of form, which makes her a better New Englander than Easterner, she has acquired a permanent following of discriminating readers through her extraordinary insight into the life of the mind and the soul. This insight is that of a latter-day Puritan, completely divorced from the outward stir of life, retiring, by preference, deeper and deeper within. Born in 1830 at Amherst, Massachusetts, she lived there all her life, and in 1886 died there. The inwardness and moral ruggedness of Puritanism she inherited mainly through her father, Edward Dickinson, lawyer and treasurer of Amherst College, a Puritan of the old type, whose heart, according to his daughter, was "pure and terrible." Her affection for him was so largely compounded with awe that in a sense they were strangers. "I have a brother and sister," she wrote to her poetical preceptor, Thomas Wentworth Higginson; "my mother does not care for thought, and father, too busy with his briefs to notice what we do. He buys me many books, but begs me not to read them, because he fears they jiggle the mind. They are religious, except me." Of course, she too was religious, and intensely so, breathing as she did the intoxicating air of Transcendentalism. In person she described herself as "small, like the wren; and my hair is bold like the chestnut burr; and my eyes, like the sherry in the glass that the guest leaves." "You ask of my companions. Hills, sir, and the sundown, and a dog large as myself." These, and not her family, were actually her companions, together with a few books and her own soul. She had an alert introspection that brought her more than the wealth of the Indies. There is no better example of the New England tendency to moral revery than this last pale Indian-summer flower of Puritanism. She is said literally to have spent years without passing the doorstep, and many more years without leaving her father's grounds. After the death of her parents, not to mention her dog Carlo, she retired still further within herself, till the sounds of the everyday world must have come to her as from a previous state of existence.

"I find ecstasy in living," she said to Higginson, and spoke truly, as her poems show. In an unexpected light on orchards, in a wistful mood of meadow or wood-border held secure for a moment before it vanished; in the few books that she read—her Keats, her Shakespeare, her *Revelation;* in the echoes, obscure in origin, that stirred within her own mind and soul, now a tenuous melody, now a deep harmony, a haunting question, or a memorable affirmation;—everywhere she displayed something of the mystic's insight and joy. And she expressed her experience in her poems, forgetting the world altogether, intent only on the satisfaction of giving her fluid life lasting form, her verse being her journal. Yet the impulse to expression was probably not strong, because she wrote no poems, save one or two, as she herself asserts, until the winter 1861–62, when she was over thirty years old. In the spring of 1862 she wrote a letter to Higginson beginning, "Are you too deeply occupied to say if my verse is alive? The mind is so near itself it cannot see distinctly, and I have none to ask." Discerning the divine spark in her shapeless verse, he welcomed her advances, and became her "preceptor," loyally listened to but, as was inevitable, mainly unheeded. Soon perceiving this, Higginson continued to encourage her, for many years, without trying to divert her lightning-flashes. In "H. H."—Helen Hunt Jackson, herself a poetess of some distinction, and her early schoolmate at Amherst—she had another sympathetic friend, who, suspecting the extent of her production, asked for the post of literary executor. At length, in 1890, a volume edited by Higginson and Mabel Loomis Todd was published, *Poems by Emily Dickinson,* arranged under various heads according to subject. The book succeeded at once, six editions being sold in the first six months; so that a second series, and later a third, seemed to be justified. From the first selection to the third, however, there is a perceptible declension.

The subject division adopted by her editors serves well enough: Life, Love, Nature, Time and Eternity. A mystical poetess sequestered in a Berkshire village, she naturally concerned herself with neither past nor present, but with the things that are timeless. Apparently deriving no inspiration from the war to which Massachusetts, including her preceptorial colonel, gave itself so freely, she spent her days in brooding over the mystery of pain, the true nature of success, the refuge of the tomb, the witchcraft of the bee's murmur, the election of love, the relation of deed to thought and will. On such subjects she jotted down hundreds of little poems.

Though she had an Emersonian faith that fame, if it belonged to her, could not escape her, she cared nothing at all about having it; like not a few Transcendentalists, she might have written on the lintels of her door-post, *Whim*. That was her guiding divinity. Whim in a high sense: not unruliness, for all her impishness, but complete subjection to the inner dictate. She obeyed it in her mode of life, in her friendships, in her letters, in her poems. It makes her poetry eminently spontaneous—as fresh and artless as experience itself—in spite of the fact that she was not a spontaneous singer. The ringing bursts of melody that are characteristic of the born lyrical poet, such as Burns, she was incapable of; but she had insight, and intense, or rather tense, emotion, and expressed herself with an eye single to the truth. Something she derived from her reading, no doubt, from Emerson, the Brownings, Sir Thomas Browne; but rarely was poet less indebted. From her silent thought she derived what is essential in her work, and her whole effort was to state her findings precisely. She could not deliberately arrange her thoughts; "when I try to organize," she said, "my little force explodes and leaves me bare and charred." If she revised her work, as she did industriously, it was to render it not more attractive but truer.

Her poems are remarkable for their condensation, their vividness of image, their delicate or pungent satire and irony, their childlike responsiveness to experience, their subtle feeling for nature, their startling abruptness in dealing with themes commonly regarded as trite, their excellence in imaginative insight and still greater excellence in fancy. Typical is such a poem as that in which she celebrates the happiness of a little stone on the road, or that in which she remarks with gleeful irony upon the dignity that burial has in store for each of us—coach and footmen, bells in the village, "as we ride grand along." Emily Dickinson takes us to strange places; one never knows what is in store. But always she is penetrating and dainty, both intimate and aloof, challenging lively thought on our part while remaining, herself, a charmingly elfish mystery. Her place in American letters will be inconspicuous but secure.

ROBERT HILLYER (1895–1961), poet, critic, and teacher, was first a professor of English at Trinity College, then Boylston Professor of Rhetoric and Oratory at Harvard. His *Collected Verse* (1933) won the Pulitzer Prize. Hillyer's essay is the first of an increasing number by prominent literary figures of the 1920's who came to regard Emily Dickinson as not merely an "interesting" poet but a great one.

Emily Dickinson

ROBERT HILLYER

"If fame belonged to me, I would not escape her; if she did not, the longest day would pass me on the chase, and the approbation of my dog would forsake me then. My barefoot rank is better." Fame? It is doubtful that Emily Dickinson will ever be famous. She is not the sort of poet to be drummed and trumpeted to the people, nor yet the sort to be respectably dissected in the college classroom. She has been fortunate enough to escape all categories, popular and scholastic:

> I'm nobody! Who are you?
> Are you nobody, too?
> Then there's a pair of us—don't tell!
> They'd banish us, you know.
>
> How dreary to be somebody!
> How public, like a frog
> To tell your name the livelong day
> To an admiring bog!

It would be incongruous to read her aloud to a large group, however sympathetic. All the pompous absurdity of election to any Hall of Fame would have convulsed her with laughter, unless directed at herself—in which case she would have fled, panic-stricken. Yet year by year knowledge of the secret spreads, as friend whispers to friend and confides the inimitable poet to a new lover. Her first admirers feel somewhat ashamed of the patronizing or apologetic tone they once adopted towards her writing, and speak in bolder phrases. "Quaint,"

From *The Freeman,* VI (October 18, 1922), 129–31.

"whimsical," "obscure," "eccentric," these words no longer encompass an appraisal of her work, and the lazy minded who once applied them to her have now either given her up altogether or have been piqued by a second reading to closer attention.

Eccentric is the most difficult characterization to dispel, and, of course, the most unjust. The highest sanity, imagination, is so consistently ignored by exponents of the "normal," that the imaginative or contemplative life must always seem to them warped and unnatural. What relation to reality had this New England spinster, who year by year retreated farther from the world, until she could boast to a correspondent, "I do not cross my father's ground to any house or town"? Her own answer is sufficient: "Of shunning men and women—they talk of hallowed things, aloud, and embarrass my dog." For every apparent eccentricity of life or style she presents the sane, the final explanation. Reclusiveness in her case was no ignominious flight from the world; it was rather a safe perspective from which she could look around and choose her intimates.

> The soul selects her own society,
> Then shuts the door;
> On her divine majority
> Obtrude no more....
>
> I've known her from an ample nation
> Choose one;
> Then close the valves of her attention
> Like stone.

For a variety of reasons, Emily Dickinson's scope has been sadly underestimated. Her brevity has been mistaken for smallness, her love of detail for mere whimsy. Certainly she followed Blake's injunction

> To see a world in a grain of sand,
> And heaven in a wild flower;
> Hold infinity in the palm of your hand,
> And eternity in an hour.

Her expression is so succinct and plausible that she often completes her statement before a sluggish-minded reader has grasped her phraseology. Her poems rarely exceed a dozen lines; they are epigrammatic and packed. The neatness of her expression is baffling to those who look for the usual padding that gives a reader time to catch up with the poet's meaning. There are no "thank-you-ma'ams" on Emily Dickinson's road; her pace is full speed, and up hill at that. But her itinerary follows a road; she makes no sudden jumps into cosmos. Always she begins her voyage in a familiar New England country-side, and if she lead you into the realm of immortality, that, too, is New England country-side, where the only strangeness is the absence of Death.

> Eden is that old-fashioned House
> We dwell in every day,
> Without suspecting our abode
> Until we drive away.
> How fair, on looking back, the Day
> We sauntered from the door,
> Unconscious our returning
> Discover it no more.

Yet her mystical second sight has in no way diminished her careful observation of external details. The New England country-side of her poems is exact as well as transfigured. Every changing aspect is noted with exquisite rapture, and every seasonable stir becomes miraculous before her eyes. She was no recluse who could look out of her window and see illimitable fields and hills stretching away beyond the horizon of death. It is only occasionally that we find her pausing perplexedly before that horizon. Finality, mortal defeat, is a rare theme with her:

> This quiet Dust was Gentlemen and Ladies,
> And Lads and Girls;
> Was laughter and ability and sighing,
> And frocks and curls.
> This passive place a Summer's nimble mansion,
> Where Bloom and Bees
> Fulfilled their Oriental Circuit,
> Then ceased like these.

More often she looks beyond her mortal landscape with a strangely solemn gaiety; her gaze is never directed towards Death, but through Death, with a sort of tiptoe expectancy of the best:

> The overtakelessness of those
> Who have accomplished Death

Majestic is to me beyond
The majesties of Earth.

The soul her 'not at Home'
Inscribes upon the flesh,
And takes her fair aerial gait
Beyond the hope of touch.

The immortality towards which Emily Dickinson turns so decisively is no mystical merging of the many into the One—that subterfuge of the weak-spirited. Identity is the greatest boon, its preservation the soul's fiercest function. It is the "Single Hound" which attends the soul through the immense adventure of Life. Moreover, she distrusted abstractions, and saw eternity, as she saw the world which lay around her, in terms of things and individuals.

This revolt against abstract ideas of God and Heaven led her, and probably others, to believe that she was not religious. Any conception of Paradise apart from the Oriental Circuit of well-loved vistas was impossible to her; an absentee God was beyond the acceptance of her healthy imagination. Speaking of her family, she writes: "They are all religious, except me, and address an eclipse, every morning, whom they call their 'Father.'" All the emphasis she could bring to bear stressed the Heaven that lies about us, the God who walks in gardens in the cool of the evening, the immortality that perfects the delights of earth. She could not preoccupy herself with churchliness as she saw it round her; one passing glimpse of scorn or of pity, and she was off to the fields again. "There is what is called an 'awakening' in the church, and I know of no choicer ecstasy than to see Mrs. —— roll out in crêpe every morning, I suppose to intimidate the Antichrist; at least it would have that effect on me.... Spring is a happiness so beautiful, so unique, so unexpected, that I don't know what to do with my heart. I dare not take it, I dare not leave it—what do you advise?"

Every Sabbath morning, the rest of the Dickinson family went piously to church; Emily stayed at home with her robins and her flowers, because, she explained, it was the more economical method, as it saved going to Heaven.

Some keep the Sabbath going to church;
I keep it staying at home,
With a bobolink for a chorister,
And an orchard for a dome....

God preaches, a noted clergyman,
And the sermon is never long;
So instead of getting to Heaven at last,
I'm going all along!

Another element that cut her off from the orthodoxy of her day was a total ignorance of evil. Sorrow she knew—not, generally, as an intruder, rather as a background to her serene joy; but evil was non-existent as far as she was concerned. The grim strife against the ghostly foe, so picturesque a part of New England belief even as late as her time, was inexplicable to her. "When much in the woods, as a little girl, I was told that the snake would bite me, that I might pick a poisonous flower, or goblins kidnap me; but I went along and met no one but angels, who were far shyer of me than I could be of them—so I haven't that confidence in fraud which many exercise." Her letters during the Civil War reflect no burning enthusiasm for any abstract cause, but merely a tender admiration for friends of hers who gave their lives—individual heroes individually loved and mourned. For the war itself she has just one comment: "War feels to me an oblique place." This was neither blindness nor heartlessness, but an unworldly innocence which could not comprehend the survival of monsters on an Elysian earth. "We read in a tremendous book about 'an enemy,' and armed a confidential fort to scatter him away. The time has passed, and years have come, and yet not any 'Satan.' I think he must be making war upon some other nation."

All these utterances of hers, whether of slightest or profoundest import, are fraught with a whimsicality of expression that some have called deliberate, even perverse. I can not believe it. Emily Dickinson paradoxically achieves the highest art by the artlessness of her method; consciously, she neither revolts nor conforms. Many of her phrases that seem conscious are short cuts to significance, such as "the soul her 'not at Home' inscribes upon the flesh"; others are natural outbursts of a delightfully naughty humour with which she sometimes tempered satire and sometimes incongruously mingled high seriousness. She was loyal to the child-hearted of the world, and children themselves were her most desired comrades. "Blessed are they that play, for theirs is the kingdom of Heaven." The industrious and disapproving were objects of scorn to be avoided when possible, and reviled when necessary.

The butterfly obtains
But little sympathy,
Though favourably mentioned
In Entomology.
Because he travels freely
And wears a proper coat,
The circumspect are certain
That he is dissolute....

Nor is she afraid to carry playfulness to the very gates of Heaven. Why not? ... There is a saucy appreciation, but no impertinence, in her commending Him for the orderliness of his routine:

Lightly stepped a yellow star
To its lofty place,
Loosed the Moon her silver hat
From her lustral face.
All of evening softly lit
As an astral hall—
'Father,' I observed to Heaven,
'You are punctual.'

If she invoke her Father's attention to the rat, she is simply taking him at his word concerning his care of all his creatures:

Papa above! Regard a Mouse
O'erpowered by the Cat;
Reserve within thy kingdom
A 'Mansion' for the Rat!

Snug in seraphic cupboards
To nibble all the day,
While unsuspecting cycles
Wheel pompously away.

Who, in the presence of these amazing poems, would wish a single twisted syllable straightened to ensure the comprehension of mediocre minds or the applause of pedants?

It is a strange combination of delights that Emily Dickinson has left to us, so direct as to seem obscure, so loving as to seem brusque, so simple as to seem eccentric. Living amid the velvet hush of American Victorianism, she blew clarion notes of the shocking truth; a daughter of Puritanism, she pushed past the rigid image of Fear and took her God confidently by the hand. The vast love that was her being was never squandered in such sentimental abstractions as Humanity, Nature, and Religion; it was profitably, if wantonly, poured out for the individuals and objects that she knew, her family, her friends, the hired man, all children, her garden, and the visible symbols of life everlasting. Pomposity and show were known to her only as absurdities to be shunned; and always, in every word she wrote, we find that sense of proportion, too significant to be called a sense of humour, which gave to her most solemn statements an unvarying charm.

As I look out of my window over the drowsy New England landscape, I catalogue the myriad details of beauty that I see, wondering if any of them escaped her gleeful comment. Not one; they are all in the fields outside; they are all in the book under my hand; and in both is the mystery of recurring life, the happy sense of everyday reality made eternal through love. It is something to have been the laureate of an entire country-side. Beauty is not always clearly articulate, and even these happy fields would be less familiar had she not interpreted their speech.

But was she a great poet? The question startles us back into technicalities. I can not rely on the word poet; it has suffered sad changes; I am not sure I should like to call anyone I respect a poet any more. Something strange has come over the world; it is half blighted like the sun in partial eclipse. She certainly discovered a magic idiom of her own, which is hers only and can never be imitated. She interpreted New England and Eternity—but both these lands have fallen in favour. Perhaps I had best turn to her own criterion of poetry as she expressed it to Colonel Higginson, who called it a "crowning extravaganza": "If I read a book and it makes my whole body so cold no fire can ever warm me, I know that is poetry. If I feel physically as if the top of my head were taken off, I know that is poetry. These are the only ways I know it. Is there any other way?" One other way, at least, Emily Dickinson; and I am not sure I can define it. I hear much talk about the Greatest American Poet, with Poe and Whitman in the foreground. I read them both; I admire one of them. But there is only one American writer who, I am certain, can never, in any place, or in any manner, be subjected to comparison; and perhaps that is another way of knowing poetry.

MARTIN ARMSTRONG (1882–), a British man of letters born near Newcastle-on-Tyne and educated at Cambridge University, became a free-lance journalist after his return from service in World War I. Between 1922 and 1924 Armstrong was associate editor of the *Spectator*, as well as a contributor to other magazines. *Exodus and Other Poems* (1912) was the first of an extensive list of verse, novels, and stories which he has written. His 1923 essay on Emily Dickinson indicates that her rising stature as a poet among American critics was paralleled among the British. In both instances her faults may still be remarked, but with a significantly different critical attitude toward them.

The Poetry of Emily Dickinson

MARTIN ARMSTRONG

Emily Dickinson was born at Amherst, Massachusetts, on December 10th, 1830, and died there at the age of fifty-five on May 15th, 1886. She lived, it seems, a life of seclusion. Her father, a leading lawyer of the place and treasurer of the College, was in the habit of giving a large annual reception attended by the leading people of Amherst and the families connected with the College. At these receptions, it is reported, Emily played the hostess with perfect self-possession and then, when the yearly event was over, retired again into her obscurity until the next.

Her poems were not written for publication but for herself or, more rarely, for friends. They were found, after her death, by her sister. "Most of the poems," we are told, "had been carefully copied on sheets of notepaper and tied in little fascicules, each of six or eight sheets. While many of them bear evidence of having been thrown off at white heat, still more have received careful revision.... They should be regarded in many cases as merely the first stray, suggestive sketches of an artist, intended to be embodied at some time in the finished picture."

So much it is of interest and importance to know. Her poetry is that of a recluse and mystic, but a recluse without any trace of the morbid

From the *Spectator*, CXXX (January 6, 1923), 22–23.

or the inhuman and a mystic only in the free sense in which Blake may be called so. She loved and studied nature in its largest and smallest [aspects] and possessed a wonderful power of accurate description both for the thing seen or heard and for the feeling—the atmosphere—of the poetic moment, and with these there is mingled at times a quaint and quiet humour. Nothing could be more sharply seen than her description of a bat as a "small umbrella, quaintly halved," and her emotional accuracy is shown in a poem which wonderfully transcribes the impression of the house opposite, where a death has just occurred:

The neighbours rustle in and out,
The doctor drives away.
A window opens, like a pod,
Abrupt, mechanically. . . .

and in that more marvellous poem in which—as so often—she imagined herself dying. Friends stand round her bed; she wills away her keepsakes,

and then
There interposed a fly,
With blue, uncertain, stumbling buzz,
Between the light and me;
And then the windows failed, and then
I could not see to see.

We find her continually on the threshold of wonder, standing detached in the sudden realization of the greatness of little things, the littleness of great, glimpsing for a moment a vast, elusive significance in the common things of life. Like Blake, whom so often she recalls, she sees a world in a grain of sand, and a heaven in a wild flower. That attitude is beautifully shown in a poem of four lines:

Where every bird is bold to go,
And bees abashless play,
The foreigner before he knocks
Must thrust the tears away.

Sometimes she is the pantheist, whose mind discovers the divine in the natural world:

The red upon the hill
Taketh away my will;
If anybody sneer,
Take care, for God is here,
That's all.

The breaking of the day
Addeth to my degree;
If any ask me how,
Artist, who drew me so,
Must tell.

In other poems, as in a close-packed little poem on the Oriole, she holds that nature gains all its significance from mind. The Oriole sings from the tree, but the reality of its song is only in the mind of the listener:

The fashion of the ear
Attireth that it hear
In dun or fair.

So whether it be rune,
Or whether it be none,
Is of within;

'The tune is in the tree,'
The sceptic showeth me;
'No, sir! In thee!'

Emily Dickinson is difficult to criticize. At her best she writes poems which are quite perfect. But on the flawless poet, detached from date or personal idiosyncracy, the little New England spinster is perpetually intruding with her charming, narrowly dated, demure yet humorous Quakerishness. It peeps out in the "No, sir! In thee!" of the Oriole poem and the "That's all" of the other poem which I quoted earlier, and again in such phrases as "You cannot fold a flood And put it in a drawer," or "The twilight stood as strangers do With hat in hand." Frequently, too, in a conventional stanzaic form she will suddenly dismay you by dropping out the rhyme so that the expected effect falls dead like a fiddlestring which suddenly slackens and goes flat. How far this is calculated it is difficult to say; the fact remains that as we grow familiar with her poetry in the aggregate these imperfections come to seem things appropriate and attractive, just as an imperfection of accent or awkwardness of gesture becomes an added charm in a charming personality. The last two stanzas of a poem called "Charlotte Brontë's Grave" illustrate both sides, the first stanza so packed and so impressive, the second to our modern ears so comical:

> Gathered from many wanderings,
> Gethsemane can tell
> Through what transporting anguish
> She reached the asphodel.
>
> Soft fall the sounds of Eden
> Upon her puzzled ear;
> Oh, what an afternoon for heaven,
> When Brontë entered there.

Occasionally—a less venial sin—she will drop into flattest prose, as in the last line in this verse from a poem on a deathbed:

> We noticed smallest things,
> Things overlooked before,
> By this great light upon our minds
> Italicized, as 't were.

The first verse of a two-verse poem on "Lost Faith" illustrates the same thing and also her occasional curious omission of the expected rhyme:

> To lose one's faith surpasses
> The loss of an estate,
> Because estates can be
> Replenished—faith cannot.

Nothing could well be worse; but it is unfair to attach great importance to such lapses, for we must remember that they may have been no more than notes, written—as she often wrote—continuously as prose without any indication of line-endings and now edited into stanzas.

Emily Dickinson would gain enormously by careful selection. I have no doubt that a volume of selected poems would reveal the fact that her poetry, as Mr. Conrad Aiken in his recent anthology of *Modern American Poets* claims, is "perhaps the finest, by a woman, in the English language." I quarrel only with his "perhaps."

I cannot, in a brief article, deal very fully with her work, but I can at least indicate some of its qualities. Two of the most characteristic—or rather two aspects of one typical quality—are great concentration of meaning and a gift for arresting and dynamic epithets and verbs—a short-circuiting, as it were, of emotion and meaning. The concentration was evident in the verse I quoted from "Charlotte Brontë's Grave," and it appears in the last line of one of her finest poems:

> I've seen a dying eye
> Run round and round a room
> In search of something, as it seemed,
> Then cloudier become;
> And then, obscure with fog,
> And then be soldered down,
> Without disclosing what it be
> 'T were blessed to have seen.

The quality which I suggested by "dynamic" is seen there too, where the eyes are "soldered down" by death. Elsewhere Death "nails" the eyes, and in a poem about the sound of wind in the trees she speaks of one who "never heard that *fleshless* chant Rise solemn in the tree."

The essence of greatness or perfection is that it cannot be analysed, but when it comes it is unmistakable, and we hear it unmistakably in such an opening as this:

> Safe in their alabaster chambers,
> Untouched by morning and untouched by noon,
> Sleep the meek members of the resurrection,
> Rafter of satin, and roof of stone....

We hear it, too, in this poem, included by Mr. Aiken in his anthology:

> My life closed twice before its close;
>   It yet remains to see
> If Immortality unveil
>   A third event to me,
>
> So huge, so hopeless to conceive,
>   As these that twice befell.
> Parting is all we know of heaven,
>   And all we need of hell.

The woman who could write that poem is, for me, without question a great poet.

As early as 1924 CONRAD AIKEN (1889–) had edited *Selected Poems of Emily Dickinson,* with an introductory essay reprinted here. By then his own poetry had earned him a solid reputation. In 1930 he was awarded the Pulitzer Prize for *Selected Poems.* His subsequent work has ranged widely over poetry, fiction, drama, and criticism. Aiken's careful selection of Dickinson poems and his balanced account of her life and work did much to stimulate reappraisal of Emily Dickinson in the 1920's, especially in England.

Emily Dickinson

CONRAD AIKEN

Emily Dickinson was born in Amherst, Massachusetts, on December 10th, 1830. She died there, after a life perfectly devoid of outward event, in 1886. She was thus an exact contemporary of Christina Rossetti, who was born five days earlier than she, and outlived her by eight years. Of her life we know little. Her father, Edward Dickinson, was a lawyer, and the Treasurer of Amherst College; and it is clear that what social or intellectual life was in that bleak era available, was available for her. That she did not choose to avail herself of it, except in very slight degree, is also clear; and that this choice, which was gradually to make of her life an almost inviolable solitude, was made early, is evident from her Letters. In a letter dated 1853, when she was twenty-three years old, she remarked, "I do not go from home." By the time she was thirty, the habit of sequestration had become distinct, a subject on which she was explicit and emphatic in her letters to T. W. Higginson —editor of the *Atlantic Monthly* at that time. She made it clear that if there was to be any question of a meeting between them, he would have to come to Amherst—she would not go to Boston. Higginson, as a matter of fact, saw her twice, and his record of the encounter is practically the only record we have of her from any "literary" personage of her lifetime. Even this is meagre—Higginson saw her superficially,

From *Selected Poems of Emily Dickinson,* edited, with an Introduction, by Conrad Aiken (London: Jonathan Cape, 1924), 5–22.

as was inevitable. Brave soldier, courtly gentleman, able editor, he was too much of the old school not to be a little puzzled by her poetry; and if he was fine enough to guess the fineness, he was not quite fine enough wholly to understand it. The brief correspondence between these two is an extraordinary document of unconscious irony—the urbanely academic editor reproaching his wayward pupil for her literary insubordination, her false quantities, and reckless liberties with rhyme; the wayward pupil replying with a humility, beautiful and pathetic, but remaining singularly, with unmalleable obstinacy, herself. "I saw her," wrote Higginson, "but twice, face to face, and brought away the impression of something as unique and remote as Undine or Mignon or Thekla." When, thirty years after the acquaintance had begun, and four after Emily Dickinson's death, he was called upon to edit a selection from her poetry, practically none of which had been published during her lifetime, his scruples were less severe, and he spoke of her with generosity and insight. "After all," he then wrote, "when a thought takes one's breath away, a lesson on grammar seems an impertinence." Again, "In many cases these verses will seem to the reader like poetry torn up by the roots." And again, "a quality more suggestive of the poetry of Blake than of anything to be elsewhere found —flashes of wholly original and profound insight into nature and life."

Thus began and ended Emily Dickinson's only important connexion with the literary life of her time. She knew, it is true, Helen Hunt Jackson, a poetess, for whose anthology, *A Masque of Poets,* she gave the poem "Success," one of the few poems she allowed publication during her life. And she knew the Bowles family, owners and editors of the *Springfield Republican,* at that time the *Manchester Guardian* of New England—which, as she put it mischievously, was one of "such papers . . . as have nothing carnal in them." But these she seldom saw; and aside from these she had few intimates outside of her family; the circle of her world grew steadily smaller. This is a point of cardinal importance, but unfortunately no light has been thrown upon it. It is apparent that Miss Dickinson became a hermit by deliberate and conscious choice. "A recluse," wrote Higginson, "by temperament and habit, literally spending years without setting her foot beyond the doorstep, and many more years during which her walks were strictly limited to her father's grounds, she habitually concealed her mind, like her person, from all but a very few friends; and it was with great difficulty that she was persuaded to print, during her lifetime, three or four poems." One of the co-editors of *Poems: Second Series* assures us that this voluntary hermitage was not due to any "love-disappointment," and that she was "not an invalid." "She had tried society and the world, and had found them lacking." But this, of course, tells us nothing. Her letters show us convincingly that her girlhood was a normally "social" one—she was active, high-spirited, and endowed with a considerable gift for extravagant humour. As a young woman she had, so Mrs. Bianchi, a niece, informs us in the preface to *The Single Hound,* several love-affairs. But we have no right, without other testimony, to assume here any ground for the singular psychological change that came over her. The only other clue we have, of any sort, is the hint from one of her girlhood friends, that perhaps, *"she was longing for poetic sympathy."* Perhaps! But we must hope that her relatives and literary executors will eventually see fit to publish *all* her literary remains, verse and prose, and to give us thus, perhaps, a good deal more light on the nature of her life. Anecdotes relating to her mischievousness, her wit, her waywardness, are not enough. It is amusing, if horrifying, to know that once, being anxious to dispose of some kittens, she put them on a shovel, carried them into the cellar, and dropped them into the nearest jar—which, subsequently, on the occasion of the visit of a distinguished judge, turned out to have been the pickle-jar. We like to know too, that even when her solitude was most remote she was in the habit of lowering from her window, by a string, small baskets of fruit or confectionery for children. But there are other things we should like to know more.

There seems, however, little likelihood of our being told, by her family, anything more; and if we seek for the causes of the psychic injury which so sharply turned her in upon herself. we can only speculate. Her letters, in this regard, give little light, only showing us again and again that the injury was deep. Of the fact that she suffered acutely from intellectual drought, there is evidence enough. One sees her vividly here—but one sees her, as it were, perpetually in retreat; always discovering anew, with dismay, the intellectual limitations of her correspondents; she is discreet, pathetic, baffled, a little humbled, and draws in her horns; takes sometimes a perverse pleasure in indulging more than ever, on the occasion of such a disappointment, in her love of a cryptic style—a delicate bombardment of parable and whim which she perfectly knows will stagger; and then again retreats to the safe ground of the superficial. It is perhaps for this reason that the letters give us so remarkably little information about her literary interests. The meagreness of literary allusion is astounding. The Brontës and the Brownings are referred to—she thought Alexander Smith "not very coherent"—Joaquin Miller she "could not care about." Of her own work she speaks only in the brief unsatisfactory correspondence with Higginson. To him she wrote in 1862, "I wrote no verse, but one or two, until this winter." Otherwise, no scrap of her own literary history: she appears to have existed in a vacuum. Of the literary events, tremendous for America, which were taking place during her most impressionable years, there is hardly a mention. Emerson was at the height of his career, and living only sixty miles away: his poems came out when she was seventeen. When she was twenty, Hawthorne published *The Scarlet Letter;* and *The House of the Seven Gables* the year after. The same year, 1851, brought out Melville's *Moby Dick*. The death of Poe took place in 1849—in 1850 was published the first collected edition of his poems. When she was twenty-four, Thoreau's *Walden* appeared; when she was twenty-five, *Leaves of Grass.* One can say with justice that she came to full "consciousness" at the very moment when American literature came to flower. That she knew this, there cannot be any question; nor that she was stimulated and influenced by it. One must assume that she found in her immediate environment no one of her own stature, with whom she could admit or discuss such things; that she lacked the energy or effrontery to voyage out into the unknown in search of such companionship; and that lacking this courage, and wanting this help, she became easily a prey to the then current Emersonian doctrine of mystical Individualism. In this connexion it is permissible to suggest that her extreme self-seclusion and secrecy was both a protest and a display—a kind of vanity masquerading as modesty. She became increasingly precious, of her person as of her thought. Vanity is in her letters—at the last an unhealthy vanity. She believes that anything she says, however brief, will be of importance; however cryptic, will be deciphered. She enjoys being something of a mystery, and she sometimes deliberately and awkwardly exaggerates it. Even in notes of condolence—for which she had a morbid passion—she is vain enough to indulge in sententiousness: as when she wrote, to a friend whose father had died on her wedding-day, "Few daughters have the immortality of a father for a bridal gift."

When we come to Emily Dickinson's poetry, we find the Emersonian individualism clear enough, but perfectly Miss Dickinson's. Henry James observed of Emerson:

> The doctrine of the supremacy of the individual to himself, of his originality and, as regards his own character, *unique* quality, must have had a great charm for people living in a society in which introspection, thanks to the want of other entertainment, played almost the part of a social resource.... There was...much relish for the utterances of a writer who would help one to take a picturesque view of one's internal possibilities, and to find in the landscape of the soul all sorts of fine sunrise and moonlight effects.

This sums up admirably the social "case" of Miss Dickinson—it gives us a shrewd picture of the causes of her singular introversion, and it suggests that we are perhaps justified in considering her the most perfect flower of New England Transcendentalism. In her mode of life she carried the doctrine of self-sufficient individualism farther than Thoreau carried it, or the naïve zealots of Brook Farm. In her poetry she carried it, with its complement of passionate moral mysticism, farther than Emerson: which is to say that as a poet she had more genius than he. Like Emerson, whose essays must greatly have influenced her, and whose poetry, especially his gnomic poems, only a little less, she was from the outset, and remained all her life, a singular mixture of Puritan and freethinker. The problems of good and evil, of life and death, obsessed her; the nature and destiny of the human soul; and Emerson's theory of compensation. Towards God, as one of her earliest critics is reported to have said, "she exhibited an Emersonian self-possession." Indeed, she did not, and could not, accept the Puritan God at all. She was frankly irreverent, on occasion, a fact which seems to have made her editors a little uneasy—one hopes that it has not resulted in the suppression of any of her work. What she was irreverent to, of course, was the Puritan conception of God, the Puritan attitude toward him.

Heavenly father, take to thee
The supreme iniquity,
Fashioned by thy candid hand
In a moment contraband.
Though to trust us seems to us
More respectful,—we are dust,
We apologize to thee
For thine own Duplicity.

This, it must be repeated, is Emily Dickinson's opinion of the traditional and anthropomorphic "God," who was still, in her day, a portentous Victorian gentleman. Her real reverence, the reverence that made her a mystic poet of the finest sort, was reserved for Nature, which seemed to her a more manifest and beautiful evidence of Divine Will than creeds and churches. This she saw, observed, loved, with a burning simplicity and passion which nevertheless did not exclude her very agile sense of humour. Her Nature poems, however, are not the most secretly revelatory or dramatically compulsive of her poems, nor, on the whole, the best. They are often of extraordinary delicacy —nearly always give us, with deft brevity, the exact in terms of the quaint. But, also, they are often superficial, a mere affectionate playing with the smaller things that give her delight; and to see her at her best and most characteristic and most profound, one must turn to the remarkable range of metaphysical speculation and ironic introspection which is displayed in those sections of her posthumous books which her editors have captioned Life, and Time and Eternity. In the former sections are the greater number of her set "meditations" on the nature of things. For some critics they will always appear too bare, bleak and fragmentary. They have no trappings, only here and there a shred of purple. It is as if Miss Dickinson who, in one of her letters uttered her contempt for the "obtrusive body," had wanted to make them, as nearly as possible, disembodied thought. The thought is there, at all events, hard, bright, and clear; and her symbols, her metaphors, of which she could be prodigal, have an analogous clarity and translucency. What is also there is a downright homeliness which is a perpetual surprise and delight. Emerson's gnomic style she tunes up to the epigrammatic—the epigrammatic she often carries to the point of the cryptic; she becomes what one might call an epigrammatic symbolist.

Lay this laurel on the one
Too intrinsic for renown.
Laurel! veil your deathless tree,—
Him you chasten, that is he!

This, from *Poems: Second Series,* verges perilously on the riddle. And it often happens that her passionate devotion to concise statement in terms of metaphor left for her readers a small rich emblem of which the colours tease, the thought entices, but the meaning escapes. Against this, however, should be set her capacity, when occasion came, for a granite simplicity, any parallel to which one must seek in the Seventeenth Century. This, for example, called Parting.

My life closed twice before its close;
It yet remains to see
If Immortality unveil
A third event to me,

So huge, so hopeless to conceive,
As these that twice befell.
Parting is all we know of heaven
And all we need of hell.

Or this, from *The Single Hound:*

Not any sunny tone
From any fervent zone
Finds entrance there.
Better a grave of Balm
Toward human nature's home,
And Robins near,
Than a stupendous Tomb
Proclaiming to the gloom
How dead we are.

Both these poems, it will be noted, deal with death; and it must be observed that the number of poems by Miss Dickinson on this subject is one of the most remarkable things about her. Death, and the problem of life after death, obsessed her. She seems to have thought of it constantly—she died all her life, she probed death daily. "That bareheaded life under grass worries one like a wasp," she wrote. Ultimately, the obsession became morbid, and her eagerness for details, after the death of a friend—the hungry desire to know *how* she died—became almost vulture-like. But the preoccupation, with its horrible uncertainties—its doubts about immortality, its hatred of the flesh, and its many reversals of both positions—gave us her sharpest work. The theme was inexhaustible for her. If her poetry seldom became "lyrical," seldom departed from the colourless sobriety of its bare iambics and toneless assonance, it did so most of all when the subject was death. Death profoundly and cruelly invited her. It was most of all when she tried "to touch the smile," and dipped her "fingers in the frost," that she took full possession of her genius.

Her genius was, it remains to say, as erratic as it was brilliant. Her disregard for accepted forms or for regularities was incorrigible. Grammar, rhyme, metre—anything went by the board if it stood in the way of thought or freedom of utterance. Sometimes this arrogance was justified; sometimes not. She did not care in the least for variety of effect—of her six hundred-odd poems practically all are in octosyllabic quatrains or couplets, sometimes with rhyme, sometimes with assonance, sometimes with neither. Everywhere, when one first comes to these poems, one seems to see nothing but a colourless dry monotony. How deceptive a monotony, concealing what reserves of depth and splendour; what subtleties of mood and tone! Once adjust oneself to the spinsterly angularity of the mode, its lack of eloquence or rhetorical speed, its naïve and often prosaic directness, one discovers felicities of thought and phrase on every page. The magic is terse and sure. And ultimately one simply sighs at Miss Dickinson's singular perversity, her lapses and tyrannies, and accepts them as an inevitable part of the strange and original genius she was. The lapses and tyrannies become a positive charm—one even suspects they were deliberate. They satisfied her—therefore they satisfy us. This marks, of course, our complete surrender to her highly individual gift, and to the singular sharp beauty, present everywhere, of her personality. The two things cannot be separated; and together, one must suppose, they suffice to put her among the finest poets in the language.

PERCY LUBBOCK (1879–) is probably best known as the author of *The Craft of Fiction* (1921), a landmark in the theory of the modern novel, though he has written biography, history, and fiction as well. *Samuel Pepys* (1909), *Roman Pictures* (1923), and more recently, *Portrait of Edith Wharton* (1947) suggest something of the time-span and range of interests which have characterized Lubbock's literary career. His judgment of Emily Dickinson's poetry as, at its best, brilliantly unique indicates how far, by 1924, her reputation in England had advanced from the general judgment of "eccentric" in the 1890's.

Determined Little Anchoress

PERCY LUBBOCK

The life of Emily Dickinson, "the most perfect flower of New England transcendentalism," is a riddle, and she clearly meant it to be a riddle. She was born in 1830, in a small country-town of Massachusetts. Her father was a leading man of the place, she had a comfortable home. Apparently with a good deal of charm and wit, certainly with an inquisitive and adventurous mind, she lived a normal sociable life till she was grown a woman. Her youthful letters to her brother are delightfully natural, easy, vivid. Once she made a little journey and paid some visits in Philadelphia and Washington. But she was still in her twenties when she began to turn herself into a mystery. She shut herself up in her father's house, she cut off very nearly every relation with the world without, she developed a tortured style of expression, in her letters to the few people whom she allowed to be her friends, that grew more darkly oracular year by year. She wrote her strange little poems and posted them to the rare elect; but they were denied with almost unbroken firmness to the profaning world. For thirty years and more she never crossed her doorstep, save only to flit like a sprite to

From the *Nation and Athenaeum*, XXXVI (October 18, 1924), 114. A review of *The Life and Letters of Emily Dickinson* by Martha Dickinson Bianchi (London: Jonathan Cape, 1924); *Selected Poems of Emily Dickinson*, edited, with an Introduction, by Conrad Aiken (London: Jonathan Cape, 1924).

her brother's house, at the bottom of the garden, and back again. And that was all; she died in 1886.

What did it mean? Was there some wound or woe of her youth that had scared her once for all into herself? A wound there was, an unhappy love-affair of early days, which may have begun the habit of seclusion. But Mrs. Bianchi, her niece, though inclined to be almost breathlessly discreet, appears to say that this memory was no lasting or embittering terror. There it was, that was Emily's way: her family, finger on lip, can say no more. Mr. Conrad Aiken takes a freer line, and perhaps a more sensible. It all happened a long time ago, and Emily Dickinson is a figure of interest, and we may certainly put our questions if we choose. Mr. Aiken, without pretending to be positive, suggests an explanation that rings like the true one. She found nobody immediately near her of her own measure; she had not the energy to look further away for companionship; and the line of least resistance was to adopt, and to find pride in adopting, the famous "Emersonian doctrine of mystical individualism," all-pervading in the air of her day and her place, which made the possession of one's soul in solitude an adventure and a career in itself. And then it is easy to see that she enjoyed the enigma she presented. Mr. Aiken roundly declares that she was vain of it; and he is right, her letters show it. Their tormented preciosity, steadily growing with the years, is the voice of vanity; she makes at last an almost open parade of her tantalizing, mystifying aloofness above the world. It is a pity; a fine spirit was spoilt, without any manner of need, for want of exposure to a little common earthly weather. Her family would have thrust her firmly out into the rain; but they were far too much in awe of her oracles for a thought so gross.

As for her strange little poems, they too suffered in the end from the perverse artificiality of her life. Their cryptic harshness, their bad rhymes and wild grammar—Emily came to believe, perhaps, that these were a mark of her originality and sincerity, disdaining rule. Her friends believed so, at any rate, and she hardly encountered the criticism of any but her friends. In a more natural atmosphere she might have been better at ease with her own sincerity, which would have been none the worse for good writing and good rhymes. As it is, the extraordinary flashes of beauty in her verse are too often merely baffled and frustrated; they shine out suddenly and are stifled in the tight clumsiness of her speech. So much a wholesome judgment will surely admit, without trying (as even Mr. Aiken tries) to think her clumsiness a peculiar grace. And it is easily admitted; for there remains enough to fill a volume with verse in which her genius moves as it should, revealing itself for the singular, exquisite thing that it truly was. Acute sensibility of feeling, swift audacity of mind—they were her gifts; when she was stirred, her thought would be off like lightning, to snatch an image and return again before another would have time to blink. And when the stars were kind, when the first words that occurred to her were also the right words, she produced a little poem that of its kind is alone in poetry. Nothing else is like it; for even the obvious influence of Emerson, the "gnomic sententiousness" of manner that she certainly caught from him, is only of the surface. Emily was no poetic moralist; she darted straight at the idea that struck her for its beauty, she did not work towards it through any argument or debate. It was always hit or miss with her; and at the happy moment she could hit with a metaphor, a figure, a word even, a vanishing impression that in another second would have passed like a streak. She saw these sudden and desirable apparitions everywhere. To this determined little anchoress, so carefully shut up in her provincial cell, nothing was sacred and nothing daunting; she made as free with heaven and hell, life and death, as with the daisies and butterflies outside her window. She was small, she was obstinate, she was not as wise as she ended by thinking herself; but her voice was unique, and she flung out the short cry of her joy or pain or mockery with a note that cannot be forgotten. It is much to say in a world where voices are so many.

Not only was HAROLD MONRO (1879–1932) a poet of some reputation, he was also well known as editor, publisher, and general source of encouragement for other writers. His first verse, simply titled *Poems*, appeared in 1906. Nine volumes of verse followed, and the *Collected Poems* was published posthumously in 1933. Monro founded three different poetry reviews and managed London's celebrated Poetry

Bookshop. His rejection of Emily Dickinson is reminiscent of the 1890's, but in 1925 it was a minority opinion.

Emily Dickinson—Overrated

HAROLD MONRO

At a first impression Emily Dickinson's tiny lyrics appear more like the jottings of a half-idiotic schoolgirl than the grave musings of a fully educated woman. This kind of verse, I thought to myself, may go down in America, but, when imported to England, we inevitably apply to it the test of comparison with the poems of Emily Brontë, Christina Rossetti, Mary Coleridge, Michael Field. Her poems are splendid blunders. How much better they could have been if she had specialized in her craft. She was intellectually blind, partially deaf, mostly dumb, to the art of poetry. Consequently seven out of ten of her lyrical jottings are plainly failures.

Emily Dickinson has been overrated, but not so far overrated as a first survey of her selected poems might indicate. Her style is clumsy; her language is poor; her technique is appalling, and there is no excuse (except that very excuse of faulty technique) for the frequent elementary grammatical errors. There is only one rhyme (and that a doubtful one) in the poem which ends with the line—

Flinging the problem back at you and I

so that one almost feels that her editor might have taken it upon himself to correct so elementary and unnecessary a mistake.

Some twentieth-century authors, we know, ignore the rules of grammar just for fun, or as a little surprise to their readers; but there is no reason to suspect these motives in Miss Dickinson. No twentieth-century levity in her. Moreover, her lyrics have been described as "the finest poetry by a woman in the English language."

She died about forty years ago. About four decades is the average period required by the civilized human intelligence to recognize its poets. In the modern world the true bards sit alone in their rooms chanting to themselves: they court no publicity. The ancient bard was

From *The Criterion,* III (January, 1925), 322–24. A review of *Selected Poems of Emily Dickinson,* edited, with an Introduction, by Conrad Aiken (London: Jonathan Cape, 1924).

a public figure. But the modern poet's voice echoes slowly from library to library in unfamiliar esoteric tone.

It would be ridiculously easy to belittle Emily Dickinson by unfavorable quotation. At her worst she is positively comic; but her worst is as distant from her best as the half-idiotic schoolgirl from, let us say, Keats. There are very few lyrics quite flawless, but as we progress in the art of understanding her, we begin to find even in many of the flaws a kind of large splendid awkwardness, something innocently audacious, grotesque, and abnormal. The woman who wrote the following:

AFTERMATH

The bustle in a house
The morning after death
Is solemnest of industries
Enacted upon earth,—

The sweeping up the heart,
And putting love away
We shall not want to use again
Until eternity.

(clumsy enough, but redeemed entirely by a magic of pathos and loveliness), could also allow (to choose only one from many possible examples) the following to stand:

But I, grown shrewder, scan the skies
With a suspicious air,—
As children, swindled for the first,
All swindlers be, infer.

She seems to be afraid. She dwelt in seclusion, social, physical, and psychological. She gives the impression of wanting to keep some secret. Clarity of thought is constantly veiled in obscurity of expression. She was not candid; she does not seem to have been moved by any overruling instinct for truth. And we compare her unavoidably with her contemporary, Emily Brontë, whose infatuated desire to be faithful to her every aspect of truth overcame all timidity.

Little is known publicly about SUSAN MILES, pseudonym of an occasional contributor to London literary journals. Sir John Squire, founder and editor of the *London Mercury* and a friend of Susan Miles, stated that she was "the extremely lively, humorous, and devoted wife and 'helpmeet' of a central London Vicar, who was that vague thing a Christian Socialist." This essay is from an article replying to Harold Monro's pronouncement that Emily Dickinson's poetry was plainly "overrated."

The Irregularities of Emily Dickinson

SUSAN MILES

Emily Dickinson's rhymes are from the conventional point of view so hopeless that it appears to me incredible that they should be due to incompetence. There is, however, wide divergence of opinion as to the significance which should be attached to her irregularities. Mr. Harold Monro, in the January issue of *The Criterion,* writes with extreme severity. "At a first impression," he begins, "Emily Dickinson's tiny lyrics appear more like the jottings of a half-idiotic schoolgirl than the grave musings of a fully educated woman.... Her style is clumsy; her language is poor; her technique is appalling." But after sending in this apparently unsatisfactory report, Mr. Monro half-withdraws his first impression, surprising us by a sentence which, if it means anything, means that he puts her best work on a level with that of Keats. Must we then understand that had it been *Hyperion* that Mr. Monro was introducing today to a public ignorant for the most part even of the author's name, it too would have been dismissed with a curt notice wholly derogatory save for three or four phrases of grudging commendation? Mr. Monro tells us that "Emily Dickinson has been over-rated, but not so far over-rated as a first survey of her selected poems might indicate," and that "as we progress in the art of understanding her we find in many of her flaws a kind of large splendid awkwardness, something innocently audacious, grotesque and abnormal." He then goes on to quote a lyric which he describes as "clumsy enough, but redeemed entirely by a magic of pathos and

From the *London Mercury,* XIII (December, 1925), 145–50; 157–58.

loveliness." After a final rebuke, to which I shall revert at the close of this article, Mr. Monro turns to *The Thirteenth Caesar,* regretting that "justice cannot be done to Mr. Sitwell in a short notice of this kind." It is a short notice; but it is considerably longer than that allotted to Emily Dickinson.

Others among Emily Dickinson's critics consistently make light of her irregularities, deliberately disregarding them as a mother might the lisp of a precocious child, or a legatee a sprinkle of misspellings in a will that made him rich. "It would be ungracious to carp when given a good gift," these critics seem to exclaim, "even if the bearer, large and flat of foot, has trodden on our toes," adding perhaps, "especially if she apologises as meekly as Emily Dickinson to the editor of *The Atlantic Monthly.*"

But most of the critics who refuse to scold, sigh. Few seem prepared to go so far as the writer in *The Times Literary Supplement,* who asserts that "in a great deal of her work there is a kind of perfection in imperfection which, if it sometimes reveals the limits of her technical resources, does honor to her judgment," and who speaks of her use in one poem of a "rhyme which is not a rhyme" as "a kind of imaginative triumph." *

Yet even this critic writes grudgingly. He admits by implication that the rhyme in defeating the ear's expectation fulfills the imagination's need—why then assert that "if perfection was unattainable it is the right kind of imperfection"? If a full rhyme would have been less expressive, wherein lies the imperfection of the Dickinsonian rhyme? Why speak of the Dickinsonian technique as "*almost* a device"? Why "a *kind* of imaginative triumph"?

My aim in writing this article is to claim quite explicitly, and without any apology, that Emily Dickinson's irregularities have a definite artistic significance. I believe that could we—*per impossibile*—without altering her vocabulary, substitute full rhymes for Dickinsonian, nothing would be gained by the substitution and, in many cases, much would be lost.

I do not, of course, intend to suggest that there is any intrinsic merit in a rhyme-scheme which arouses expectation and then defeats it. The device is a piece of technique which may be justified or may not. It is

* "An American Poetess," *The Times Literary Supplement,* Oct. 30, 1924, 673–74.—Editors' note.

wholly a question of what it is that the artist using it wishes to express. If he wishes to give expression to a consistent belief in a world where not a worm is cloven in vain and not a moth with vain desire is shrivelled in a fruitless fire, he does artistically well to construct a volume of neat stanzas where "sin" rhymes with "in," "fall" with "all," "night" with "light," and "ill" with "will." If he has had an impression of a universe where all discord is harmony not understood, all partial ill is universal good, he will adequately express that impression in trim heroic couplets, rhyming "be" with "me" and "curse" with "worse" in undeviating regularity. As a matter of fact, neither Pope nor Tennyson nor any other poet ever had a wholly consistent impression of such a world. And when these poets were not actively believing in a dove-tailed universe their rhymes ceased to resemble a game of ping-pong played by expert and cautious children. When his impressions demanded such expression, Tennyson rhymed "death" with "faith," "home" with "masterdom," "move" with "love," "wood" with "blood," and "heath" with "death"; Pope rhymed "food" with "blood," "mourns" with "burns," and "rest" with "beast." These are not full rhymes; but critics pass them without question, partly perhaps because they find them in the work of poets with an established reputation for orthodoxy, partly, no doubt, because they have some sense of what is artistically seemly. Ping-pong rhyming is consistently practised only by such writers as Ella Wheeler Wilcox, who labels her verses *Poems of Optimism* and plasters her pages with the tags "Ignore Misfortune" and "Be indifferent to evil."

But the universe as Emily Dickinson envisaged it was very different from the universe as pictured by Ella Wheeler Wilcox. Emily Dickinson viewed a world made up of pieces which often did not dove-tail, and it was her impression of this world that she sought to express in her poetry. The annual resurrection in field and forest was to her extremely odd. Experience for her was a precarious gait. A splinter very often seemed to swerve in her brain while the brains of other people ran evenly and true within their grooves. She pondered a tremendous scene, and a little madness in her rhymes was part of her expression of it. Sometimes that expression demanded a three-quarters rhyme, that is, an echo of the final consonant (if any), and the substitution of a long for a corresponding short vowel, or of a short for a corresponding long; sometimes the expression demanded a half-rhyme, that is, an echoing vowel and a contrasting consonant, or an echoing consonant and a contrasting vowel;

sometimes a non-rhyme, that is, a sound which echoes neither final consonant nor vowel, but which clangs out its contrast to both....

I do not wish to labor my thesis in detail; it may easily be tested by reference to such poems as: "He dropped so low in my regard," "I never hear the word 'escape,'" "I know that he exists," "The heart asks pleasure first," "Pain has an element of blank," "The brain within its groove," "She rose to his requirement," and "The sun kept setting, setting still."

As we might expect, the irregularities of rhyme are less frequent in the poems that deal with inanimate nature than in those concerned with humanity.

> It makes no difference abroad,
> The seasons fit the same,
> The mornings blossom into noons,
> And split their pods of flame.
>
> Wild-flowers kindle in the woods,
> The brooks brag all the day;
> No blackbird bates his jargoning
> For passing Calvary.

Here the significance of the part-rhyme in the second stanza is as obvious as is that of the full rhyme in the first.

And consider "A lady red upon the hill." Here in the first three stanzas which describe the imminence of spring, the rhymes come pat as Pope's. It is only in the last stanza that an irregularity of rhyme is called for by the thought:

> A lady red upon the hill
> Her annual secret keeps;
> A lady white within the field
> In placid lily sleeps!
>
> The tidy breezes with their brooms
> Sweep vale, and hill, and tree!
> Prithee, my pretty housewives!
> Who may expected be?
>
> The neighbours do not yet suspect!
> The woods exchange a smile—
> Orchard, and buttercup, and bird—
> In such a little while!
>
> And yet how still the landscape stands,
> How nonchalant the wood,
> As if the resurrection
> Were nothing very odd!

We have only to substitute the following to see by contrast how far from clumsy is the poet's technique.

> And yet how still the landscape stands,
>   How nonchalant the vale,
> As if the resurrection
>   Were commonplace and stale.

If we seek to enrich what Mr. Monro regards as the poverty of Emily Dickinson's language by substituting, let us say, "silent lies" for "nonchalant" and "coming of the spring" for "resurrection," the ruin will be completed.

> And yet how still the landscape stands,
>   How silent lies the vale,
> As if the coming of the spring
>   Were commonplace and stale.

Let us turn to "The sky is low," another nature poem which includes a rhyme that, in defeating the ear, echoes the implication of defeat in the thought.

> The sky is low, the clouds are mean,
> A travelling flake of snow
> Across a barn or through a rut
> Debates if it will go.
>
> A narrow wind complains all day
> How some one treated him;
> Nature, like us, is sometimes caught
> Without her diadem.

Here again, it is a flash of the human that cleaves the thought and leaves a pair of ragged edges demanding representation in the rhyme. "Nature, like us. . . ." Change the second stanza to:

> An icy wind complains all day
> Like angry men who frown,
> Nature like us is sometimes caught
> Without her golden crown.

and it is evident that the virtue has departed almost as obviously through the patness of the substituted rhyme as through the flatness of the substituted words.

It would be interesting, by the way, to know how "again" was pronounced in Amherst by Emily Dickinson's circle. To pronounce it "agen," in the following poem is to end on a more harmonious and a less wistful note than that given us by "agane."

> A train went through a burial gate,
> A bird broke forth and sang,
> And trilled, and quivered, and shook his throat
> Till all the churchyard rang;
>
> And then adjusted his little notes,
> And bowed and sang again.
> Doubtless, he thought it meet of him
> To say good-bye to men.

For that reason "agane" is the pronunciation I should favor; the more so, perhaps, in view of this couplet from "An altered look about the hills":

> A flippant fly upon the pane;
> A spider at his trade again,

where the sense seems to demand a full rhyme.

I have said that there is obviously no intrinsic merit in rhymes which defeat the ear. It is equally obvious, of course, that no system of consistently irregular rhymes is possible. There must be expectation to be defeated. Except in the nonsense verses written for her brother's children, in which she seems to be writing quite carelessly, I cannot recall any instances in Emily Dickinson's poems of irregular rhymes which have no artistic significance....

In conclusion, I should like to turn to the final paragraph of Mr. Monro's criticism: "She seems," he writes, "to have been afraid. She dwelt in seclusion; social, physical and psychological. She gives the impression of wanting to keep some secret. Clarity of thought is constantly veiled in obscurity of expression. She was not candid; she does not seem to have been moved by any over-ruling instinct for truth. And we compare her unavoidably with her contemporary, Emily Brontë, whose infatuated desire to be faithful to her every aspect of truth overcame all timidity."

But Emily Dickinson is surely one of the comparatively few poets—

Thomas Hardy is another—who have achieved an aesthetic impression of a cleft and unmatching world. Artistic necessity is too often confused with logical necessity—surely Mr. Abercrombie is, at any rate verbally, guilty of this confusion in the final chapter of his *Theory of Poetry*—and I can see no reason for assuming that the artistic necessity which compelled the "perfection in imperfection" of Emily Dickinson's technique had any connection with a wish-fulfilment for a logical necessity such as might compel the existence of a universe spiritually co-ordinated in spite of apparent inco-ordination. I do not agree with Mr. Abercrombie that "every poem is an ideal version of the world we most profoundly desire; and that by virtue of its form." His is an ingenious, and an intriguing theory, but I doubt whether it is more than plausible. It seems to me to be the case that whereas aesthetic activity purges us of desire, in the case of artistic activity desire is irrelevant. It does not appear to me that Emily Dickinson was using her art as a means of escape from life; but that on the other hand art such as Emily Dickinson's must necessarily involve preliminary courage in the envisaging of life. In the eyes of many who are not poets the world fails to fit, but in most the emotion of fear, or bewilderment, or pity, or disgust is too devastating for the detachment of an artist to be possible. To achieve detachment when envisaging a fissure on the edge of which we ourselves are clinging needs surely a supreme courage. Had Emily Dickinson become a social worker, or even a journalist, in Boston, would she have been credited with more independence and fortitude? A leisured life at Amherst could call for courage from the woman who wrote "that bareheaded life under grass worries one like a wasp."

HART CRANE'S (1899–1932) most striking poetic achievement was the long Whitmanesque poem, *The Bridge* (1930). The poem addressed to Emily Dickinson is itself a kind of critical appreciation of a poet whom Crane had consistently admired.

To Emily Dickinson

HART CRANE

You who desired so much—in vain to ask—
Yet fed your hunger like an endless task,
Dared dignify the labor, bless the quest—
Achieved that stillness ultimately best,

Being, of all, least sought for: Emily, hear!
O sweet, dead Silencer, most suddenly clear
When singing that Eternity possessed
And plundered momently in every breast;

—Truly no flower yet withers in your hand,
The harvest you descried and understand
Needs more than wit to gather, love to bind.
Some reconcilement of remotest mind—

Leaves Ormus rubyless, and Ophir chill.
Else tears heap all within one clay-cold hill.

THEODORE SPENCER (1902–49), teacher, scholar, and poet, became Boylston Professor of Rhetoric and Oratory at Harvard in 1946. Reviewing *Further Poems of Emily Dickinson,* edited by Martha Dickinson Bianchi and Alfred Leete Hampson (1929), Spencer significantly assumes, rather than proposes, the poet's greatness. But he enunciates a serious problem already apparent in Emily Dickinson's published

From *The Collected Poems of Hart Crane* (New York: Liveright Publishing Corporation, 1933).

work: the need for informed, responsible establishment of the texts of the poems.

Concentration and Intensity

THEODORE SPENCER

It is a commonplace among students of the English language that there have survived in New England a number of words, pronunciations, and twists of speech which have long since disappeared in England itself. One wonders whether the same thing—so dependent is thought on vocabulary—has not occurred with regard to the mind. There are turns of thought in Emerson that remind us of the great sermon writers of the English seventeenth century; it is not only in the way he writes, but also sometimes in the way he thinks, that Melville shows his affinity with Urquhart and Sir Thomas Browne. So with Emily Dickinson; her poetry has none of that mirror-like cultural relation with her contemporaries that limited Longfellow's appeal so largely to his own age; her genius went deeper, and by its very isolation blossomed from the roots of the New England mind; she is mentally related, not to Tennyson, but to the metaphysical poets of two centuries before. Had she lived in the seventeenth century, her position would have been, I imagine, somewhere between Herbert and Donne. I quote one of the best poems in this new volume:

I make his crescent fill or lack.
His nature is at full
Or quarter—as I signify,
His tides do I control.

He holds superior in the sky
Or gropes at my command
Behind inferior clouds, or round
A mist's slow colonnade.

But since we hold a mutual disc,
And front a mutual day,
Which is the despot neither knows,
Nor whose the tyranny.

From the *New England Quarterly*, II (July, 1929), 498–501. A review of *Further Poems of Emily Dickinson*, edited by Martha Dickinson Bianchi and Alfred Leete Hampson (Boston: Little, Brown and Co., 1929).

There is here the same development of thought through imagery, the same use of metaphor in a structural, not merely an ornamental, manner which we associate with metaphysical verse. The moon is to this poem just what the pair of compasses is to Donne's "Valediction Forbidding Mourning." Without the image the thought and emotion would not be fused into unity; the image is both a poetic mortar and a short cut to communication.

These two metaphors, indeed, help us to identify the qualities in Emily Dickinson's poetry which make it valuable. Her poems are hard, sharply defined, packed with meaning. She is more stark than the poets of the seventeenth century; all extraneous luxuriance is stripped away. Perhaps this is the result of two centuries of Puritanism; it is more probably the consequence of her own character and the personal renunciation which seems to have sharpened it; the poems in this volume, written apparently after she had sent her lover away, are terrible with despair. But she achieves, as the result of this bareness, an epigrammatic quality which her seventeenth-century prototypes frequently lack. She excels at definition, and many of her poems have an aphoristic pregnancy: like those dry Japanese flowers which blossom out when put in water, her condensed preservations of experience spread and expand in the reader's mind.

This concentration and intensity are the characteristics of Emily Dickinson's poetry which rightly place her among the two or three greatest women poets. By no means all her writing, however, is of the same high standard; there are many verses in this volume which it is doubtful if she would have liked to see in print. Her use of images is frequently private, and her turns of phrase are sometimes merely trick. For instance, the final effect of an otherwise very beautiful poem on page one hundred and forty-five of the present volume is spoilt for the reviewer by a phrase at the end which has only a verbal cleverness:

> Love, thou art veiled, a few behold thee
> Smile and alter and prattle and die;
> Bliss were an oddity without thee,
> Nicknamed by God eternity.

But this very application of a homely and familiar word ("nicknamed") to unknown and illimitable things ("eternity") is one of the individualizing features of Emily Dickinson's style, and when it is successful, is responsible for some of her most vital and moving poems. Taken as a whole, this volume, with its successes and its failures, is thoroughly representative of her work, and it would be a loss to our literature if we did not have it.

It would, however, be unfair to Emily Dickinson's memory not to remark on the way in which these poems have been handled by her editors. As every one acquainted with her work knows, she wrote almost entirely in the simplest verse forms, and in those forms her poems should be printed. This, Mrs. Bianchi and Mr. Hampson have not done. Disregarding the most obvious indications of meter and rhyme, they have distorted nearly every poem into an arbitrary shape of their own invention; what should plainly be one line is printed as two, what should be two is printed as one, until we have an exasperating hybrid which is neither quatrain nor free verse. To give an example; the second stanza of the poem about the moon quoted above is printed, not as there reproduced, but as follows:

> He holds superior in the sky
> Or gropes at my command
> Behind inferior clouds,
> Or round a mist's slow colonnade.

Obviously the words "or round" belong to the third line; not to put them there is to prevent the poem from making its proper effect on the reader. And this is not the only or the most flagrant example. One can discover similar stupidities on every page. In addition, several of the poems are so punctuated (and with Emily Dickinson, punctuation is part of the editor's business) as to be meaningless. Further, we are told nothing about why these poems were withheld from previous publication or where they have been, or how they were discovered. The preface consists only of sloppy sentiment. Have these poems been known all along, and are there others yet to come? The whole proceeding is suspicious.

There have, indeed, been many incompetent editions in the world, but it is to be doubted if there is any other which so disregards the primary functions of an editor as this. While we must be grateful to Mrs. Bianchi and Mr. Hampson for giving us these poems, we can only deplore the fact that in doing so, they have contrived to mar the art of the poet they apparently intended to honor.

EDMUND BLUNDEN (1896–) has had a varied career as poet, critic, scholar, and teacher. He has published a substantial body of poetry (he was awarded the Hawthornden Prize in 1922 and the Queen's Gold Medal for Poetry in 1956). His teaching assignments have ranged as widely as Merton College, Oxford, and the University of Hong Kong. The year 1930 was the centenary of Emily Dickinson's birth and on both sides of the Atlantic the occasion called forth fresh assessments of her work. Blunden's "An Unguessed Poetry" suggests the growth of her reputation in England by 1930.

An Unguessed Poetry

EDMUND BLUNDEN

A hundred years since Emily Dickinson was born; impossible! To those who know her, the most living, contemporary, mockingly future of poets, this chronological fact is a little dust blown by the wind; and "to celebrate her centenary" would sound like a parade of Ruritanian generals saluting a snowdrop. Yet the occasion will serve as well as any other to point out that—there is Emily Dickinson. It will not be easy to do much more. There are spirits moving in verse who never did and never will provide satisfactory "matter" for the constructors of theses; what could a dozen volumes do to make the light of Emily Brontë, or Christina Rossetti, or Charlotte Mew, or Emily Dickinson more entertaining and impressive? My excuse for a few paragraphs on Emily Dickinson, whose secret must be listened for in her poetry, is merely that of the doorkeeper, or signpost. Passions like hers are not for immodest circulations, and there is something in the sad saying that you can never tell a secret to him who knew it not. But I am sure that there are many who would respond to Emily Dickinson if merely the "letter she wrote to the world" could be delivered.

What accessible abundance of an unguessed poetry awaits those who have not yet opened the *Complete Poems* and *Further Poems* of Emily

From the *Nation and Athenaeum,* XLVI (March 22, 1930), 863. A review of *The Complete Poems of Emily Dickinson,* 1928. (London: Secker, 10s.6d.); *Further Poems of Emily Dickinson,* 1929. (London: Secker, 10s.6d.).

Dickinson! Perhaps the word "unguessed" is speaking beyond warrant, for later writers have caught something of the same quick vibration and communicated it to us. Nor would I go as far as the niece of the poet, who is also her editor, and challenge the analysts of poetic mode with a statement that "As to the modern lyric as we know it, the important thing is that she did it first." Emily Dickinson may have missed the poems of Herman Melville, but she was well aware of the Brontës and the strange secluded victory of their laconic lyrical confessions. Moreover, Emerson had been heard through America, and his poetry had worked out its curious track. It would be possible almost to describe the verse of Emily Dickinson with expressions, *mutatis mutandis,* drawn from Oliver Wendell Holmes's chapter on Emerson's poems. "This little planet could not provincialize such a man.... One cannot help feeling that he might have dropped in upon us from some remote centre of spiritual life, where, instead of addition and subtraction, children were taught quaternions, and where the fourth dimension of space was as familiarly known to everybody as a foot-measure or a yard-stick is to us.... There is something in his verse which belongs, indissolubly, sacredly, to his thought. Who would decant the wine of his poetry from its quaint and antique-looking *lagena?* ... In his exquisite choice of descriptive epithets he reminds me of the *tenui-rostrals.* His subtle selective instinct penetrates the vocabulary for the one word he wants, as the long, slender bill of those birds dives deep into the flower for its drop of honey."

That is something like a technical account of Emily Dickinson's poetry, of which one may add one or two characteristics. It is as a rule a lyrical epigram, sudden, soon cut short, colloquial, celestial. It follows more or less the expectation of stanza-form and even of rhyme, but almost invariably in its rapid transit the greatest thoughts are expressed, or scenes created, with unusual decisions of accent and word. It is by her extraordinary, inexhaustible, and oracular control of words like hieroglyphs that Emily Dickinson perfects her poems. With an illusory easiness, even raggedness, she sends out each little squadron of verses to storm some formidable and complex-surrounded thought—and one, or two, or three of her phrases blow the trumpet that brings the walls crashing down. You had hardly thought anything was about to happen. You missed the costly and far-flung preparations for victory. And then the flags are seen in the central redoubt. Yet,

I found the phrase to every thought
  I ever had, but one;
And that defies me,—as a hand
  Did try to chalk the sun

To races nurtured in the dark;—
  How would your own begin?
Can blaze be done in cochineal,
  Or noon in mazarin?

The possible difference between the poets of this period and those of the past lies in physical perceptions, or in the willingness to let them find expression, no matter how odd and rare they may seem. Life has been less minutely regarded in ages less toilsome. Great-sized monsters, especially theological ones, have demanded the faculties of the imaginative. And now we are in a time of sensations rather than of thoughts. The life of Emily Dickinson must have been an acuteness of sensation accompanying, or instantly creating, a newness of thought. "Her body thought":—

There came a wind like a bugle;
It quivered through the grass,
And a green chill upon the heat
So ominous did pass
We barred the windows and the doors
As from an emerald ghost....

Her sense is delicate indeed, and makes its statement of elemental recognitions with the aid of an independent fancy. She is content at times to regard Nature's qualities, and is happy to give them their eulogy in their reflection:

The rat is the concisest tenant.
He pays no rent,—
Repudiates the obligation,
On schemes intent....

A sepal, petal, and a thorn
Upon a common summer's morn,
A flash of dew, a bee or two,
A breeze,
A caper in the trees,—
  And I'm a rose.

She honours almost all things imaginable with her paradox: will speak of "that pale sustenance, Despair"; argues of routine with, "Capacity to terminate Is a specific Grace." Yet the precious element in her is not named yet. It no doubt "comes under the heading" of the mystical intuition. Whatever you call this unconfinable, adventuring, divining presence, it invests her poems with their own glory; it says the last word for her in composition, it decides the pulsation and variation of the verse.

GEORGE F. WHICHER (1889–1954) published *This Was a Poet* in 1938, one of the earlier full-length critical studies of Emily Dickinson and still one of the best. A teacher at Columbia, Johns Hopkins, and Amherst at various times, Whicher was throughout his career a close student of American literature. The essay printed here appeared in 1930, the centenary year of Emily Dickinson's birth. It cogently summarizes the main lines of interest a student of Emily Dickinson will follow: the relevant facts of her life; the vagaries of her reputation as a poet from 1890 to 1930; her place in and contribution to the American literary heritage; and especially the distinctive merits of her poetic art.

A Centennial Appraisal

GEORGE F. WHICHER

A list of the writings about Emily Dickinson, approaching completeness more nearly than any yet compiled, reveals how surely she has become the "somebody" that she refused to be in life. Since the publication forty years ago of a first selection from her poems there have been many eager to tell her name to a widening circle of admirers. Though all this evidence of worldly success can add nothing to the triumph "too intrinsic for renown" that she must have realized in her soul's polar privacy, yet she would perhaps have felt a secret satisfaction—however hidden under expressions of ironical dismay—had she foreseen the

From *Emily Dickinson: A Bibliography* (Amherst: the Jones Library, 1930), with a foreword by George F. Whicher, 9–15.

amount of her public acclaim. At least we may be gratified for her sake, and poetry's, that her work is no longer in danger of being overlooked.

Her centennial year has been marked by numerous celebrations. It has also seen the publication of two full-length biographies, two volumes of reminiscences, a new edition of her poems, many articles and reviews, a bibliography more partial than the one here given, and a novel further exploiting as avowed fiction the family version of her thwarted love affair.

It is more reassuring to dwell upon the amount of attention that Emily Dickinson as person and poet has received than to investigate its quality, as may now be done most conveniently in the large collection of material gathered by The Jones Library. A few competent writers have studied her life and mind with intuitive understanding, but the mass of comment constitutes a monument of critical ineptitude. Its vacillations are amusing. In the decade of the publication of her poetry, she was typically regarded as a nine days' wonder, piquant, daring, even verging on the sacrilegious; ten years later she was a "forgotten poetess." In 1915 a responsible historian of letters characterized her verse as lifeless and overrated; in 1922 a fellow-poet called it "perhaps the finest by a woman in the English language," and yet another enthusiast was found to quarrel with the word "perhaps." Her inadvertences and slipshod lapses have been soberly defended as beauties beyond the comprehension of the vulgar, and her name has been invoked to support the favorite predilections of her critics for movements in verse that she could never have heard of. All these judgments cannot be true; read *en masse* they cancel each other out, leaving vacuity.

And this vacuity tends to be filled by the romantic legend of Emily the Elusive.

> Others abide our question. Thou art free.

The intended compliment, however, is equivocal. Really elusive minds are those that society keeps shut up in institutions. Emily Dickinson, though she followed subtle ways, did not shrink from speaking her mind with fullness and precision. Her letters to her neighbors, in later life especially, were couched in a personal idiom often startlingly condensed and sometimes obscure, but her "letter to the world" was the clear message of a poet, not the mumbling of a pythoness. Like other sensitive and profound artists she felt language in the round, making words convey implications that are more than the sum of their meanings laid end to end; and in consequence her work may be glimpsed by readers in a variety of aspects. Her poetry is not the formal mask of a personality, but a living face vibrant with expressiveness. If any momentous facts about her are shrouded, the veil that has been so sedulously drawn over them, and latterly so seductively raised about the edges, was none of her devising. Though many looking into the well of her being have seen only the distorted image of their own desires, a free mind may discern beneath the surface her true form and substance. If it were not so, she would be a poet of no significance.

Instead of claiming her at once as a "mystic akin to Emerson" or "the feminine Walt Whitman," let us have the patience to study her own pattern. The simple and central fact about her is that she lived in Amherst during the middle years of the nineteenth century. This meant that she came into a Puritan heritage at the moment when it was becoming invalid. Edwards was dissolving in Emerson. The Puritan habit of mind remained with its amazing gift of inward seeking; but what had once been a quest across the verge of consciousness to the feet of the Almighty had altered into a rather aimless tour of man's mental and moral nature. The old confidence in ultimates was waning fitfully. Emily Dickinson detected and distrusted the insincerity of conventional religious formulas, but the need of a faith was still strong in her. In certain moods, more frequently expressed in her letters than in her poems, she almost kindles to mystic rapture and leans eager-eyed toward heaven. At other moments she is frankly sceptical or derisive. As someone has charmingly put it, she delighted in being alternately God's child and God's little rascal. But she seldom reckoned so ill as to leave God out.

The larger and better part of her poetry, however, is psychological rather than religious or irreligious. We have few more candid and penetrating records of what Henry James has called "the landscape of the soul" than she has left us. In her preoccupation with states of consciousness, her exactitude of observation, her impersonal awareness of what she was personally undergoing, she reveals a genius in introspection remarkable even in New England. Other writers, such as Jonathan Edwards in his treatises on the will and the religious affections and Emerson in his musings on the sources of spiritual power, had trenched upon the same field, but always with ulterior motives. Emily Dickinson, on the contrary, was not concerned to demonstrate the sovereignty of God or the beneficence of Nature. Her desire was simply to present a faithful, uncolored report of her mental experiences.

She was an instinctive artist. In her swift, breathless poems she found an instrument perfectly suited to her need, a form capable of containing with the utmost economy a single idea at a time. While Emerson was struggling to join "sentences like infinitely repellent particles" in the mosaic of his essays, thereby achieving an aesthetic *tour de force,* her hands grew deft in the finer "gem tactics" of her verse. Other critics besides Colonel Higginson have deplored the inexactness of her rhymes, as though a poet's main business were with the rhyming dictionary. She knew better. She was inattentive to superficial polish, but at a time when poetry was like furniture put together with putty, gilded, and heavily upholstered, she preserved in her writing the same instinct of sound workmanship that made the Yankee clipper, the Connecticut clock, and the New England doorway objects of beauty.

The most striking theme of her poetry is the Puritan theme of renunciation. It recurs again and again studied from many angles, sometimes clasped passionately to the heart, sometimes twirled ironically on a finger. No writer has so deeply and piercingly laid bare that quality in the New England character which enables it to invert suffering into a kind of joy, to welcome defeat for the sake of the increment thereby added to the soul, and to project satisfaction beyond the bounds of life.

Finally, her poetry is saturated with the atmosphere of the countryside where she lived. She is not a local poet in the obvious sense that Burns or Whittier are local. Alps, Chimborazo, and "Himmaleh" find a place in her verse to the exclusion of the Holyoke Range and Mount Tom. But the favorite characters of her poems are the bee, the breeze, and the butterfly of the Dickinson meadow and the birds and flowers of her garden. All the mutations of Connecticut Valley climate are recreated in her words. The boy who passes whistling, the dog with feet of "intermittent plush," the panoply of funerals are the common sights and sounds of her village. And from the "little toil of love" of her household routine she draws quaint and expressive symbols.

It is necessary to insist on the evidences of time and place in relation to Emily Dickinson because the accident of delayed publication has made her seem almost our contemporary. It is only by an effort that we remember that she belonged to a generation which had come of age before the Civil War and was to do its work in the decades immediately following. Word has gone round that New England then entered upon a period of cultural stagnation, a verdict that might be just if we took into account only the writers who flowered and faded with the age, the Higginsons and Helen Hunts who had their meed of contemporary applause. But we have learned that the best writers of the time worked unknown, and there is reason to revise our estimate. While the democracy of America found its prophets in Whitman and Mark Twain, the other half of the American character, its power to analyze experience, to select and reject, in a word, its distinction, was maintained in the writing of two New Englanders, Henry Adams and Emily Dickinson. We cannot if we would leave them out of account. In intelligence and intensity it would be hard to match them by any other two figures in our literary history.

3

1931–TO THE PRESENT

A. C. WARD (1891–), British educator, literary historian, critic, and editor, was graduated from the University of London and taught a number of years before becoming chief editor of the Oxford University Press (1945–56). His literary works are numerous, including *American Literature: 1880–1930, Illustrated History of English Literature: Chaucer to Shaw,* studies of Lamb, Gissing, and Shaw, and critical editions of works by Austen, the Brontës, Wells, and others. His essay on Emily Dickinson acknowledges her greatness as a poet, but goes on to see her poetry as crucial in understanding both the cultural and literary history of America in the late nineteenth and early twentieth centuries.

A Major American Poet

A. C. WARD

In this survey of the nineteenth-century makings of American literature, chief attention must be given to those writers through whose work lines of development and currents of change can most vividly be seen. An apology could therefore be made for omitting any but brief reference to Emily Dickinson's poetry, since America knew nothing of it during her lifetime: and if she has helped at all to shape her country's literature, it is in the twentieth century that her influence has been felt. Upon her own time she neither left nor desired to leave any mark. But to omit her would be to omit a major American poet—perhaps next to Whitman the greatest American poet of the last century. Emily Dickinson's verse was curiously complementary to Whitman's: as if he were the positive and she the negative pole in a single circuit—the circuit of the Passionate Self. If Whitman was the path of force, Emily Dickinson was a generating chamber of reserved subtlety. She lived in and upon her Self; he lived through an abundant Self which he desired to enlarge with a kind of atomic energy until that Self should, without losing its separate identity, become an accordant member of the Universal SELF. Both of them wrote as though no one had written poetry before, and as though there were no echoes to be heard. Through these two it might be said that America was finding her soul.

From A. C. Ward, *American Literature: 1880–1930* (London: Methuen, 1932), 43–52.

The supposed enigmatic personality of Emily Dickinson will no doubt make her the victim of literary body-snatchers throughout successive generations, as the Brontës have been in England. Her father, Edward Dickinson, a member of Congress and a well-known figure in educational circles in Amherst, Mass., appears to have been a milder version of Mr. Barrett of Wimpole Street and the Rev. Patrick Brontë of Haworth. But though he was a possessive egoist in relation to his daughters, Emily was given exceptional opportunities in education, and as a young woman she displayed the normal interest in social occasions. She came into touch with most of the intellectualists, religionists, and men of affairs in Amherst, until in her mid-twenties she developed that habit of concentration upon the interior life which caused Emily Dickinson to withdraw from her former associates. She was in Philadelphia early in 1854, and is supposed to have met there the man to whom her love poems were addressed. This part of her life has remained obscure and is chiefly the subject of conjecture, though the nonsensational biographers declare that no credence is to be given to the suggestion that the Philadelphia episode wrecked her life or forced her into solitude. She was a solitary by preference, but not in the morbid sense a recluse until after her father's death in 1874. Thenceforward, for the remaining twelve years of life, Emily Dickinson practically incarcerated herself in the house at Amherst. Of what went on mentally and emotionally within this secret woman we shall never know more than her poetry tells us, because the poetry tells us everything, in the only way it can be told. Natural vulgar curiosity may incite us to peer about for information concerning externalities, but even if we should ever know the whole of the plain facts we shall know nothing more of Emily Dickinson than the poetry already conveys in essence.

Emily Dickinson's life in the physical world, then, is of no significance apart from her poetry: all that it is necessary to know concerning her is there, but there in a form which perhaps means little to the general public eye. She speaks in one poem of mirth as "the mail of anguish," a protection against those who, moved by sympathy or whatever else, might seek to invade the sufferer's privacy. The inviolability of Selfhood was the substance and refrain of almost everything she wrote, and when she employed the mail of mirth to dress her creed it was mirth that turned to corrosive wit:

How dreary to be somebody!
How public, like a frog
To tell your name the livelong day
To an admiring bog!

She speaks elsewhere of the soul as attended by "A Single Hound"—"its own Identity." J. C. Powys' commendation of "the ichthyosaurus ego" or "the lonely self" [1] is a philosophy paralleled by Emily Dickinson's, but in neither case is the lonely self to be interpreted as a voluntarily imprisoned self. The poetess was denied a woman's full experience, and this limitation was undoubtedly a source of distress to her, and the word "escape" a constant unfulfilled hope.[2] Yet her thwarted energies, turned inward, sharpened her perceptions and sensibilities, and gave her the tragic intensity of Emily Brontë tempered by the critical acuteness of Jane Austen. The presence of those two strains in Emily Dickinson's temperament prevented her from being as great as either of the English writers, since her critical sense kept her from attaining the unbalanced majesty of the one, and her intensity from sharing in the large serene wisdom of the other. But if this was disadvantageous in certain ways, it was not wholly so. Compelled to bring both her tragic and her comic sense into as harmonious a relation as possible, she learned to discipline her spirit as Emily Brontë never did, and as Jane Austen had no need to do since hers was not inclined to indiscipline. Emily Dickinson had to learn what she calls "superiority to fate," and at the same time as she is recording the possibility of obtaining that superiority, pittance by pittance, she notes with the sharp irony characteristic of her that as a reward for discipline

The soul with strict economy
Subsists till Paradise.[3]

Such strict economy in the soul's subsistence was her own achievement, but not one in which she enjoyed any inward satisfaction, nor one which she could regard as more than a mocking superiority to fate. Avid of life and intensely curious about people, she could not endure

[1] See *In Defence of Sensuality*, by J. C. Powys.
[2] See *Complete Poems* (1924), xxxvi.
[3] See *Complete Poems* (1924), lxxxv.

men and women who were no more than the husks of creatures: she required that people should have "meat within." Genuineness in others, perception and sincerity in herself, these were the terms Emily Dickinson wished to make with life—hard terms which led her to revile herself (when something or some one failed to reach the expected standard)

For entertaining plated wares
Upon my silver shelf.[1]

She was not, it is clear, a resigned and long-suffering spinster who took the world as she found it. To the world she may have appeared placid and acquiescent, because it was within her Self that the drama was played and judgements passed. Picture Emily Dickinson patient and polite at a tea-party, turning afterwards to the comfort of a pen-and-ink detonation of the explosives accumulated inside her:

What soft cherubic creatures
  These gentlewomen are!
One would as soon assault a plush
  Or violate a star.
Such *dimity convictions*
  A horror so refined
Of freckled human nature,
  Of Deity ashamed....

The contempt here expressed of "dimity convictions" is more illuminating for a portrait of Emily Dickinson than anything that could be written of her in other words than her own. She was the antithesis of the hurried pushing America which forced itself onward to unique material prosperity and had no time to stabilize its mind and soul. Living in a generation that was becoming increasingly gregarious and veering toward an idea of heaven organized chiefly for "stout fellows," "good mixers," Rotarians and Elks—a heaven, that is, of flatly generalized creatures formed in single likeness—Emily Dickinson appears to a later age as both a rock and a lighthouse withstanding and warning against an idea of heaven which has turned out to be very hell. If the United States had gone the way of Whitman and Emily Dickinson it

[1] *Complete Poems,* cxviii.

might have become one hundred per cent human, instead of (while clamouring to become one hundred per cent American) becoming neither human nor American but merely one hundred per cent bemused and stultified. The probability is, however, that even if her poems had been published while she was alive, little notice would have been taken of them; it is improbable that she would have been noticed on the rising tide of prosperity, however impressive she may seem as a portent now the tide is falling. "Dimity convictions" have had their day and done their spineless worst in an America that was perhaps less ashamed of Deity than patronizing toward Deity. As it happened, the American Jason set out in quest of the golden fleece and came back empty-handed at last to

Behold his last emolument
Upon the apple-tree.[1]

All the time, Emily Dickinson is saying that wealth and glory do not exist anywhere unless they first exist in one's Self—that the right adjustment of Self is the beginning of wisdom and the road of entrance to a proper relation with the universe. She sweeps over inessentials, surface-values and pretensions to proclaim that

The pedigree of honey
Does not concern the bee;
A clover any time to him
Is aristocracy.

This is the true principle of democracy, which America completely missed in its devotion to Babbittry; and which, indeed, it is impossible to operate in any system where democracy is rooted in a political or economic idea instead of in a metaphysical one. Emily Dickinson's real force lay in her almost contemptuously detached manner of stating truths which it would be impertinent to press, because Truth should no more be hawked in the market-place than the Majesty of God should be. She was a prophet of Time and Eternity (as her editor suggests by grouping a section of her poems under that heading), but she was not a proselyte, not a saleswoman of salvation, not a purveyor of predigested truths. Consequently her poetry is as full of meat as she wanted life

[1] *Complete Poems,* Nature, xiii.

and men and women to be; it is also full of hard sayings that make no concession to the popular taste for comforting flattery of humanity's sense of self-importance. She had enough of the mystic's sense of the unity of all Creation to draw an entirely non-homocentric picture of the universe, which would have been vastly unsympathetic to Americans and Britons, equally, at a time when man (and particularly the Anglo-Saxon variety) was still enthroned in the general mind as God's crowning achievement. It was necessary that man should be dethroned from what may be his wholly illusive position at the centre of the universe before anything vital could be done with or for man, and Emily Dickinson is a surprisingly insistent prophet of the need for that dethronement:

A toad can die of light!
Death is the common right
   Of toads and men,—
Of earl and midge
The privilege,
   Why swagger then?
The gnat's supremacy
Is large as thine.[1]

Emily Dickinson's situation in late nineteenth-century American literature is as important as it is interesting and singular. It was not so much her misfortune as her privilege to be antipathetic to the spirit of her own age; and in refraining from publication she was wise—though if she had published and had suffered either neglect or opposition it would have left her unruffled: she would not have cared. Her posthumous reward has been to find a generation fifty years ahead that was exactly ready for her, and qualified (by its painful reaction from false optimistic idealism in thought and excessive materialism in practice) to know how right she was. It is ridiculous to attempt to find parallels to her, because she had that complete originality which consists in seeing the universe quite freshly with a personal vision and of beginning the contemplation of the universe from zero: but if a parallel may be suggested, it possibly exists in A. E. Housman's poetry, though, of course, neither was influenced by the other. There is, in both, a positive almost coldly passionate severity which permits the poet to look

[1] *Complete Poems,* Time and Eternity, cxxxvii.

full in the face of Destiny without fluttering an eyelid; in both, the same capacity for building up an entirely satisfactory relation with the universe, without recourse to any of those metaphysical drugs of ultimate good—or ultimate something-or-other pleasant—desired by many. Yet it might be urged that Housman does actually fortify himself with the drug of absolute pessimism, which enables him to start by anticipating the worst and of gaining a certain degree of satisfaction whenever the universe turns out to be not entirely abhorrent. This is not true of Emily Dickinson. In the best sense, Despair is at the bottom of her metaphysic as it is at the bottom of Housman's; but she starts out with no preliminary assumptions—neither that the universe is good, nor that the universe is not good. Her initial postulate is Despair because she expects from the universe nothing but whatever it may prove to be that the universe yields and does. Housman gives the impression of looking at the universe and thinking gloomily, "This is a black and blasted sort of affair, and quite obviously sinister and malignant. Well, come on: let it do what will certainly be its altogether beastly damnedest. I'll show it that it's not going to get me down, anyhow." In a somewhat tiresomely reiterant implication this is the refrain throughout Housman's poetry; and the reader cannot be sure that the universe has not got Housman down even while the poet is declaring that it never will. The gentleman sometimes protests too much, though he appears not to be protesting at all: not only protest but fear and defeat may lie at the heart of Housman's metaphysical swagger, which in its highest moments can nevertheless be read as an admirably strong and unshakenly confident despair. No such doubts are raised by Emily Dickinson's poetry, inasmuch as she does not, by statement or implication, either gibe at or defy the universe. To her, the universe IS: to be faced and dealt with upon whatever terms it seems to impose. If it imposes anguish—there is mirth, not wailing, as the proper antidote. If humanity is less good than one would prefer it to be—all right: we must be careful not to be misled into putting plated wares among the genuine silver. If those we love die—well, we must be prepared to engage in what she calls the "solemnest of industries enacted upon earth"—

> The sweeping up the heart,
> And putting love away
> We shall not want to use again
> Until eternity.

If gnats are not inferior to men in the sight of eternity—why should they be?—man can get on quite well without his self-flattering swagger of superiority to the rest of Creation. The Universe IS and I AM. What is involved is the simple (though far from easy) problem of adjustment, without the intrusion of preconceived ideas of how that adjustment is to be conducted, and without the equally intrusive assumption that my neighbours' processes of adjustment are relevant to me. It might seem occasionally in her poetry that she wished to impose her own system upon others, though actually this is not so. When she castigates the cherubic gentlewomen for their dimity convictions, it is only because those convictions lead to an evident maladjustment between the gentlewomen and a universe which is conditioned to include freckled human nature and the Deity as well as themselves. The gentlewomen require a universe made in their own likeness, and believe, moreover, that the universe is at fault in precisely the degree to which it is so curiously unlike what they expect of it.

Emily Dickinson's original (in the sense of being wholly personal) and unexceptional attitude toward experience, gains force by its presentation in verse correspondingly original in form and idiom. Its beauty is the beauty of gems and fine gold—though it would be difficult to find a comparison which seems so obviously and infuriatingly inappropriate. It would be far more apposite to say that her poetry resembles fused quartz, if one could be sure that this picture would suggest any idea of beauty at all. The essential point is to convey the impression of verse which has been fired to a final release from softening alloy—verse which achieves full identity with Beauty without ever being demonstrably "beautiful." No doubt it is merely an unfamiliar truism to suggest that what immediately impresses our senses as beautiful is, in truth, but half-way between prettiness and beauty—an adulterant of that absolute Beauty which is too blasting to touch us caressingly: absolute Beauty and absolute Truth exist nowhere but in Deity and are manifested only in the Face of God. The nearer a poet approaches to ultimate harmony with the universe, the closer is the approach to absolute Beauty and the less likelihood is there of that harmony issuing in "beautiful" verse. It is certain, at any rate, that in Emily Dickinson the verse and the vision are one. Her apparent simplicity is as delusive as Blake's; and she uses no poetic ornamentation. When simple metrical rhyming verse serves for what she has to say, she uses that. When assonance, or half-rhymes, or a-metre serve better, she uses any or all of those devices. But always the thing-to-be-said finds the fit mould that will exactly contain it in utmost concentration—which is only to express in another way what has already been noted, namely, that her vision and her verse attain the unity which is achieved only by poets of a high order.

Poet, biographer, critic, and teacher, ALLEN TATE (1899–) has been one of the most influential figures in twentieth-century American letters. As a member of the Southern Agrarian group and one of the founders of *Fugitive,* Tate was closely associated with John Crowe Ransom in the formulation of the "New Criticism" which excited a generation of writers, critics, and students with its demand for a predominantly aesthetic, analytic approach to literature. Characteristically, Tate defines an American cultural tradition which Emily Dickinson represents, then discusses single poems as superior aesthetic expressions of that culture as Emily Dickinson embodied it.

New England Culture and Emily Dickinson

ALLEN TATE

I

Great poetry needs no special features of difficulty to make it mysterious. When it has them, the reputation of the poet is likely to remain uncertain. This is still true of Donne, and it is true of Emily Dickinson, whose verse appeared in an age unfavorable to the use of intelligence in poetry. Her poetry is not like any other poetry of her time; it is not like any of the innumerable kinds of verse written today. In still another respect it is far removed from us. It is a poetry of ideas, and it demands of the reader a point of view—not an opinion of the New Deal or of the League of Nations, but an ingrained philosophy that is fundamental, a settled attitude that is almost extinct in this eclectic age. Yet

From the *Symposium,* III (April, 1932), 206–26; reprinted in Allen Tate, *The Man of Letters in the Modern World* (New York: Meridian Books, 1955).

it is not the sort of poetry of ideas which, like Pope's, requires a point of view only. It requires also, for the deepest understanding, which must go beneath the verbal excitement of the style, a highly developed sense of the specific quality of poetry—a quality that most persons accept as the accidental feature of something else that the poet thinks he has to say. This is one reason why Miss Dickinson's poetry has not been widely read.

There is another reason, and it is a part of the problem peculiar to a poetry that comes out of fundamental ideas. We lack a tradition of criticism. There were no points of critical reference passed on to us from a preceding generation. I am not upholding here the so-called dead hand of tradition, but rather a rational insight into the meaning of the present in terms of some imaginable past implicit in our own lives: we need a body of ideas that can bear upon the course of the spirit and yet remain coherent as a rational instrument. We ignore the present, which is momently translated into the past, and derive our standards from imaginative constructions of the future. The hard contingency of fact invariably breaks these standards down, leaving us the intellectual chaos which is the sore distress of American criticism. Marxian criticism has become the latest disguise of this heresy.

Still another difficulty stands between us and Miss Dickinson. It is the failure of the scholars to feel more than biographical curiosity about her. We have scholarship, but that is no substitute for a critical tradition. Miss Dickinson's value to the research scholar, who likes historical difficulty for its own sake, is slight; she is too near to possess the remoteness of literature. Perhaps her appropriate setting would be the age of Cowley or of Donne. Yet in her own historical setting she is, nevertheless, remarkable and special.

Although the intellectual climate into which she was born, in 1830, had, as all times have, the features of a transition, the period was also a major crisis culminating in the war between the States. After that war, in New England as well as in the South, spiritual crises were definitely minor until the First World War.

Yet, a generation before the war of 1861–65, the transformation of New England had begun. When Samuel Slater in 1790 thwarted the British embargo on mill machinery by committing to memory the whole design of a cotton spinner and bringing it to Massachusetts, he planted the seed of the "Western spirit." By 1825 its growth in the East was rank enough to begin choking out the ideas and habits of living that New England along with Virginia had kept in unconscious allegiance to Europe. To the casual observer, perhaps, the New England character of 1830 was largely an eighteenth-century character. But theocracy was on the decline, and industrialism was rising—as Emerson, in an unusually lucid moment, put it, "Things are in the saddle." The energy that had built the meeting-house ran the factory.

Now the idea that moved the theocratic state is the most interesting historically of all American ideas. It was, of course, powerful in seventeenth-century England, but in America, where the long arm of Laud could not reach, it acquired an unchecked social and political influence. The important thing to remember about the puritan theocracy is that it permeated, as it could never have done in England, a whole society. It gave final, definite meaning to life, the life of pious and impious, of learned and vulgar alike. It gave—and this is its significance for Emily Dickinson, and in only slightly lesser degree for Melville and Hawthorne—it gave an heroic proportion and a tragic mode to the experience of the individual. The history of the New England theocracy, from Apostle Eliot to Cotton Mather, is rich in gigantic intellects that broke down—or so it must appear to an outsider—in a kind of moral decadence and depravity. Socially we may not like the New England idea. Yet it had an immense, incalculable value for literature: it dramatized the human soul.

But by 1850 the great fortunes had been made (in the rum, slave, and milling industries), and New England became a museum. The whatnots groaned under the load of knickknacks, the fine china dogs and cats, the pieces of Oriental jade, the chips off the leaning tower of Pisa. There were the rare books and the cosmopolitan learning. It was all equally displayed as the evidence of a superior culture. The Gilded Age had already begun. But culture, in the true sense, was disappearing. Where the old order, formidable as it was, had held all this personal experience, this eclectic excitement, in a comprehensible whole, the new order tended to flatten it out in a common experience that was not quite in common; it exalted more and more the personal and the unique in the interior sense. Where the old-fashioned puritans got together on a rigid doctrine, and could thus be individualists in manners, the nineteenth-century New Englander, lacking a genuine religious center, began to be a social conformist. The common idea of the Redemption, for example, was replaced by the conformist idea of respectability among neighbors whose spiritual disorder, not very evident at the surface, was becoming acute. A great idea was breaking up, and society was moving towards external uniformity, which is usually the measure of the spiritual sterility inside.

At this juncture Emerson came upon the scene: the Lucifer of Concord, he had better be called hereafter, for he was the light-bearer who could see nothing but light, and was fearfully blind. He looked around and saw the uniformity of life, and called it the routine of tradition, the tyranny of the theological idea. The death of Priam put an end to the hope of Troy, but it was a slight feat of arms for the doughty Pyrrhus; Priam was an old gentleman and almost dead. So was theocracy; and Emerson killed it. In this way he accelerated a tendency that he disliked. It was a great intellectual mistake. By it Emerson unwittingly became the prophet of a piratical industrialism, a consequence of his own transcendental individualism that he could not foresee. He was hoist with his own petard.

He discredited more than any other man the puritan drama of the soul. The age that followed, from 1865 on, expired in a genteel secularism, a mildly didactic order of feeling whose ornaments were Lowell, Longfellow, and Holmes. "After Emerson had done his work," says Mr. Robert Penn Warren, "any tragic possibilities in that culture were dissipated." Hawthorne alone in his time kept pure, in the primitive terms, the primitive vision; he brings the puritan tragedy to its climax. Man, measured by a great idea outside himself, is found wanting. But for Emerson man is greater than any idea and, being himself the Over-Soul, is innately perfect; there is no struggle because—I state the Emersonian doctrine, which is very slippery, in its extreme terms—because there is no possibility of error. There is no drama in human character because there is no tragic fault. It is not surprising, then, that after Emerson New England literature tastes like a sip of cambric tea. Its center of vision has disappeared. There is Hawthorne looking back, there is Emerson looking not too clearly at anything ahead: Emily Dickinson, who has in her something of both, comes in somewhere between.

With the exception of Poe there is no other American poet whose work so steadily emerges, under pressure of certain disintegrating obsessions, from the framework of moral character. There is none of whom it is truer to say that the poet *is* the poetry. Perhaps this explains the zeal of her admirers for her biography; it explains, in part at least, the gratuitous mystery that Mrs. Bianchi, a niece of the poet and her official biographer, has made of her life. The devoted controversy that Miss Josephine Pollitt and Miss Genevieve Taggard started a few years ago with their excellent books shows the extent to which the critics feel the intimate connection of her life and work. Admiration and affection are pleased to linger over the tokens of a great life; but the solution to the Dickinson enigma is peculiarly superior to fact.

The meaning of the identity—which we merely feel—of character and poetry would be exceedingly obscure, even if we could draw up a kind of Binet correlation between the two sets of "facts." Miss Dickinson was a recluse; but her poetry is rich with a profound and varied experience. Where did she get it? Now some of the biographers, nervous in the presence of this discrepancy, are eager to find her a love affair, and I think this search is due to a modern prejudice: we believe that no virgin can know enough to write poetry. We shall never learn where she got the rich quality of her mind. The moral image that we have of Miss Dickinson stands out in every poem; it is that of a dominating spinster whose very sweetness must have been formidable. Yet her poetry constantly moves within an absolute order of truths that overwhelmed her simply because to her they were unalterably fixed. It is dangerous to assume that her "life," which to the biographers means the thwarted love affair she is supposed to have had, gave to her poetry a decisive direction. It is even more dangerous to suppose that it made her a poet.

Poets are mysterious, but a poet, when all is said, is not much more mysterious than a banker. The critics remain spellbound by the technical license of her verse and by the puzzle of her personal life. Personality is a legitimate interest because it is an incurable interest, but legitimate as a personal interest only; it will never give up the key to anyone's verse. Used to that end, the interest is false. "It is apparent," writes Mr. Conrad Aiken, "that Miss Dickinson became a hermit by deliberate and conscious choice"—a sensible remark that we cannot repeat too often. If it were necessary to explain her seclusion with disappointment in love, there would remain the discrepancy between what the seclusion produced and the seclusion looked at as a cause. The effect, which is her poetry, would imply the whole complex of anterior fact, which was the social and religious structure of New England.

The problem to be kept in mind is thus the meaning of her "deliberate and conscious" decision to withdraw from life to her upstairs room. This simple fact is not very important. But that it must have been her sole way of acting out her part in the history of her culture, which made, with the variations of circumstance, a single demand upon all its representatives—this is of the greatest consequence. All pity for Miss Dickinson's "starved life" is misdirected. Her life was one of the richest and deepest ever lived on this continent.

When she went upstairs and closed the door, she mastered life by rejecting it. Others in their way had done it before; still others did it later. If we suppose—which is to suppose the improbable—that the love affair precipitated the seclusion, it was only a pretext; she would have found another. Mastery of the world by rejecting the world was the doctrine, even if it was not always the practice, of Jonathan Edwards and Cotton Mather. It is the meaning of fate in Hawthorne: his people are fated to withdraw from the world and to be destroyed. And it is one of the great themes of Henry James.

There is a moral emphasis that connects Hawthorne, James, and Miss Dickinson, and I think it is instructive. Between Hawthorne and James lies an epoch. The temptation to sin, in Hawthorne, is, in James, transformed into the temptation not to do the "decent thing." A whole world-scheme, a complete cosmic background, has shrunk to the dimensions of the individual conscience. This epoch between Hawthorne and James lies in Emerson. James found himself in the post-Emersonian world, and he could not, without violating the detachment proper to an artist, undo Emerson's work; he had that kind of intelligence which refuses to break its head against history. There was left to him only the value, the historic role, of rejection. He could merely escape from the physical presence of that world which, for convenience, we may call Emerson's world: he could only take his Americans to Europe upon the vain quest of something that they had lost at home. His characters, fleeing the wreckage of the puritan culture, preserved only their honor. Honor became a sort of forlorn hope struggling against the forces of "pure fact" that had got loose in the middle of the century. Honor alone is a poor weapon against nature, being too personal, finical, and proud, and James achieved a victory by refusing to engage the whole force of the enemy.

In Emily Dickinson the conflict takes place on a vaster field. The enemy to all those New Englanders was Nature, and Miss Dickinson saw into the character of this enemy more deeply than any of the others. The general symbol of Nature, for her, is Death, and her weapon against Death is the entire powerful dumb-show of the puritan theology led by Redemption and Immortality. Morally speaking, the problem for James and Miss Dickinson is similar. But her advantages were greater than his. The advantages lay in the availability to her of the puritan ideas on the theological plane.

These ideas, in her poetry, are momently assailed by the disintegrating force of Nature (appearing as Death) which, while constantly breaking them down, constantly redefines and strengthens them. The values are purified by the triumphant withdrawal from Nature, by their power to recover from Nature. The poet attains to a mastery over experience by facing its utmost implications. There is the clash of powerful opposites, and in all great poetry—for Emily Dickinson is a great poet—it issues in a tension between abstraction and sensation in which the two elements may be, of course, distinguished logically, but not really. We are shown our roots in Nature by examining our differences with Nature; we are renewed by Nature without being delivered into her hands. When it is possible for a poet to do this for us with the greatest imaginative comprehension, a possibility that the poet cannot himself create, we have the perfect literary situation. Only a few times in the history of English poetry has this situation come about: notably, the period between about 1580 and the Restoration. There was a similar age in New England from which emerged two talents of the first order —Hawthorne and Emily Dickinson.

There is an epoch between James and Miss Dickinson. But between her and Hawthorne there exists a difference of intellectual quality. She lacks almost radically the power to seize upon and understand abstractions for their own sake; she does not separate them from the sensuous illuminations that she is so marvelously adept at; like Donne, she *perceives abstraction* and *thinks sensation*. But Hawthorne was a master of ideas, within a limited range; this narrowness confined him to his own kind of life, his own society, and out of it grew his typical forms of experience, his steady, almost obsessed vision of man; it explains his depth and intensity. Yet he is always conscious of the abstract, doctrinal aspect of his mind, and when his vision of action and emotion is weak, his work becomes didactic. Now Miss Dickinson's poetry often runs into quasi-homiletic forms, but it is never didactic. Her very ignorance, her lack of formal intellectual training, preserved her from the risk that imperiled Hawthorne. She cannot reason at all. She can only *see*. It is impossible to imagine what she might have done with drama or fiction; for, not approaching the puritan temper and through it the puritan myth, through human action, she is able to grasp the terms of the myth directly and by a feat that amounts almost to anthropomorphism, to give them a luminous tension, a kind of drama, among themselves.

One of the perfect poems in English is "The Chariot," and it illustrates better than anything else she wrote the special quality of her mind. I think it will illuminate the tendency of this discussion:

Because I could not stop for death,
He kindly stopped for me;
The carriage held but just ourselves
And immortality.

We slowly drove, he knew no haste,
And I had put away
My labor, and my leisure too,
For his civility.

We passed the school where children played,
Their lessons scarcely done;
We passed the fields of gazing grain,
We passed the setting sun.

We paused before a house that seemed
A swelling of the ground;
The roof was scarcely visible,
The cornice but a mound.

Since then 'tis centuries; but each
Feels shorter than the day
I first surmised the horses' heads
Were toward eternity.

If the word "great" means anything in poetry, this poem is one of the greatest in the English language. The rhythm charges with movement the pattern of suspended action back of the poem. Every image is precise and, moreover, not merely beautiful, but fused with the central idea. Every image extends and intensifies every other. The third stanza especially shows Miss Dickinson's power to fuse, into a single order of perception, a heterogeneous series: the children, the grain, and the setting sun (time) have the same degree of credibility; the first subtly preparing for the last. The sharp *gazing* before *grain* instills into nature a cold vitality of which the qualitative richness has infinite depth. The content of death in the poem eludes explicit definition. He is a gentleman taking a lady out for a drive. But note the restraint that keeps the poet from carrying this so far that it becomes ludicrous and incredible; and note the subtly interfused erotic motive, which the idea of death has presented to most romantic poets, love being a symbol interchangeable with death. The terror of death is objectified through this figure of the genteel driver, who is made ironically to serve the end of Immortality. This is the heart of the poem: she has presented a typical Christian theme in its final irresolution, without making any final statements about it. There is no solution to the problem; there can be only a presentation of it in the full context of intellect and feeling. A construction of the human will, elaborated with all the abstracting powers of the mind, is put to the concrete test of experience: the idea of immortality is confronted with the fact of physical disintegration. We are not told what to think; we are told to look at the situation.

The framework of the poem is, in fact, the two abstractions, mortality and eternity, which are made to associate in equality with the images: she sees the ideas, and thinks the perceptions. She did, of course, nothing of the sort; but we must use the logical distinctions, even to the extent of paradox, if we are to form any notion of this rare quality of mind. She could not in the proper sense think at all, and unless we prefer the feeble poetry of moral ideas that flourished in New England in the eighties, we must conclude that her intellectual deficiency contributed at least negatively to her great distinction. Miss Dickinson is probably the only Anglo-American poet of her century whose work exhibits the perfect literary situation—in which is possible the fusion of sensibility and thought. Unlike her contemporaries, she never succumbed to her ideas, to easy solutions, to her private desires.

Philosophers must deal with ideas, but the trouble with most nineteenth-century poets is too much philosophy; they are nearer to being philosophers than poets, without being in the true sense either. Tennyson is a good example of this; so is Arnold in his weak moments. There have been poets like Milton and Donne, who were not spoiled for their true business by leaning on a rational system of ideas, who understood the poetic use of ideas. Tennyson tried to mix a little Huxley and a little

Broad Church, without understanding either Broad Church or Huxley; the result was fatal, and what is worse, it was shallow. Miss Dickinson's ideas were deeply imbedded in her character, not taken from the latest tract. A conscious cultivation of ideas in poetry is always dangerous, and even Milton escaped ruin only by having an instinct for what in the deepest sense he understood. Even at that there is a remote quality in Milton's approach to his material, in his treatment of it; in the nineteenth century, in an imperfect literary situation where literature was confused with documentation, he might have been a pseudo-philosopher-poet. It is difficult to conceive Emily Dickinson and John Donne succumbing to rumination about "problems"; they would not have written at all.

Neither the feeling nor the style of Miss Dickinson belongs to the seventeenth century; yet between her and Donne there are remarkable ties. Their religious ideas, their abstractions, are momently toppling from the rational plane to the level of perception. The ideas, in fact, are no longer the impersonal religious symbols created anew in the heat of emotion, that we find in poets like Herbert and Vaughan. They have become, for Donne, the terms of personality; they are mingled with the miscellany of sensation. In Miss Dickinson, as in Donne, we may detect a singularly morbid concern, not for religious truth, but for personal revelation. The modern word is self-exploitation. It is egoism grown irresponsible in religion and decadent in morals. In religion it is blasphemy; in society it means usually that culture is not self-contained and sufficient, that the spiritual community is breaking up. This is, along with some other features that do not concern us here, the perfect literary situation.

II

Personal revelation of the kind that Donne and Miss Dickinson strove for, in the effort to understand their relation to the world, is a feature of all great poetry; it is probably the hidden motive for writing. It is the effort of the individual to live apart from a cultural tradition that no longer sustains him. But this culture, which I now wish to discuss a little, is indispensable: there is a great deal of shallow nonsense in modern criticism which holds that poetry—and this is a half-truth that is worse than false—is essentially revolutionary. It is only indirectly revolutionary:

the intellectual and religious background of an age no longer contains the whole spirit, and the poet proceeds to examine that background in terms of immediate experience. But the background is necessary; otherwise all the arts (not only poetry) would have to rise in a vacuum. Poetry does not dispense with tradition; it probes the deficiencies of a tradition. But it must have a tradition to probe. It is too bad that Arnold did not explain his doctrine, that poetry is a criticism of life, from the viewpoint of its background: we should have been spared an era of academic misconception, in which criticism of life meant a diluted pragmatism, the criterion of which was respectability. The poet in the true sense "criticizes" his tradition, either as such, or indirectly by comparing it with something that is about to replace it; he does what the root-meaning of the verb implies—he *discerns* its real elements and thus establishes its value, by putting it to the test of experience.

What is the nature of a poet's culture? Or, to put the question properly, what is the meaning of culture for poetry? All the great poets become the material of what we popularly call culture; we study them to acquire it. It is clear that Addison was more cultivated than Shakespeare; nevertheless Shakespeare is a finer source of culture than Addison. What is the meaning of this? Plainly it is that learning has never had anything to do with culture except instrumentally: the poet must be exactly literate enough to write down fully and precisely what he has to say, but no more. The source of a poet's true culture lies back of the paraphernalia of culture, and not all the historical activity of an enlightened age can create it.

A culture cannot be consciously created. It is an available source of ideas that are imbedded in a complete and homogeneous society. The poet finds himself balanced upon the moment when such a world is about to fall, when it threatens to run out into looser and less self-sufficient impulses. This world order is assimilated, in Miss Dickinson, as medievalism was in Shakespeare, to the poetic vision; it is brought down from abstraction to personal sensibility.

In this connection it may be said that the prior conditions for great poetry, given a great talent, may be reduced to two: the thoroughness of the poet's discipline in an objective system of truth, and his lack of consciousness of such a discipline. For this discipline is a number of fundamental ideas the origin of which the poet does not know; they give form and stability to his fresh perceptions of the world; and he cannot shake them off. This is his culture, and, like Tennyson's God, it is nearer than hands and feet. With reasonable certainty we unearth the elements of Shakespeare's culture, and yet it is equally certain—so innocent was he of his own resources—that he would not know what our discussion is about. He appeared at the collapse of the medieval system as a rigid pattern of life, but that pattern remained in Shakespeare what Shelley called a "fixed point of reference" for his sensibility. Miss Dickinson, as we have seen, was born into the equilibrium of an old and a new order. Puritanism could not be to her what it had been to the generation of Cotton Mather—a body of absolute truths; it was an unconscious discipline timed to the pulse of her life.

The perfect literary situation: it produces, because it is rare, a special and perhaps the most distinguished kind of poet. I am not trying to invent a new critical category. Such poets are never very much alike on the surface; they show us all the varieties of poetic feeling; and, like other poets, they resist all classification but that of temporary convenience. But, I believe, Miss Dickinson and John Donne would have this in common: their sense of the natural world is not blunted by a too-rigid system of ideas; yet the ideas, the abstractions, their education or their intellectual heritage, are not so weak as to let their immersion in nature, or their purely personal quality, get out of control. The two poles of the mind are not separately visible; we infer them from the lucid tension that may be most readily illustrated by polar activity. There is no thought as such at all; nor is there feeling; there is that unique focus of experience which is at once neither and both.

Like Miss Dickinson, Shakespeare is without opinions; his peculiar merit is also deeply involved in his failure to think about anything; his meaning is not in the content of his expression; it is in the tension of the dramatic relations of his characters. This kind of poetry is at the opposite of intellectualism. (Miss Dickinson is obscure and difficult, but that is not intellectualism.) To T. W. Higginson, the editor of *The Atlantic Monthly,* who tried to advise her, she wrote that she had no education. In any sense that Higginson could understand, it was quite true. His kind of education was the conscious cultivation of abstractions. She did not reason about the world she saw; she merely saw it. The "ideas" implicit in the world within her rose up, concentrated in her immediate perception.

That kind of world at present has for us something of the fascination of a buried city. There is none like it. When such worlds exist, when such cultures flourish, they support not only the poet but all members of society. For, from these, the poet differs only in his gift for exhibiting the structure, the internal lineaments, of his culture by threatening to tear them apart: a process that concentrates the symbolic emotions of society while it seems to attack them. The poet may hate his age; he may be an outcast like Villon; but this world is always there as the background to what he has to say. It is the lens through which he brings nature to focus and control—the clarifying medium that concentrates his personal feeling. It is ready-made; he cannot make it; with it, his poetry has a spontaneity and a certainty of direction that, without it, it would lack. No poet could have invented the ideas of "The Chariot"; only a great poet could have found their imaginative equivalents. Miss Dickinson was a deep mind writing from a deep culture, and when she came to poetry, she came infallibly.

Infallibly, at her best; for no poet has ever been perfect, nor is Emily Dickinson. Her precision of statement is due to the directness with which the abstract framework of her thought acts upon its unorganized material. The two elements of her style, considered as point of view, are immortality, or the idea of permanence, and the physical process of death or decay. Her diction has two corresponding features: words of Latin or Greek origin and, sharply opposed to these, the concrete Saxon element. It is this verbal conflict that gives her verse its high tension; it is not a device deliberately seized upon, but a feeling for language that senses out the two fundamental components of English and their metaphysical relation: the Latin for ideas and the Saxon for perceptions—the peculiar virtue of English as a poetic language.

Like most poets Miss Dickinson often writes out of habit; the style that emerged from some deep exploration of an idea is carried on as verbal habit when she has nothing to say. She indulges herself:

> There's something quieter than sleep
> Within this inner room!
> It wears a sprig upon its breast,
> And will not tell its name.
>
> Some touch it and some kiss it,
> Some chafe its idle hand;
> It has a simple gravity
> I do not understand!

While simple hearted neighbors
Chat of the "early dead,"
We, prone to periphrasis,
Remark that birds have fled!

It is only a pert remark; at best a superior kind of punning—one of the worst specimens of her occasional interest in herself. But she never had the slightest interest in the public. Were four poems or five published in her lifetime? She never felt the temptation to round off a poem for public exhibition. Higginson's kindly offer to make her verse "correct" was an invitation to throw her work into the public ring—the ring of Lowell and Longfellow. He could not see that he was tampering with one of the rarest literary integrities of all time. Here was a poet who had no use for the supports of authorship—flattery and fame; she never needed money.

She had all the elements of a culture that has broken up, a culture that on the religious side takes its place in the museum of spiritual antiquities. Puritanism, as a unified version of the world, is dead; only a remnant of it in trade may be said to survive. In the history of puritanism she comes between Hawthorne and Emerson. She has Hawthorne's matter, which a too irresponsible personality tends to dilute into a form like Emerson's; she is often betrayed by words. But she is not the poet of personal sentiment; she has more to say than she can put down in any one poem. Like Hardy and Whitman, she must be read entire; like Shakespeare, she never gives up her meaning in a single line.

She is therefore a perfect subject for the kind of criticism which is chiefly concerned with general ideas. She exhibits one of the permanent relations between personality and objective truth, and she deserves the special attention of our time, which lacks that kind of truth.

She has Hawthorne's intellectual toughness, a hard, definite sense of the physical world. The highest flights to God, the most extravagant metaphors of the strange and the remote, come back to a point of casuistry, to a moral dilemma of the experienced world. There is, in spite of the homiletic vein of utterance, no abstract speculation, nor is there a message to society; she speaks wholly to the individual experience. She offers to the unimaginative no riot of vicarious sensation; she has no useful maxims for men of action. Up to this point her resemblance to Emerson is slight: poetry is a sufficient form of utterance, and her devotion to it is pure. But in Emily Dickinson the puritan world is no longer self-contained; it is no longer complete; her sensibility exceeds its dimensions. She has trimmed down its supernatural proportions; it has become a morality; instead of the tragedy of the spirit there is a commentary upon it. Her poetry is a magnificent personal confession, blasphemous and, in its self-revelation, its honesty, almost obscene. It comes out of an intellectual life towards which it feels no moral responsibility. Cotton Mather would have burnt her for a witch.

After graduation from Harvard in 1923, GRANVILLE HICKS (1901–) taught briefly at Smith College. During the depression years he became intensely interested in Marxism. For a time he was literary editor of *New Masses,* and in 1933 he published the Marxist-slanted *The Great Tradition* which immediately involved him in numerous controversies. More recently Hicks's social views have been modified in the direction of broader principles. His discussion of Emily Dickinson reflects his social emphases of the 1930's, especially in his suggestive comparisons of Dickinson and her contemporaries.

Emily Dickinson and the Gilded Age

GRANVILLE HICKS

Henry James's grandfather had made money and left his descendants free to live as they saw fit; Emily Dickinson's grandfather devoted himself to the advancement of evangelical Christianity in the Connecticut Valley and bequeathed to his family the responsibilities of that cause. Though he chose the law rather than the ministry, he was the mainstay of the local church, and his great achievement was the founding of Amherst College as a bulwark against infidelity. His son Edward inherited his father's practice along with his obligations to church and college. His failure to join the church until he had reached middle age argues, perhaps, the existence in him of some such spirit of rebellion as was to manifest itself in his daughter, but it did not prevent him

From Granville Hicks, *The Great Tradition* (New York: The Dial Press, 1933), 124–30.

from loyally serving both that institution and the college. From the first lawyers had constituted the secular arm of the Puritan theocracy, and Edward Dickinson took his duties seriously. He was chosen to Congress, and he was called Squire by his fellow-townsmen—an honor probably as pleasing to him as any within their power to bestow.

By the time Emily was born the Puritan theocracy had made its last stand; it was no longer able, as the Unitarian schism showed, to dominate New England. Its foundations were tottering: the cultivation of the land to the westward struck at the prosperity of its small farmers; its merchants were losing their power at sea. The building of textile factories in Lowell and Lawrence marked the beginning of a new era. Yet Amherst, in 1830, was still a Puritan village, with its life centered in the church and the church-controlled college. The new currents of life had thus far left it untouched; Edward Dickinson, stalwart defender of the old order, was largely responsible for the coming of the railroad in 1853.

In such an environment Emily naturally occupied her young mind with religion, and her early letters bear much testimony to the seriousness of her affirmations and her doubts. At the age of sixteen she was lamenting her failure to make her peace with God and asking a friend to pray for her. After a college revival she regretted that she "did not give up and become a Christian," and the death of Leonard Humphrey filled her with solemn thoughts of the hereafter. With her reflections there mingled, it is true, both suggestions of doubt and touches of mild irreverence; but it may be questioned whether, either in her pious or her profane moods, she greatly differed from other young women of her day. Certainly thoughts of religion did not darken her life; she could be gay and even giddy. She engaged in such social life as Amherst afforded, and even the most intuitive of her friends must have believed that she would, in due season, marry some minister, lawyer, or teacher, and settle down in conventional domesticity.

By some event, still a mystery, that path was closed to her. In one sense what happened does not matter. Reading the letters we can see that, as Colonel Higginson observed, "the mystic and bizarre Emily is born at once between two pages," and that is enough to confirm the tradition that somehow love was aroused and frustrated. How Emily would have adjusted herself to domesticity we cannot surmise; it may have been well both for her and for poetry that the adjustment did not have to be made. As it was, she turned to solitude. There were inner resources for her to rely upon, fortunately for us, for otherwise she would have been one more New England old maid, of the kind Mrs. Freeman so often described, instead of the most distinguished poet of her generation.

For a person of Emily Dickinson's intensity no compromise was possible: either she accepted the active life of the average woman of her day, or she lived in and for herself. For her as a poet, in other words, solitude was imperative. The spirit of her age, of those momentous years between 1850 and 1880, could only have interfered with such an imagination as hers. In other ages, perhaps even in the period of Emerson, she could have found some nourishment in the life about her, but by the time her poetic powers were ripe, that was impossible. Presumably, after her love had proven fruitless, she wanted to live as she did live and write as she did write; it is, however, worth observing that, whether she knew it or not, she had no choice.

If we want proof, we need only turn to the work of those poets who were in the public eye in the post-war years. They enjoyed their popularity and went to their graves believing they had enriched the literature of the world. To be their kind of poet in the Gilded Age was not to live in a garret; on the contrary, Americans were eager, as Henry James pointed out, to bow down and worship the man of letters. If poetry was musical, graceful, and easily understood, if it reflected the current morality, if it sounded like Tennyson, and if it avoided the expression of personal passion, the promulgation of religious heresy, and the use of any theme that had not been sanctified by at least two generations of poetic tradition, its author was highly esteemed and well rewarded. The appreciation of art had become a mark of social distinction. The church was no longer at the center of American life; politics had been debauched; business was not quite respectable. Poetry helped the moderately prosperous Americans who read it to forget the gross struggle for material goods, and yet it did not hinder their participation in that struggle. So long as it was completely removed from the great affairs of the day, poetry had an enormous appeal, even reaching, at one end of the scale, some of the malefactors of great wealth and, at the other, some of their humble victims.

Plenty of persons appeared to meet this demand for polite poetry, foremost among them Thomas Bailey Aldrich, with Taylor, Stoddard,

Stedman, and Gilder not far behind. Precocious, talented, genteel, Aldrich devoted himself to enamelling discreet trifles and, on occasion, to voicing in portentous odes his faith in the righteousness of the Republican Party and the superiority of the Anglo-Saxon race. The others were as willing slaves as he, and their poetry like his never shook off its chains.

By contrast the homely humor and pathos of the dialect poets are a relief. The popularity of Bret Harte, the success of John Hay's handful of Pike County ballads, and the long-continued vogue of James Whitcomb Riley suggest that the polite poets may have been praised more than they were read. And it can at least be said for these men that they sometimes spoke with authenticity of life as it was being lived. Riley, like the urban poets, voiced a complacency based on ignorance, blindness, and self-deceit, but his sympathies were with the common people, and he gave little comfort to those who wanted to be convinced of their own superiority.

For a person with a capacity for original perception and a longing for individual expression, neither the genteel poetry of the city nor the self-consciously rude poetry of the country could have been attractive. E. R. Sill, for example, though he leaned towards respectability, was driven by self-distrust out of the beaten paths of the Aldriches and Gilders, and wrestled in solitude with his own problems. Sidney Lanier, perhaps because he was a southerner, was outspokenly critical of commercialism. He could declare,

> If business is battle, name it so:
> War-crimes less will shame it so,
> And widows less will blame it so.

But all he could propose was to substitute love of art for love of money. In practice that meant that poetry should be a refuge from the pressing problems of life, and as if to justify this evasion, Lanier elaborated his theories of the parallel between poetry and music. His own verse is musical enough, but too often it is nothing else.

The qualities that raised Sill and Lanier above such artificers as Aldrich were the qualities that made Emily Dickinson tower over the other poets of the period. Since she was forced into solitude, as we have seen, her age spoke in her poems only negatively, only in their omissions. The positive content comes from Emily herself, from her observations and from the influences of her childhood, which was of another age. Many of her poems are undistinguished: her loneliness did not nourish a capacity for self-criticism, and she left not only much work that is crude in expression but also some that is conventional in conception. But she reminds one, nonetheless, of the great poets: her experience, though limited, was intense; her perceptions, though active in but a small field, were original.

Emily Dickinson's theology has, obviously, little significance to-day, but her religious experiences are not without interest, simply because she describes and interprets them so personally and honestly. In her poems one feels the vitality of both Puritanism and the revolt against Puritanism; they are alive for us because they were alive for her. Emerson's doctrine of self-reliance takes on substance by virtue of its immediate reality for a real person, even though self-reliance meant for that person merely an isolated life in Amherst, Massachusetts. And what is true of her religious experiences is true of all the others that figure in her poems. Like Thoreau she could find importance in the simplest events of nature, and she was perhaps even more successful than he in communicating her sensitive perceptions to her readers. The limited observations of field and garden furnished themes for many poems and images for many more. And there was, of course, a whole field of experience, closed to Thoreau, that Emily returned to time after time in her poetry. We may not know who her lover was or why she never married him, but surely no American poet has written so movingly of love and renunciation. Sometimes she spoke with the utmost simplicity; sometimes passion merged with religious aspiration in a cry of fierce and almost agonizing intensity. The exaltation of the mystic is in most of her poems, whether her theme is life or death, heaven or hell; but that exaltation rests upon a singularly intense response to altogether human joys and fears.

To compare Emily Dickinson's poetry with the verse of her contemporaries is almost to deal with incommensurables. Though her themes are often metaphysical, her poems contain none of the platitudinous discourses on philosophy that Lowell introduced into his odes. Not only are her love poems free from sentimentality; they never suggest the slightest awareness of the romantic, prudish doctrines of contemporary respectability. She wrote of birds and flowers as if no one had ever written of them before. Literary conventions did not exist for her; as a poet she was quite untroubled by public opinion. Everything in her work is immediate, personal, and honest.

And yet the poetry of Emily Dickinson is undeniably fragile and remote. The discovery of her work is, for any sensitive reader, an exciting event; one responds eagerly to so complete a revelation of personal experience. But, close as her life comes to the lives of her readers, it touches them at very few points. It is as true of her as it is of Sarah Orne Jewett or Henry James that her strength is her weakness. The fact that she would not publish her poems in her own lifetime, though she was not unwilling to have them published after her death, indicates, among other things, that she was aware of the impossibility of coming to terms with her own age. By this gesture she severed herself from the Gilded Age more effectively than Miss Jewett could do in her Maine village or James in his home at Rye. This permitted her to avoid all the contamination of an era of uncertainty and of false values, but at the same time it meant that she could have none of the vigor that is found in an artist for whom self-expression is also the expression of the society of which he is part.

As Henry James somehow complements Howells, so that, as Emerson once said of Hawthorne and Alcott, the two of them might make one real man, so Emily Dickinson complements Walt Whitman, and the two of them, one feels, might make one poet. Where Whitman was merely expansive Emily Dickinson was intensive, but where she was narrow he was broad. And, though she did what she set out to do more effectively than he, just as James wrought more finely than Howells, the future was not with her, nor with James, but with Howells and Whitman. As one weighs the faults and the merits on both sides, one sighs with Emerson, "So many promising youths and never a finished man!"

SIR HERBERT READ (1893–) is an art historian, a literary critic, and a poet, who has written extensively on poets and poetry. Read's assumption in 1933 that all of Emily Dickinson's poems were finally collected and edited points up again the problem of complete and definitive texts of the poems, a problem not to be clarified until the 1950's. Sir Herbert's consequent difficulty in assessing the entire Dickinson canon is apparent.

The Range of Emily Dickinson

HERBERT READ

This is the definitive complete edition of Emily Dickinson's poems, so it is now possible for anyone to come to final critical terms with her work. Whether such a final estimate will be higher than the vague one that most of us have formed from a few anthology pieces is doubtful. It is a mistake to think that a poet gains from mere bulk. Most of the great poets have, it is true, been prolific, but there is no law to be deduced from that fact. The survival of such poets as Skelton, Marvell, Gray and Blake is guaranteed by a very few poems, whereas some of the major poets—Spenser, the later Milton and Browning, for example—tend to sink unread just because their genius is so consistently even and fluent. We do not work out poetic averages; we judge by the absolute attainment. Genius is always various; only talent is dependable.

Seen singly, as I have always hitherto seen them, the poems of Emily Dickinson are sufficiently intriguing to arouse a general interest in her work. One does not immediately accept them as beautiful or great; but one wonders if their eccentricity is the sign of an exceptional gift, which would yield fresh and accumulative interest when explored. My own experience of this volume has been one of great disappointment. I approached her poetry in the best critical mood—with interest but without any prepossessions which a knowledge of the poet's life and circumstances might give me, and with an expectation of enjoyment. To begin with, I was surprised at the actual number of the poems—there

From the *Spectator,* CLI (December 29, 1933), 971. A review of *The Poems of Emily Dickinson* (London: Secker, 1933).

are nearly eight hundred. Many of them are very short—four or six lines only—but what, in combination with their quantity, is so disturbing, is their sameness. It is a sameness that amounts to a poverty of technique. It would not be unfair to compare these poems with the works of a painter who had all his life painted small pictures of similar subjects in one colour with one texture. The eccentricity of technique, when we see it in bulk, is evidently not one of design, but rather of incapacity, of insensitiveness, of incredible naïvety in thought and expression. There are literally scores of poems of the following kind:

Surgeons must be very careful
When they take the knife!
Underneath their fine incisions
Stirs the culprit—Life!

Most of the verses are quite bathetic in their lack of any poetic, or even rhythmic, quality:

Undue significance a starving man attaches
To food
Far off; he sighs, and therefore hopeless,
And therefore good.

Partaken, it relieves indeed, but proves us
That spices fly
In the receipt. It was the distance
Was savory.

The poems in this edition are arranged in substantial sections, labelled "Life," "Nature," "Love," "Time and Eternity," and perhaps such an arrangement accentuates the general monotony. The best section is, I think, the shortest—the one labelled "Love." Here a sense of personal tragedy adds poignancy to the triteness:

Heart, we will forget him!
  You and I, to-night!
You may forget the warmth he gave,
  I will forget the light.

When you have done, pray tell me,
  That I my thoughts may dim;
Haste! lest while you're lagging,
  I may remember him!

The one technical excellency which Emily Dickinson may be said to have exploited is a kind of cryptic economy of statement, and since economy is always conducive to poetic expression, a poetic quality is sometimes achieved. Perhaps the following example will illustrate my meaning:

Title divine is mine
The Wife without
The Sign.
Acute degree
Conferred on me—
Empress of Calvary.
Royal all but the
Crown—
Betrothed, without the swoon
God gives us women
When two hold
Garnet to garnet,
Gold to gold—
Born—Bridalled—
Shrouded—
In a day
Tri-Victory—
'My Husband'
Women say
Stroking the melody,
Is this the way?

The nearest parallel to her poetry is Emily Brontë's, but there is no equality of stature. Too much that is childish and immature has been published under Emily Bronte's name, too much that was never meant for publication. But even the childish poems have lyric feeling, whereas the mature poems (such as "Often rebuked, yet always back returning," and "No coward soul is mine") reach an intensity and a largeness that are far beyond the range of Emily Dickinson. One cannot help feeling that in her case there has been too much anxiety to make a public display of a private talent. Something exquisite and real has been buried underneath a monument of mistaken devotion.

GAY WILSON ALLEN (1902–), professor of English at New York University since 1946, has devoted himself chiefly to the study of Walt Whitman. In *American Prosody* (1935) Allen systematically analyzed Emily Dickinson's prosody, clarifying much that had been thought problematic since the 1890's, and describing authoritatively the precise character of her poetic form.

Emily Dickinson's Versification

GAY WILSON ALLEN

1. Introduction

Contrary to popular belief, Miss Dickinson's poetry had many devotees before the twentieth century,[1] but the present generation of critics and poetry lovers likes to feel that it really "discovered" her, and recently the adoration of her technique has become almost a cult. As a consequence, many bitter literary battles have been fought in her name, for there are still some "die-hards," like Professor Pattee,[2] who refuse to accept her as a star leading to a new Jerusalem.

Thus our first problem in the study of Emily Dickinson's versification is whether her poetry is sufficiently important to deserve analysis. The judging of her work as poetry necessarily involves literary standards, aesthetics, and philosophical or thought content, none of which belong to the special subject of poetic technique. Whether or not her poetry is *great,* therefore, is not our problem, at least at present. Yet it does not seem that any one who is familiar with her influence on recent American poets could doubt the importance of her versification. Though she never wrote a word specifically on prosody, so far as we know (one never knows what new manuscripts her relatives may turn up!), her own technique has been accepted by the later poets (especially the *vers librists*) as a challenge to the established conventions of English versification.[3] And her versification is also important as a link between Emerson and the "New Poetry."

[1] Cf. Anna Mary Wells, "Early Criticism of Emily Dickinson," *American Literature* (November, 1929), I, No. 3, 243–259.

[2] Fred Lewis Pattee, *A History of American Literature since 1870* (New York, 1915), p. 341.

From Gay Wilson Allen, *American Prosody* (New York: American Book Co., 1935), 307–19.

2. The Textual Problem

There is a great stumbling block for the student of Miss Dickinson's technique, namely, that we have no adequate text for a study of her method. The first edition of her poetry made its appearance posthumously in 1890, followed by the "Second" and "Third Series" in 1891 and 1896. These were edited by Miss Dickinson's friends, Mrs. Mabel Loomis Todd and Col. T. W. Higginson. In 1924 the poet's niece, Martha Dickinson Bianchi, edited *The Complete Poems of Emily Dickinson;* but in 1929 this edition was supplemented by *Further Poems of Emily Dickinson,* which had been "Withheld from publication by her sister Lavinia."

Mrs. Todd has explained the chief difficulties of the editors.[4] Emily did not write her poems for publication, and left her manuscripts in no condition for the printer. She wrote on scraps of paper, backs of old envelopes, bits of wrapping paper, and whatever was convenient. Some of her improvisations appear to have been revised, but these revisions often consist of several substitute words and phrases, no preference being indicated. Naturally the line divisions were erratic, sometimes the shape and size of the scrap of paper making it impossible for the poet to indicate clearly her divisions (if, indeed, she would have bothered with them anyway); and the editors tell us that her main punctuation mark was the dash. The handwriting itself offered the editors many difficulties, but also some aid, since we are told that the chronology of the poems can be fairly accurately judged from the handwriting—though unfortunately for the student of versification, no attempt has been made in the various editions to indicate chronology in any way.

The most serious of all textual problems, however, is the skepticism of some scholars regarding the editors' readings of the manuscripts, which, it is to be regretted, have not been made generally accessible to scholars. Professor Prescott has questioned especially the editing of *Further Poems.* He quotes the following poem:

> Too much of proof affronts
> Belief.
> The Turtle will not try
> Unless you leave him;
> Then return—
> And he had hauled away,

---

[3] Miss Amy Lowell, for instance, says that, "thirty years after her death the flag under which she fought had become a great banner, the symbol of a militant revolt." *Poetry and Poets* (Boston, 1930), p. 89.

[4] *Harper's Magazine* (March, 1930), CLX, 463–471.

Adding: "The line division is so inexpressive of the obvious rhythm—the 'common measure' in which nine-tenths of all Emily's poems are written—that one suspects the editors of having made six lines out of four (ending respectively *belief, try, return,* and *away*). This suspicion is strengthened by other considerations: 1. This same poem when quoted in the Introduction is divided not into six, but into five lines. 2. Where other poems appear (in part) in both Introduction and text the two in almost every case disagree, in line division, punctuation, or wording. Sometimes these changes alter at least the suggestion of the poems. 3. Many pages in the manuscripts, the editors tell us, are "difficult to read"—the writing often "so bold that there are but two words on a line." Have the editors read correctly? [5]

There can be no justification of these inconsistencies which Professor Prescott points out, but there are many people who believe that Emily Dickinson's irregular line divisions were intentional and that they are more expressive than a regular arrangement could be. This latter class, including many of the *vers librists,* is not disturbed by the textual arrangement which we have at present. But until we have at least further proof that the editors have "read correctly," or a more general agreement regarding the arrangements of Emily Dickinson's poems, no definitive exposition of her versification can be given; for the irregular line division is one of the two most important innovations in her verse technique (the other regards rime, see § 4). What we really need is a complete edition edited by several competent, and preferably well-known, scholars, a sort of jury to decide upon the Emily Dickinson canon. Until something like that is done, our analyses and conclusions regarding her versification must be tentative, given with the understanding that further manuscript studies of her poems may modify our interpretations, inasmuch as changes in line divisions, in punctuation, and in wording affect rhythm very fundamentally.

3. The Question of Irregular Meter

In the Preface to the first volume of Emily Dickinson's *Poems,* Colonel Higginson says, "Though curiously indifferent to all conventional rules, [she] had yet a rigorous literary standard of her own, and

[5] F. C. Prescott, "Emily Dickinson's *Further Poems,*" *American Literature* (November, 1929), I, No. 3, 306–307.

often altered a word many times to suit an ear which had its own tenacious fastidiousness."[6] Indifference to *all* conventional rules is pretty sweeping, as well as ambiguous, though the Colonel apparently meant indifference to the "classical" rules of versification. The last clause of the quotation, however, indicates that he did not understand her technique, for the vague assertion that she was careful in her choice of words is exactly the kind of statement that Whitman's loyal but puzzled admirers made about his craftsmanship. But when the Colonel adds that Emily's "words and phrases" were "often set in a seemingly whimsical or even rugged frame," he errs absurdly, since *rugged* is the last word that ought to be applied to Emily Dickinson's versification. "Fragile," "lace-like," "delicately-carved" are far more accurate; certainly never "rugged."

Mrs. Todd's Preface is better: "Like impressionist pictures, or Wagner's rugged music, the very absence of conventional form challenges attention . . . her verses all show a strange cadence of inner rhythmical music. Lines are always daringly constructed, and the 'thought-rhyme' appears frequently,—appealing, indeed, to an unrecognized sense more elusive than hearing."[7]

Here we have the word "rugged" again, and "thought-rhyme" is also puzzling, as Amy Lowell admitted.[8] But this last phrase may mean that parallel words are substituted for rime; and the influence of biblical rhythms upon Emily Dickinson's work is obvious, though as her niece says, not "obtrusive."[9]

Nevertheless, it is to be regretted that both of these early editions so greatly emphasized the metrical irregularities; for it must have been, however they attempted to define it, their failure to recognize conventional meters (and rimes) in her verse that made them regard the technique as "rugged." We say this emphasis was regrettable because the truth is that, aside from rimes, Emily Dickinson's versification is not a great deal more irregular than Emerson's. Her poetry was startlingly original for her age, but its originality lies more in the thought than in the metrical technique.

Some of her rhythms are irregular, yet the majority of them are

[6] *Poems by Emily Dickinson* (Boston, 1890).

[7] *Poems by Emily Dickinson,* Second Series (Boston, 1897).

[8] Amy Lowell, *Poetry and Poets* (Boston, 1930), p. 95.

[9] *The Poems of Emily Dickinson,* ed. by Martha Dickinson Bianchi and Alfred Leete Hampson (Boston, 1930), p. viii.

surprisingly regular for the epigrammatic diction and thought. We have already cited "Too much of proof affronts belief" in Professor Prescott's criticism of the editors. Arranged as "common meter," the poem scans as follows:

> Too múch of próof affrónts belíef.
> The Túrtle wìll not trý
> Unléss you léave hìm; thén retúrn
> And hé has háuled awáy.

Another representative example is "I fit for them," which is printed as a nine line poem, in irregular verses and exceedingly puzzling rimes. But this poem is also nothing but common meter, and if arranged as four regular 4 + 3 quatrains even the rimes are less irregular: "fit" in the second line riming with "sweet" in the fourth, and "them" in the second line of the second quatrain riming with "aim" in the fourth line. These consonant-rimes are a usual practice with Emily Dickinson (see § 4). The first two lines of the poem show how the irregular verses straighten out when arranged to indicate the natural rhythms in which the poem was written:

> (1) I fít for thém,
> I séek the dárk till Ì am thórough fít.
> (2) I fít for thém, I séek the dárk
> Till Ì am thórough fít.

It is interesting that some very fine specimens of "common meter," arranged as irregular-length lines, are quoted by Miss Lowell in an essay in which she cites Emily Dickinson as a forerunner of Miss Lowell's own "school." "They bothered the critics dreadfully," says Miss Lowell, "these original, impossible poems where form (conventional form) was utterly disregarded..."[10] From *The Single Hound,* the following poems are quoted, all of which, supposedly, "utterly dis-

[10] Amy Lowell, *op. cit.,* p. 93.

regard conventional form." No. LXVI is printed in nine lines, but if lines seven and eight (each two-stress) are combined, we have two 4 + 3 quatrains. No. XLII is in ten lines, but if the two final lines (each composed of two phrases) are broken up, we have three trimeter quatrains, each ending with a period, and riming *abcd*. No. XXX is simply a seven-stress couplet, which of course is metrically the same as a quatrain of "common meter." No. LXVII is printed as eleven lines, but is simply two 4 + 3 quatrains, with *abcd* rimes, the first quatrain rimes being conventional, "street" and "beat," and the second quatrain having final consonant rimes, "steed" and "played." As the poem is printed, the rimes are without order, but in ballad quatrains, they come at the right places.

Despite her own statements that the poems utterly disregarded conventional form, Miss Lowell acknowledges the fact that "Emily Dickinson had no conscious idea of any form of verse other than the metrical ... she did her best to cram her subtle rhythmic sense into a figure of even feet and lines." [11] But she thought that Emily's "genius revolted," carrying her "over into cadence in spite of herself." Miss Lowell also believed that her own doctrine [12] of "verse based upon a unit of time instead of a unit of accent ... would have liberated Emily Dickinson from the bonds against which she chafed." [13]

There was undoubtedly a conflict of some sort in Emily Dickinson's technique, for some of her poems do seem to hang between regular meters and "free verse"; yet her few irregular poems appear to have blinded many people to the fact that the majority are in regular meters. Professor Prescott's estimate of nine-tenths "common meter" seems a little bit high, though it is safe to say that two-thirds of her poems are in this measure. Conrad Aiken was mistaken when he said that of six hundred poems practically all were in octosyllabic quatrains or couplets; [14] however, a large number are, and the regular trimeter quatrain is also used a good deal. Emily Dickinson hardly ever used pentameter, but we do find it occasionally (cf. III in *The Single Hound,* a regular five-stress quatrain). Even the irregular poems are mainly four- and

[11] *Ibid.*, pp. 105–106.
[12] *Ibid.*, p. 106.
[13] *Ibid.*, p. 106.
[14] Conrad Aiken, "Emily Dickinson," *Dial* (April, 1924), LXXVI, 308.

three-stress, and in many cases "common meter" is obviously the underlying pattern.

We must conclude, therefore, that Emily Dickinson's metrical irregularities have been grossly exaggerated, the mistaken conception being based mainly on the irregular line divisions. And in view of the reported condition of her manuscripts, it is impossible to decide whether she had any intention of substituting "cadence" for meter in her versification. But no matter how the lines are printed on the page, when the poems are read aloud the conventional iambic rhythmical patterns are plainly discernible.

4. Emily Dickinson's Rime

Some of the early critics assumed that Emily Dickinson's erratic rimes were the result of a faulty ear for sounds, yet it seems very unlikely that a person with her sense of rhythm would be unable to distinguish a good rime from a bad one, though a recent critic in *Poetry* still refers to her "almost comic gaucherie in the finding of rhyme." [15]

It does seem certain, however, that while Emily at no time completely and intentionally abandoned rime, she did not hesitate to sacrifice accurate rimes whenever they stood in the way of the expression of her thought, as was so often the case. Her practice, then, stands somewhere between the unrimed verses of Emerson's notebooks and the approximate rimes of Emerson's revised poems. And this comparison is more than an analogy, for her manuscripts are probably little more than mere notes; and whereas Emerson suppressed the spontaneity of his notebooks in favor of revisions in more conventional forms, she appears to have found increasingly greater satisfaction in her most natural and uncurbed manner.

Miss Susan Miles had an interesting theory that Emily Dickinson's irregular rimes have an artistic and psychological significance, and in nine cases out of ten express or imply defeat, struggle, frustration, suspense, failure, disillusion, etc. This theory leads Miss Miles to work out a classification of Emily's rimes:

(1) "Sometimes the expression demanded a three-quarters rhyme, that is an echo of the final consonant (if any) and the substitution

[15] Edward Sapir, in a review of the *Complete Poems* and the *Life and Letters, Poetry* (1925), XXVI, 99.

of a long for a corresponding short vowel, or of a short for a corresponding long;

(2) "sometimes the expression demanded a half-rhyme, that is, an echoing vowel and a contrasting consonant, or an echoing consonant and a contrasting vowel;

(3) "sometimes a non-rhyme, that is, a sound which echoes neither final consonant nor vowel, but which clangs out its contrast to both."[16] [And probably this was what Mrs. Todd meant by "thought rhyme."]

There appears to be some justification for this theory, and it is in no way invalidated by the suspicion that Emily Dickinson was probably unconscious of the artistic significance of the three-fourths, half-, and non-rimes which Miss Miles points out. But the theory must be accepted, if at all, only as a working principle. Miss Miles herself inadvertently demonstrates that it cannot be applied with reliable accuracy. For instance, she cites the poem "I felt a clearing in my mind," the rimes in the first quatrain being "split" and "fit," and those in the second quatrain being "before" and "floor." Then she points out the appropriateness of the first accurate rime and the second "three-quarters rhyme." But why are "before" and "floor" not "full" rimes? The final consonant is repeated, and in both words the *o* is long. Or at least it is in American speech, if not in Miss Miles's English pronunciation (thus illustrating one of the dangers in theories and critiques on the subject of rime).

And yet whatever we may think of the aesthetic and psychological aspects of this theory of Emily Dickinson's rimes, Miss Miles's classification is a convenient one. Without it, we would have difficulty in labeling the rimes in "Some have resigned the Loom":

...Loom a
...tomb a
...employ b
...feet c
...gate, c
...[at you and] I. b

The rimes marked "a" are "full" or accurate rimes, those marked "c" are half-rimes ("an echoing consonant and a contrasting vowel"), and

[16] Susan Miles, "The Irregularities of Emily Dickinson," *London Mercury* (1925–1926), XIII, 145–158.

there is a suggestion of assonance in "employ" and "I" (though we might add a fourth classification and call it a one-fourth rime). This poem, however, is uncharacteristic in the rime-scheme indicated above, for Emily Dickinson's usual scheme is, as we have noticed, *abcd*. This is significant because the scheme itself reduces rime to a minimum.

Of course the final rime in this poem would be less far-fetched if the line were grammatical, "at you and me." Just how the defenders of Emily Dickinson's every practice would justify this phrase is difficult to see, for it does not seem that the bad grammar serves any artistic or poetic purpose. The truth probably is that here, as in many other places, she was simply careless in composing the verse and too indifferent to revise it carefully afterward.

Further illustrations of her half-rimes (the most numerous variety of her inaccurate ones) have already been referred to as "final consonant rimes" in the preceding section on meter. For example, in "I fit for them" the rimes are "fit" and "sweet," "Them" and "Aim"; in "Like Brooms of Steel," "Street" and "heat" is a full rime, but "Steed" and "played" is only a half-rime. In "I bet with every Wind that blew," there is another half-rime, "chagrin" and "Balloon."

In "Of tribulation these are they," the rimes of all four quatrains repeat only the final consonant (or two consonants, as once in the second quatrain): "white" and "designate," "times" and "palms," "soil" and "mile," "road" and "Saved."

Among the "full" rimes, the light-ending (i.e., rime on a final unaccented syllable) is found frequently, as, for instance, "bee" and "revery" in "To make a prairie." Wherever a poem contains triplet rimes (rare but used occasionally), some of them are almost certain to be "light." "A Spider sewed at night" is a good illustration. The first three lines end with "night," "light," and "white"; then follow the half-rimes "dame," "gnome," and "inform"; and finally these lines:

> Of immortality
> His strategy
> Was physiognomy.

Sometimes the repetition of a word and not rime gives form and symmetry to the poem. The reiteration may take place anywhere in the line, but the initial position is frequently used. In "Glowing is her Bonnet," No. LXI in *The Single Hound,* the phrase "glowing is her" is repeated three times in the first quatrain, and the second quatrain has similar repetitions.

The parallelism, however, in most of Emily Dickinson's poems is more subtle and irregular than in this poem, and the reiteration (a natural concomitant of parallelism) does not usually extend over so many lines, though in "Bring me the sunset in a cup," all four of the six-line stanzas are marked out by the repetition of phrases,

> Tell me how far the morning leaps,
> Tell me what time the weaver sleeps, etc.

In fact, this sort of parallelism of both thought and words is used extensively in the sections of poems which the editors call "Life" and "Nature," the latter containing more parallelism than the former (cf. "The Wind began to rock the grass").

But parallelism and reiteration in Emily Dickinson's versification do not crowd out meter and rime. They help to form patterns and to reinforce the metrical rhythms, yet they are not, as with Whitman's verse, rhythmical principles in themselves.

5. The Link Between Emerson and "Imagism"

The resemblance of Emily Dickinson's rhythms and imperfect rimes to Emerson's is important, but is superficial in comparison to the deeper and more significant relationships of style and epigrammatic manner. Of course Emily's fractures of grammatical rules and dictionary pronunciations are hardly ever paralleled in Emerson's verse, but even these faults are not difficult to reconcile with Emerson's doctrines of spontaneity and individualism of poetic technique. Conrad Aiken has made a still more important comparison: "The thought is there" in Emily Dickinson's poems, he says, "hard, bright, and clear; and her symbols, her metaphors, of which she could be prodigal, have all analogous clarity and translucency ... Emerson's gnomic style she tunes up to the epigrammatic—the epigrammatic she often carries to the point of the cryptic, she becomes what one might call an epigrammatic symbolist." [17]

The epigram is so packed with meaning that the thought becomes of far more importance than rhythm, rime, and word-music. There is

[17] Conrad Aiken, *op. cit.*, p. 306.

some beautiful music in Emily Dickinson's poems, yet in reading them we are usually far more conscious of the thought than the music. This fact probably explains why her versification has been so puzzling to some critics. She often had to sacrifice versification for a closely-packed metaphor or a barbed epigram, not because she had any intention of breaking the conventional rules but because what she had to say did not precisely fit the accentuation and form which the conventional scheme demanded. This is especially true in those poems which Professor Elliott calls too "Emersonianly enlightened, to arrive." [18]

As we have seen, her irregularities of meters are more likely to consist of uneven-length lines rather than erratic accentuation; but the line-divisions have been taken up by the "free versifiers" as a valuable precedent for them. And Mr. Aiken's characterization of her thought as "hard, bright, and clear" is the central ideal of the "Imagists." Finally, Emily Dickinson's poetic style is ejaculatory, suggestive rather than completely formed, and it is perhaps in this respect most of all that she is a link between Emerson and the "Imagists." [19]

[18] G. R. Elliott, in a book review of *Further Poems, American Literature* (January, 1930), I, No. 4, 442.

[19] "Imagism" is the self-styled name given to a group of English and American poets who in 1914 decided to "reform" their native prosody. The Americans were Miss Amy Lowell (the chief organizer and spokesman), Mr. John Gould Fletcher, and "H.D." (Hilda Doolittle). In 1915 they published an anthology called *Some Imagist Poets,* with a preface setting forth the "creed" of the movement. The following is a condensed version of the creed: (1) "To use the language of common speech, but to employ always the exact word," (2) "To create new rhythms as the expression of new moods—and not to copy old rhythms, which merely echo old moods," (3) "absolute freedom in the choice of the subject," (4) "To present an image . . . and not deal in vague generalities, however magnificent and sonorous," (5) "To produce poetry that is hard and clear, never blurred nor indefinite," (6) "concentration is of the very essence of poetry." The Imagists insisted upon the freedom to use "free verse" if they chose to do so, but their movement only partly coincides with the free verse tendencies of the times. References: Amy Lowell, *Tendencies in Modern American Poetry.* Boston: Houghton Mifflin Company, 1917. Glenn Hughes, *Imagism and the Imagists.* Stanford University Press, 1931.

YVOR WINTERS (1900–) has held a critical point of view at once stimulating and exasperating to modern readers. The focus of his literary career has been teaching, since 1927 at Stanford University. The content and method of his criticism are clearly set forth in *Maule's Curse* (1938) and *In Defense of Reason* (1947). Winters' final judgment of Emily Dickinson is that "she is one of the greatest lyric poets of all time," but his essay deals rigorously with what he regards as her defects and her virtues.

Emily Dickinson and the Limits of Judgment

YVOR WINTERS

Antiquest felt at noon
When August, burning low,
Calls forth this spectral canticle,
Repose to typify.

When the poems of Emily Dickinson first began to appear, in the years shortly following her death, she enjoyed a period of notoriety and of semi-popularity that endured for perhaps ten years; after about ten years of semi-obscurity, her reputation was revived with the publication of *The Single Hound,* and has lasted unabated to the present day, though with occasional signs that it may soon commence to diminish. A good many critics have resented her reputation, and it has not been hard for them to justify their resentment; probably no poet of comparable reputation has been guilty of so much unpardonable writing. On the other hand, one cannot shake off the uncomfortable feeling that her popularity has been mainly due to her vices; her worst poems are certainly her most commonly praised, and as a general matter, great lyric poetry is not widely read or admired.

The problem of judging her better poems is much of the time a subtle one. Her meter, at its worst—that is, most of the time—is a kind of stiff sing-song; her diction, at its worst, is a kind of poetic nursery jargon;

From Yvor Winters, *Maule's Curse* (Norfolk, Connecticut: New Directions, 1938), 149–65; reprinted in Yvor Winters, *In Defense of Reason* (University of Denver Press, n.d.), 283–99.

and there is a remarkable continuity of manner, of a kind nearly indescribable, between her worst and her best poems. The following poem will illustrate the defects in perfection:

I like to see it lap the miles,
And lick the valleys up,
And stop to feed itself at tanks;
And then, prodigious, step

Around a pile of mountains,
And, supercilious, peer
In shanties by the sides of roads;
And then a quarry pare

To fit its sides, and crawl between,
Complaining all the while
In horrid, hooting stanza;
Then chase itself down hill

And neigh like Boanerges;
Then, punctual as a star,
Stop—docile and omnipotent—
At its own stable door.

The poem is abominable; and the quality of silly playfulness which renders it abominable is diffused more or less perceptibly throughout most of her work, and this diffusion is facilitated by the limited range of her metrical schemes.

The difficulty is this: that even in her most nearly perfect poems, even in those poems in which the defects do not intrude momentarily in a crudely obvious form, one is likely to feel a fine trace of her countrified eccentricity; there is nearly always a margin of ambiguity in our final estimate of even her most extraordinary work, and though the margin may appear to diminish or disappear in a given reading of a favorite poem, one feels no certainty that it will not reappear more obviously with the next reading. Her best poems, quite unlike the best poems of Ben Jonson, of George Herbert, or of Thomas Hardy, can never be isolated certainly and defensibly from her defects; yet she is a poetic genius of the highest order, and this ambiguity in one's feeling about her is profoundly disturbing. The following poem is a fairly obvious illustration; we shall later see less obvious:

I started early, took my dog,
And visited the sea;

The mermaids in the basement
Came out to look at me,

And frigates in the upper floor
Extended hempen hands,
Presuming me to be a mouse
Aground, upon the sands.

But no man moved me till the tide
Went past my simple shoe,
And past my apron and my belt,
And past my bodice too,

And made as he would eat me up
As wholly as a dew
Upon a dandelion's sleeve—
And then I started too.

And he—he followed close behind;
I felt his silver heel
Upon my ankle,—then my shoes
Would overflow with pearl.

Until we met the solid town,
No man he seemed to know;
And bowing with a mighty look
At me, the sea withdrew.

The mannerisms are nearly as marked as in the first poem, but whereas the first poem was purely descriptive, this poem is allegorical and contains beneath the more or less mannered surface an ominously serious theme, so that the manner appears in a new light and is somewhat altered in effect. The sea is here the traditional symbol of death; that is, of all the forces and qualities in nature and in human nature which tend toward the dissolution of human character and consciousness. The playful protagonist, the simple village maiden, though she speaks again in the first person, is dramatized, as if seen from without, and her playfulness is somewhat restrained and formalized. Does this formalization, this dramatization, combined with a major symbolism, suffice effectually to transmute in this poem the quality discerned in the first poem, or does that quality linger as a fine defect? The poem is a poem of power; it may even be a great poem; but this is not to answer the question. I have never been able to answer the question.

Her poetic subject matter might be subdivided roughly as follows: natural description; the definition of moral experience, including the definition of difficulties of comprehension; and mystical experience, or the definition of the experience of "immortality," to use a favorite word, or of beatitude. The second subdivision includes a great deal, and her best work falls within it; I shall consider it last. Her descriptive poems contain here and there brilliant strokes, but she had the hard and uncompromising approach to experience of the early New England Calvinists; lacking all subtlety, she displays the heavy hand of one unaccustomed to fragile objects; her efforts at lightness are distressing. Occasionally, instead of endeavoring to treat the small subject in terms appropriate to it, she endeavors to treat it in terms appropriate to her own temperament, and we have what appears a deliberate excursion into obscurity, the subject being inadequate to the rhetoric, as in the last stanza of the poem beginning, "At half-past three a single bird":

> At half-past seven, element
> Nor implement was seen,
> And place was where the presence was,
> Circumference between.

The stanza probably means, roughly, that bird and song alike have disappeared, but the word "circumference," a resonant and impressive one, is pure nonsense.

This unpredictable boldness in plunging into obscurity, a boldness in part, perhaps, inherited from the earlier New Englanders whose sense of divine guidance was so highly developed, whose humility of spirit was commonly so small; a boldness dramatized by Melville in the character of Ahab; this congenital boldness may have led her to attempt the rendering of purely theoretic experience, the experience of life after death. There are numerous poems which attempt to express the experience of posthumous beatitude, as if she were already familiar with it; the poetic terms of the expression are terms, either abstract or concrete, of human life, but suddenly fixed, or approaching fixation, as if at the cessation of time in eternity, as if to the dead the living world appeared as immobile as the dead person appears to the living, and the fixation frequently involves an element of horror:

> Great streets of silence led away
> To neighborhoods of pause;
> Here was no notice, no dissent,
> No universe, no laws.

By clocks 'twas morning, and for night
The bells at distance called;
But epoch had no basis here,
For period exhaled.

The device here employed is to select a number of terms representing familiar abstractions or perceptions, some of a commonplace nature, some relatively grandiose or metaphysical, and one by one to negate these terms; a number of statements, from a grammatical point of view, have been made, yet actually no concrete image emerges, and the idea of the poem—the idea of the absolute dissidence of the eternal from the temporal—is stated indirectly, and, in spite of the brevity of the poem and the gnomic manner, with extraordinary redundancy. We come painfully close in this poem to the irresponsible playfulness of the poem about the railway train; we have gone beyond the irresponsible obscurity of the poem about the bird.

This is technically a mystical poem: that is, it endeavors to render an experience—the rapt contemplation, eternal and immovable, which Aquinas describes as the condition of beatitude—which is by definition foreign to all human experience, yet to render it in terms of a modified human experience. Yet there is no particular reason to believe that Emily Dickinson was a mystic, or thought she was a mystic. The poems of this variety, and there are many of them, appear rather to be efforts to dramatize an idea of salvation, intensely felt, but as an idea, not as something experienced, and as an idea essentially inexpressible. She deliberately utilizes imagery irrelevant to the state with which she is concerned, because she cannot do otherwise; yet the attitude toward the material, the attitude of rapt contemplation, is the attitude which she presumably expects to achieve toward something that she has never experienced. The poems are invariably forced and somewhat theoretical; they are briskly clever, and lack the obscure but impassioned conviction of the mystical poems of Very; they lack the tragic finality, the haunting sense of human isolation in a foreign universe, to be found in her greatest poems, of which the explicit theme is a denial of this mystical trance, is a statement of the limits of judgment.

There are a few curious and remarkable poems representing a mixed theme, of which the following is perhaps the finest example:

Because I could not stop for Death,
He kindly stopped for me;

The carriage held but just ourselves
And Immortality.

We slowly drove, he knew no haste,
And I had put away
My labor, and my leisure too,
For his civility.

We passed the school where children played
At wrestling in a ring;
We passed the fields of gazing grain,
We passed the setting sun.

We paused before a house that seemed
A swelling of the ground;
The roof was scarcely visible,
The cornice but a mound.

Since then 'tis centuries; but each
Feels shorter than the day
I first surmised the horses' heads
Were toward eternity.

In the fourth line we find the familiar device of using a major abstraction in a somewhat loose and indefinable manner; in the last stanza there is the semi-playful pretence of familiarity with the posthumous experience of eternity, so that the poem ends unconvincingly though gracefully, with a formulary gesture very roughly comparable to that of the concluding couplet of many an Elizabethan sonnet of love; for the rest the poem is a remarkably beautiful poem on the subject of the daily realization of the imminence of death—it is a poem of departure from life, an intensely conscious leave-taking. In so far as it concentrates on the life that is being left behind, it is wholly successful; in so far as it attempts to experience the death to come, it is fraudulent, however exquisitely, and in this it falls below her finest achievement. Allen Tate, who appears to be unconcerned with this fraudulent element, praises the poem in the highest terms; he appears almost to praise it for its defects: [1] "The sharp *gazing* before *grain* instils into nature a kind of cold vitality of which the qualitative richness has infinite depth. The content of death in the poem eludes forever any explicit definition . . . she has presented a typical Christian theme in all its final irresolution, without making any final statement about it." The poem ends in irresolution in

[1] *Reactionary Essays on Poetry and Ideas,* by Allen Tate. Scribners, 1936. The essay on Emily Dickinson. [See pp. 160–61 in this anthology.—Editors' note.]

the sense that it ends in a statement that is not offered seriously; to praise the poem for this is unsound criticism, however. It is possible to solve any problem of insoluble experience by retreating a step and defining the boundary at which comprehension ceases, and by then making the necessary moral adjustments to that boundary; this in itself is an experience both final and serious, and it is the experience on which our author's finest work is based.

Let me illustrate by citation. The following poem defines the subject which the mystical poems endeavor to conceal: the soul is taken to the brink of the incomprehensible, and is left there, for retreat is impossible, and advance is impossible without a transmutation of the soul's very nature. The third and fourth lines display the playful redundancy of her weaker poems, but the intrusion of the quality here is the result of habit, and is a minor defect; there is nothing in the conception of the poem demanding a compromise. There is great power in the phrasing of the remainder of the poem, especially in the middle stanza:

Our journey had advanced;
Our feet were almost come
To that odd fork in Being's road,
Eternity by term.

Our pace took sudden awe,
Our feet reluctant led.
Before were cities, but between
The forest of the dead.

Retreat was out of hope,—
Behind, a sealëd route,
Eternity's white flag before,
And God at every gate.

She is constantly defining the absolute cleavage between the living and the dead. In the following poem the definition is made more powerfully, and in other terms:

'Twas warm at first, like us,
Until there crept thereon
A chill, like frost upon a glass,
Till all the scene be gone.

The forehead copied stone,
The fingers grew too cold

To ache, and like a skater's brook
The busy eyes congealed.

It straightened—that was all—
It crowded cold to cold—
It multiplied indifference
As Pride were all it could.

And even when with cords
'Twas lowered like a freight,
It made no signal, nor demurred,
But dropped like adamant.

The stiffness of phrasing, as in the barbarously constructed fourth and twelfth lines, is allied to her habitual carelessness, yet in this poem there is at least no triviality, and the imagery of the third stanza in particular has tremendous power.

The poem beginning, "The last night that she lived," treats the same theme in more personal terms; the observer watches the death of a friend, that is follows the friend to the brink of the comprehensible, sees her pass the brink, and faces the loss. The poem contains a badly mixed figure and at least two major grammatical blunders, in addition to a little awkward inversion of an indefensible variety, yet there is in the poem an immediate seizing of terrible fact, which makes it, at least fragmentarily, very great poetry:

And we, we placed the hair,
And drew the head erect;
And then an awful leisure was,
Our faith to regulate.

Her inability to take Christian mysticism seriously did not, however, drive her to the opposite extreme of the pantheistic mysticism which was seducing her contemporaries. The following lines, though not remarkable poetry, are a clear statement of a position consistently held:

But nature is a stranger yet;
The ones that cite her most
Have never passed her haunted house,
Nor simplified her ghost.

To pity those that know her not
Is helped by the regret

That those who know her, know her less
The nearer her they get.

Nature as a symbol, as Allen Tate has pointed out in the essay to which I have already referred, remains immitigably the symbol of all the elements which corrupt, dissolve, and destroy human character and consciousness; to approach nature is to depart from the fullness of human life, and to join nature is to leave human life. Nature may thus be a symbol of death, representing much the same idea as the corpse in the poem beginning " 'Twas warm at first, like us," but involving a more complex range of association.

In the following poem, we are shown the essential cleavage between man, as represented by the author-reader, and nature, as represented by the insects in the late summer grass; the subject is the plight of man, the willing and freely moving entity, in a universe in which he is by virtue of his essential qualities a foreigner. The intense nostalgia of the poem is the nostalgia of man for the mode of being which he perceives imperfectly and in which he cannot share. The change described in the last two lines is the change in the appearance of nature and in the feeling of the observer which results from a recognition of the cleavage:

Farther in summer than the birds,
Pathetic from the grass,
A minor nation celebrates
Its unobtrusive mass.

No ordinance is seen,
So gradual the grace,
A pensive custom it becomes,
Enlarging loneliness.

Antiquest felt at noon
When August, burning low,
Calls forth this spectral canticle,
Repose to typify.

Remit as yet no grace,
No furrow on the glow,
Yet a druidic difference
Enhances nature now.

The first two lines of the last stanza are written in the author's personal grammatical short-hand; they are no doubt defective in this respect, but the defect is minor. They mean: There is as yet no diminution of beauty, no mark of change on the brightness. The twelfth line employs a meaningless inversion. On the other hand, the false rhymes are employed with unusually fine modulation; the first rhyme is perfect, the second and third represent successive stages of departure, and the last a return to what is roughly the stage of the second. These effects are complicated by the rhyming, both perfect and imperfect, from stanza to stanza. The intense strangeness of this poem could not have been achieved with standard rhyming. The poem, though not quite one of her most nearly perfect, is probably one of her five or six greatest, and is one of the most deeply moving and most unforgettable poems in my own experience; I have the feeling of having lived in its immediate presence for many years.

The three poems which combine her greatest power with her finest execution are strangely on much the same theme, both as regards the idea embodied and as regards the allegorical embodiment. They deal with the inexplicable fact of change, of the absolute cleavage between successive states of being, and it is not unnatural that in two of the poems this theme should be related to the theme of death. In each poem, seasonal change is employed as the concrete symbol of the moral change. This is not the same thing as the so-called pathetic fallacy of the romantics, the imposition of a personal emotion upon a physical object incapable either of feeling such an emotion or of motivating it in a human being. It is rather a legitimate and traditional form of allegory, in which the relationships between the items described resemble exactly the relationships between certain moral ideas or experiences; the identity of relationship evoking simultaneously and identifying with each other the feelings attendant upon both series as they appear separately. Here are the three poems, in the order of the seasons employed, and in the order of increasing complexity both of theme and of technique:

I

A light exists in spring
Not present in the year
At any other period.
When March is scarcely here

A color stands abroad
On solitary hills

That science cannot overtake,
But human nature feels.

It waits upon the lawn;
It shows the furthest tree
Upon the furthest slope we know;
It almost speaks to me.

Then, as horizons step,
Or noons report away,
Without the formula of sound,
It passes, and we stay:

A quality of loss
Affecting our content,
As trade had suddenly encroached
Upon a sacrament.

2

As imperceptibly as grief
The Summer lapsed away,—
Too imperceptible, at last,
To seem like perfidy.

A quietness distilled,
As twilight long begun,
Or Nature, spending with herself
Sequestered afternoon.

The dusk drew earlier in,
The morning foreign shone,—
A courteous, yet harrowing grace,
As guest who would be gone.

And thus, without a wing,
Or service of a keel,
Our summer made her light escape
Into the beautiful.

3

There's a certain slant of light,
On winter afternoons,
That oppresses, like the weight
Of cathedral tunes.

Heavenly hurt it gives us;
We can find no scar,

But internal difference
Where the meanings are.

None may teach it anything,
'Tis the seal, despair,—
An imperial affliction
Sent us of the air.

When it comes, the landscape listens,
Shadows hold their breath;
When it goes, 'tis like the distance
On the look of death.

In the seventh, eighth, and twelfth lines of the first poem, and, it is barely possible, in the seventh and eighth of the third, there is a very slight echo of the brisk facility of her poorer work; the last line of the second poem, perhaps, verges ever so slightly on an easy prettiness of diction, though scarcely of substance. These defects are shadowy, however; had the poems been written by another writer, it is possible that we should not observe them. On the other hand, the directness, dignity, and power with which these major subjects are met, the quality of the phrasing, at once clairvoyant and absolute, raise the poems to the highest level of English lyric poetry.

The meter of these poems is worth careful scrutiny. The basis of all three is the so-called Poulter's Measure, first employed, if I remember aright, by Surrey, and after the time of Sidney in disrepute. It is the measure, however, not only of the great elegy on Sidney commonly attributed to Fulke Greville, but of some of the best poetry between Surrey and Sidney, including the fine poem by Vaux on contentment and the great poem by Gascoigne in praise of a gentlewoman of dark complexion. The English poets commonly though not invariably wrote the poem in two long lines instead of four short ones, and the lines so conceived were the basis of their rhetoric. In the first of the three poems just quoted, the measure is employed without alteration, but the short line is the basis of the rhetoric; an arrangement which permits of more varied adjustment of sentence to line than if the long line were the basis. In the second poem, the first stanza is composed not in the basic measure, but in lines of eight, six, eight, and six syllables; the shift into the normal six, six, eight, and six in the second stanza, as in the second stanza of the poem beginning, "Farther in summer," results in a subtle and beautiful muting both of meter and of tone. This shift she employs elsewhere, but especially in poems of four stanzas, to which it appears to have a natural relationship; it is a brilliant technical invention.

In the third poem she varies her simple base with the ingenuity and mastery of a virtuoso. In the first stanza, the two long lines are reduced to seven syllables each, by the dropping of the initial unaccented syllable; the second short line is reduced to five syllables in the same manner. In the second stanza, the first line, which ought now to be of six syllables, has but five metrical syllables, unless we violate normal usage and count the second and infinitely light syllable of *Heaven,* with an extrametrical syllable at the end, the syllable dropped being again the initial one; the second line, which ought to have six syllables, has likewise lost its initial syllable, but the extrametrical *us* of the preceding line, being unaccented, is in rhythmical effect the first syllable of the second line, so that this syllable serves a double and ambiguous function—it maintains the syllable-count of the first line, in spite of an altered rhythm, and it maintains the rhythm of the second line in spite of the altered syllable-count. The third and fourth lines of the second stanza are shortened to seven and five. In the third stanza the first and second lines are constructed like the third and fourth of the second stanza; the third and fourth lines like the first and second of the second stanza, except that in the third line the initial unaccented syllable is retained; that is, the third stanza repeats the construction of the second, but in reverse order. The final stanza is a triumphant resolution of the three preceding: the first and third lines, like the second and fourth, are metrically identical; the first and third contain seven syllables each, with an additional extrametrical syllable at the end which takes the place of the missing syllable at the beginning of each subsequent short line, at the same time that the extrametrical syllable functions in the line in which it is written as part of a two-syllable rhyme. The elaborate structure of this poem results in the balanced hesitations and rapid resolutions which one hears in reading it. This is metrical artistry at about as high a level as one is likely to find it.

Emily Dickinson was a product of the New England tradition of moral Calvinism; her dissatisfaction with her tradition led to her questioning most of its theology and discarding much of it, and led to her reinterpreting some of it, one would gather, in the direction of a more nearly Catholic Christianity. Her acceptance of Christian moral concepts was unimpaired, and the moral tone of her character remained immitigably Calvinistic in its hard and direct simplicity. As a result of this Calvinistic temper, she lacked the lightness and grace which might have enabled her to master minor themes; she sometimes stepped without hesitation into obscurantism, both verbal and metaphysical. But also as a result of it, her best poetry represents a moral adjustment to certain major problems which are carefully defined; it is curious in the light of this fact, and in the light of the discussion which they have received, that her love poems never equal her highest achievement—her best work is on themes more generalized and inclusive.

Emily Dickinson differed from every other major New England writer of the nineteenth century, and from every major American writer of the century save Melville, of those affected by New England, in this: that her New England heritage, though it made her life a moral drama, did not leave her life in moral confusion. It impoverished her in one respect, however: of all great poets, she is the most lacking in taste; there are innumerable beautiful lines and passages wasted in the desert of her crudities; her defects, more than those of any other great poet that I have read, are constantly at the brink, or pushing beyond the brink, of her best poems. This stylistic character is the natural product of the New England which produced the barren little meeting houses; of the New England founded by the harsh and intrepid pioneers, who in order to attain salvation trampled brutally through a world which they were too proud and too impatient to understand. In this respect, she differs from Melville, whose taste was rich and cultivated. But except by Melville, she is surpassed by no writer that this country has produced; she is one of the greatest lyric poets of all time.

RICHARD P. BLACKMUR (1904–   ) has exercised significant influence in contemporary criticism. *The Double Agent* (1935) and *The Expense of Greatness* (1940) stand at the beginning of a distinguished bibliography of essays, editions, reviews—and volumes of his own poetry. Blackmur has been associated with Princeton as resident fellow in creative writing and as professor of English. His essay on Emily Dickinson is one of the most searching, especially in its concern to focus and clarify the major claims for and against her greatness.

Emily Dickinson: Notes on Prejudice and Fact

R. P. BLACKMUR

The disarray of Emily Dickinson's poems is the great obvious fact about them as they multiply from volume to volume—I will not say from edition to edition, for they have never been edited—just as a kind of repetitious fragmentariness is the characterizing fact of her sensibility. No poet of anything like her accomplishment has ever imposed on the reader such varied and continuous critical labor; and on few poets beyond the first bloat of reputation has so little work been done. Few poets have benefited generally, and suffered specifically, from such a handsome or fulsome set of prejudices, which, as they are expressed, seem to remove the need for any actual reading at all.

The barriers to critical labor are well known, and some of them are insuperable. No text will be certain so long as the vaults at Amherst remain closed. Without benefit of comparative scholarship it is impossible to determine whether a given item is a finished poem, an early version of a poem, a note for a poem, a part of a poem, or a prose exclamation. Worse, it is impossible to know whether what appear to be crotchets in the poems as printed are correctly copied. The poet's handwriting was obscure, loose, and run-over; hence it is plain that unskilled copyists cannot be relied on in matters of punctuation, line structure, and the terminal letters of words. It is plainer still, if suspicion be in case, that many examples of merely irritating bad grammar—mistakes that merely hinder the reader—may well represent systematic bad guessing by the copyist. Perhaps it is not plain, but it is plausible, to imagine that a full and open view of the manuscripts would show the poet far less fragmentary and repetitious than the published work makes her seem. Most poets have a desk full of beginnings, a barrel of fragments and anything up to an attic full of notes. The manner of notation, if it were known, might make a beginning at the establishment of a canon. With the obvious fragments cut out, or put in an appendix, a clean, self-characterizing, responsive, and responding body of poetry, with limits and a fate and a quaking sensibility, might then be made to show itself.

Then is not now. This essay cannot enact a prophecy. This disarray of fragments, this mob of verses, this din of many motions, cannot be made to show itself in its own best order—as the strong parade we hoped

From *Southern Review*, III (Autumn, 1937), 323–47.

it really was. This essay proposes, in lieu of adumbrating a complete criticism, first to examine a set of prejudices which are available as approaches to Emily Dickinson, and then to count—and perhaps account for—a few staring facts: obvious, animating, defacing facts about the verses as they now appear. If the essay has a good eye for the constitution of poetic facts, the affair of counting will be adventurous, a part of the great adventure of sensibility which consists, one sometimes thinks, in an arduous fealty to facts. If the fealty is sound, perhaps the vestiges of a complete criticism will be there too, or at least a bias, a prejudice, in that direction.

For it takes a strong and active prejudice to see facts at all, as any revolutionist will tell you. And just as the body must have a strong prejudice, which is its wisdom, about the nature of time in order to wake up exactly *before* the alarm goes off—an affair of counting, if ever—so the sensibility must have a pretty firm anterior conviction about the nature of poetry in order to wake up to a given body of poetry at all. We suddenly realize that we have, or have *not*—which in a very neat way comes to the same thing—counted some of these facts before. We know where we are in terms of where we thought we were, at home, lost, or shaking: which is when the alarm goes off. To depend on prejudice for the nature of time or poetry may seem a little willful and adventitiously mysterious. But it is a method that allows for mistakes, and in the present condition of Emily Dickinson's poetry, it is imperative to allow for continuous error, both in the facts and in their counting—in the prejudices by which we get at them.

Most prejudices are frivolous to the real interests concerned, which is why they are so often made to appear as facts instead of mere keys to facts. That Emily Dickinson is a great poet, "with the possible exception of Sappho, the greatest woman poet of all time," or the author of poetry "perhaps the finest by a woman in the English language," or that in one of the volumes of her verse "there are no dregs, no single drop can be spared,"—these are variations upon an essentially frivolous prejudice. Only the last variation is dangerous, because by asserting perfection it makes the poet an idol and removes her from the possibility of experience. On the whole, statements of this order are seldom taken seriously, but are felt as polite salutations and farewells. The trouble is that it is hard to persuade oneself actually to read work towards which one has accomplished gestures so polite. If not a drop can be spared, let us not risk spilling any; let us say, rather, here is great poetry—we know what *that* is like! A chalice, a lily, a sea-change. Old memories are mulled. We have the equivalent of emotion. And equivalents, like substitutes, though not so good as what you asked for, are often, for sensibilities never exercised enough to have been starved, a full meal.

It would be unfair, though, to leave the prejudice of Emily Dickinson's magnitude so naked. Politeness may conceal a legitimate wish that dare not put itself in bald speech. I am convinced that Conrad Aiken, in referring to Emily Dickinson's poetry as "perhaps the finest by a woman in the English language," had the legitimate wish to condition the reader with a very good fundamental prejudice—which we shall come to—about Emily Dickinson to the effect that there was something exciting or vital or amusing in her work. It is a kind of flag-waving; it reminds you of what you ought to be able to feel. Most readers of poetry are flag-wavers, and in order to get them to be more, you have to begin by waving a flag. I cannot imagine Mr. Aiken, or any other reader, addressing a Dickinson poem as "perhaps the finest by a woman in the English language." That is only how he addresses other people, hoping that they will thus be prejudiced into responding to the poem as he actually does, in terms of the words and the motions of the words which make it up: which are the terms (not the thing itself) of magnitude. I too would like to begin and end with the idea that in some such sense Emily Dickinson is sometimes a great poet.

There is a more dangerous but no less frivolous type of prejudice in the following sentence. "Her revolt was absolute; she abandoned rhyme altogether when she chose, and even assonance, writing in meter alone, like a Greek." There is a Spanish proverb that if God does not bless you with children, the devil will send you nieces. As a literary critic, if not as a niece, Mme. Bianchi, who is responsible for the sentence quoted, is thoroughly diabolic; as idolaters are by rule. The idea is to make you feel that the slips and roughnesses, the truncated lines, false rhymes, the inconsistencies of every description which mar the majority of Emily Dickinson's poems are examples of a revolutionary master-craftsman. Only the idol is served here; no greater disservice could be done to the poetry the reader reads than to believe with however great sincerity that its blemishes have any closer relation than contrast to its beauty. Emily Dickinson never knew anything about the craft of verse well enough to exemplify it, let alone revolt from it. If, where you are autonomous as in the *practice* of verse, you revolt first, you only revolve in a vacuum; and you will end as Emily Dickinson did in many of her failures by producing chaotic verses which have no bearing on the proper chaos of their subject—the life where precisely, as Emily Dickinson well enough knew, you are not autonomous but utterly dependent and interlocked.

As for Mme. Bianchi's specific terms: if the ear and arithmetic of this essay are right, Emily Dickinson did not abandon rhyme so much as she failed to get that far—her lines strike *as if* they intended to end in rhyme; and her assonances seem frequently incomplete substitutes for rhyme and not assonances at all. She did not write in meter alone; her meters were most often exiguous or overrun proximations of common English meter—or again they met the pattern of meter in syllabification miter-perfect without meeting the enlivening movement of meter. And as for writing like a Greek it would be more nearly correct, metrically, to say that she wrote like an Italian with recurring pairs of stressed syllables. I do not refer here to the successful meters in Emily Dickinson, but only to the variously deficient meters.

But Mme. Bianchi is not half so dangerous in idealizing her aunt's technical inadequacy as absolute, as Ludwig Lewisohn is in magnifying her intellectual and mystical force—a composition of magnitudes not commonly come by outside Dante. "She can be," says Mr. Lewisohn, "of a compactness of expression and fullness of meaning not less than Goethean in Goethe's epigrammatic mood... She can soar like the intense mystical poets of the seventeenth century." This is the method of instilling prejudice by means of the unexpanded comparison. We are assumed to have the American poet in front of us and to know what she is; then our knowledge of her is heightened by a comparison with Goethe's epigrams, which are probably not in front of us except by reputation. As we think, we suddenly realize that the cognate qualities in Emily Dickinson are not with us either. They are precisely as far off as Goethe. Mr. Lewisohn has compared abstracted qualities for a concrete effect: the effect, I take it, of vivid moral insight; but he has not *made* the comparison. He has not shown us what it is in either poet that he is talking about. If he expanded and did show us, he might prove right; I do not at the moment say he is wrong—although I suspect an intolerable identification: the target of insight for the two poets could hardly have been the same. What I want to emphasize is merely this:

Mr. Lewisohn is actually only saying that Emily Dickinson's poetry possesses moral insight. What he pretends to do is to put her insight on the level of the supreme type of moral insight—by mentioning Goethe's name. He would have done better to distinguish the *difference* between the achieved qualities in the epigrams of the two poets—the difference between insight as wisdom, say, and insight as vision.

Mr. Lewisohn's other comparison, with the intense mystical poets of the seventeenth century, is equally unexpanded and equally misleading. He does not say which poets nor in what respects; and what we actually get out of his comparison is the idea that Emily Dickinson was intensely mystical in an exciting and inexpensive way. The spread of such a prejudice may multiply readers, but it fosters bad reading. Poetic mysticism, as the term is loosely used, is a kind of virus that gets about through the medium of the printed page, and its chief effect is to provide a matchless substitute for the discipline of attention in incapable minds. By making ultimate apprehension of God—or matter—free in words, it relieves the poet of the necessity to make his words first apprehend the *manifestation*—what is actually felt—in this world; and it relieves the reader of the obligation to apprehend anything at all when everything may always be apprehended at once. To exercise this sort of prejudice on a really interesting poet is to carry politeness too far—and far beyond, as it happens, Emily Dickinson's poems' own idea of their operative reach and willed intention. I quote, as facts worth counting in this connection, the following lines and phrases: they illuminate Mr. Lewisohn's prejudice by reducing it to the actual scope of the poems.

> The missing All prevented me
> From missing minor things . . .
>
> Almost we wish the end
> Were further off—too great it seems
> So near the Whole to stand . . .
>
> Was the Pine at my window a "Fellow"
> Of the Royal Infinity?
> Apprehensions are God's introductions
> Extended inscrutably.

These lines are, I think, characteristic of the general "mystical" attitude in the poems. It is not mysticism itself. It is an attitude composed partly of the English Hymnal, partly of instinctive protestant transcendentalism, partly of instinctively apprehended Puritan theology, and partly of human sensibility bred with experience to the point of insight. There is besides an element of composition at work, which is the most important of all the distinguishable elements, and which makes the lines quoted, at least in their contexts, into poetry.

Admittedly this language is as loose as Mr. Lewisohn's, and as open to reduction; but I, too, am dealing with initial prejudice. My prejudice is that Emily Dickinson is a mid-nineteenth century New England Christian poet. Christianity moved her, and experience moved through her poems upon the machinery of Christianity, which is a machinery for the worship of God in all his works, and, among other things, for the redemption, which is to say the completion, of the soul. Christianity in action, especially in poetry, often looks to the outsider like an exercise in mysticism; and that is perhaps the mistake Mr. Lewisohn makes—just as so many have made a similar mistake about Gerard Manley Hopkins, or, for that matter, about Herbert and Vaughan. All these poets approached the mystery of God which is unity, but they approached it in human terms; they did what every Christian must; but they never seized or lost themselves in the unity of God as St. Francis and St. Theresa seemed to do—or as the great cathedrals and the great Church music, to the lay imagination, indubitably did. Put another way, there is nothing in the poems of Hopkins or Emily Dickinson which passes the willing understanding; if their poems sometimes confront the supersensible—and they mostly do not—it is always on the plane of the rational imagination, never in the incomprehensible terms of the mystical act. The mystery is there, but like the mystery of physical death the relation of the poetry to it is heuristic—an affair of discovery of which the very excitement, promise, and terror are that it never takes place, yet may, indeed momently, must.

Those who persist in calling this relationship mystical underestimate the scope of rational imagination working in language and in the face of mystery. That scope is exhausted only in the instance; the mystery is never exhausted merely by being expressed; and the mystery, as a fact, is always the same. When Shakespeare, who never troubled directly about God, mastered the emotion of jealousy in *Othello,* he was precisely as rational or precisely as "mystical" in his approach to mystery—and the same mystery, the mystery of the actual—as Emily Dickinson was in her deliberate approach to God in terms of nature and death.

What differs is the machinery, or sometimes the formula, of approach.

Here we come on a different type of prejudice, in its own way as general and as beyond the point if taken too solemnly as those we have been discussing, but with an air of specificity about it which is disarming. This is the prejudice about the poet in relation to his time, where the poet is taken as a fatal event in cultural history. The time produced the poet, we say, and the poet crowned the time—crowned it with its own meaning. If we go far enough on this line, the time, or the age, tends to disappear in the meaning—as for many of us early Greece disappears in Homer; which is only a way of bringing the time up to date, of telescoping all the coördinates rashly into the one image of meaning. Mr. Allen Tate has in an admirable essay (in his *Reactionary Essays*) performed this labor upon Emily Dickinson, with the further labor that when he has got his image all made he proceeds to sort out its component parts. It is hard to separate what Mr. Tate found in Emily Dickinson as traces or inklings from what he brought with him on his own account; which is all in his favor if you like what he says, as I do, and if the combination illuminates and enlivens Emily Dickinson, as I believe it does. Mr. Tate as a critic has the kind of rightness that goes with insight, and not at all the kind of wrongness that goes with sincerity—which is perhaps how we should characterize Mr. Lewisohn.

At any rate, Mr. Tate builds up a pretty good historical prejudice and makes it available in the guise of insight. Emily Dickinson came, he says, exactly at the dying crisis of Puritan New England culture—not at the moment of death, but at the moment—it was years long—when the matrix began to be felt as broken. Spiritual meaning and psychic stability were no longer the unconscious look and deep gesture worn and rehearsed lifelong; they required the agony of doubt and the trial of deliberate expression in specifically, wilfully objective form. Faith was sophisticated, freed, and terrified—but still lived; imagination had suddenly to do all the work of embodying faith formerly done by habit, and to embody it with the old machinery so far as it could be used. There was no other machinery available. Thus the burden of poetry was put upon the New England version of the Christian sensibility.

It is arguable that Greek tragedy came at the analogous moment in Athenian history, when the gods were seen as imaginative instead of magical myths. The advantage for the poet is in both instances double and pays in poetry for the burden. There is the advantage of the existing machinery of meaning in the specific culture, which is still able to carry any weight and which is universally understood; and there is the advantage of a new and personal plasticity in the meanings themselves. Faith, in the agonized hands of the individual, becomes an imaginative experiment of which all the elements are open to new and even blasphemous combinations, and which is subject to the addition of new insights. It is no longer enough to repeat prayers and to rehearse Mass or its protestant equivalent; indeed the institutional part of culture is the first to show itself as dead; faith becomes to the secularized imagination of Emily Dickinson "the Experiment of our Lord!"—which it could never have seemed, on the same foundation, half a century earlier. The great advantage for a poet to come at a time of disintegrating culture is, then, to sum up, just this: the actuality of what we are and what we believe is suddenly seen to be nearly meaningless as habit, and must, to be adequately known, be translated to the terms and modes of the imagination. Nothing can be taken for granted but the machinery, which is there, all available, and which indeed cannot help being taken for granted. These are the conditions of belief—though not the only conditions—which may produce great poetry: the conditions of spiritual necessity and mechanical freedom. It is worth adding, for proportion, that the opposite conditions—spiritual freedom (a unity of belief and discipline) and mechanical necessity—produced such a great poet as Dante; and, again, it is quite possible that Shakespeare may have been produced at the nexus of quite a different set of conditions which had more to do with the state of language than with the state of belief. Here we are concerned with the occurrence of Emily Dickinson at the precise time when it became plain that Puritan Christianity was no longer the vital force in New England culture and before any other force had recognizably relieved the slack. If we are inclined to see a causal connection it is only as a more vivid and dramatic way of seeing the association it may really and only have been.

Now I do not want to let it appear that Mr. Tate would assent to my treatment of his idea; he has his own treatment, which is certainly not so highfalutin as mine; and besides, I am not sure how far I can assent to my own remarks without a feeling that I am merely succumbing to the temptation of a bright idea, which like the idea of chance explains less and less the more you look into it. Let us take the idea provisionally, and more provisionally for me than for Mr. Tate. So taken, it indicates a source; and with the source a tragic strength, for the fund and flow of Emily Dickinson's meaning. As the Massachusetts theocracy failed, became, say, more humane and individualized, its profoundly dramatic nature—all that it had left—became sharper and plainer, until in the imagination of Hawthorne and Melville and Emily Dickinson it took in, or implied, pretty near the whole of human experience. Then it died. It fed the imagination; then it died; and at the same time that particular form of the New England imagination reached its small surfeit and died too.

In the last sentence lies buried, but not in the least dead, the fundamental prejudice we have been looking for all the time: the prejudice contained in the idea of imagination being fed and dying, or for that matter living or doing anything whatever—that is to say, a prejudice about the nature of poetry itself as the chief mode of imagination. Poetry is composed of words and whenever we put anything into poetry—such as meaning or music; whenever poetry is affected by anything—such as the pattern of a culture or the structure of a stanza; whenever anything at all happens in poetry it happens in the medium of words. It is also near enough the truth to say that whenever we take anything out of poetry, either to use it or to see just what it is, we have to take it out in the words—and then put it right back before it gets lost or useless. The greatness of Emily Dickinson is not—to review our select list of prejudices—going to be found in anybody's idea of greatness, or of Goethe, or intensity, or mysticism, or historical fatality. It is going to be found in the words she used and in the way she put them together; which we will observe, if we bother to discriminate our observations, as a series of facts about words. What is behind the words or beyond them, we cannot know as facts, as any discussion amply demonstrates. Our knowledge of implication and inkling, quite as much as our knowledge of bald sound and singing sense, will be governed solely by what we can recognize, and perhaps by a good deal that we cannot recognize, of the poetic relations of the words—that is to say, by what they make of each other. This rule, or this prejudice, applies, which is why it is mentioned at all, exactly as strongly to our method of determining the influence of a culture or a church or a philosophy, alive, dead, or dying, upon the body of Emily Dickinson's poetry. We will see what the influence did to the words, and more important, what the words did to the influence.

So far as poetry goes, then, the influence of intellectual or other abstracted considerations can be measured only as it affects the choice and arrangement of words—as it richens or impoverishes the texture of the imaginative vehicle of the poetry. The puritan theory of renunciation, for example, will be not at all the same thing in a hortatory tract, no matter how eloquent and just, as in a poem of Emily Dickinson, which might well have drawn from the tract, however loose or fragmentary the poem may be. Imagination, if it works at all, works at the level of actualized experience. Here is the example, pat to the purpose, and to other purposes as well.

> Renunciation
> Is a piercing virtue,
> The letting go
> A presence for an expectation—
> Not now.

There is no forensic here, nor eloquence, nor justness; it is a bare statement amounting to vision—vision being a kind of observation of the ideal. It has nothing to do with wisdom, there is no thinking in it; and there is no ordinary observation in it—in the sense that there is no relation between an observer and a thing observed. The lines do not prove themselves, or anything else; they make a statement. Yet it is not a naïve statement—it is not directly itself—however much it may seem to be. It rises rather out of a whole way of life—the protestant, puritan way, felt suddenly at what can be called nothing less than a supremely sophisticated level. The feeling is in the sophistication. As a religious or philosophical statement it is probably vain and tragic and an example of self-arrogation; certainly it is without humility. Perhaps I am not competent to judge, being in a worse predicament than the poet, but it is possible to say that this is the sort of thing that happens to a religious notion when one's awareness of it becomes personal and without authority, when one is driven to imagine—in words or otherwise—the situation actually felt.

We do not examine these lines with a view to calling them great poetry but in order to present a series of facts as to how they derive their being and to afford a clue to the facts about a whole species of Dickinson poems—those that deal with the renunciation of love, the death of the beloved, and the heavenly reward. The machinery of meaning remains roughly the same throughout the group; what differs is the degree or amount of experience actualized in the verse. The machinery and the experience are perhaps inseparable, or at any rate are in their varying proportions equally necessary to the production of the kind of poetry Emily Dickinson wrote. When the balance is lost, when the fusion is not made, or when resort is had to feeling alone or to machinery insufficiently felt, something less than good poetry appears. We have either a poem without mooring or a poem without buoyancy.

Let us provisionally inquire what it is in the words that makes poetry of the statement about renunciation. Let us treat the machinery, not as what we may or may not know it to be intellectually, but as an example of words in operation; and let us look at the image—what is imagined—as the emergent fact of the words in operation, indeed, as the operation itself. That is how our best reading takes poetry in its stride; here we arrest the stride or make slow motion of it. The words are all simple words, parts of our stock vocabulary. Only one, *renunciation,* belongs to a special department of experience or contains in itself the focus of a particular attitude, a department and an attitude we condition ourselves to keep mostly in abeyance. We know what renunciation is; we know it turns up as heroism or hypocrisy or sentimentality; and we do as little as possible about it. Only one word, *piercing,* is directly physical; something that if it happens cannot be ignored but always shocks us into reaction. It is the shock of this word that transforms the phrase from a mere grammatical tautology into a metaphorical tautology which establishes as well as asserts identity. Some function of the word *pierce* precipitates a living intrinsic relation between renunciation and virtue; it is what makes the phrase incandesce. The two adjectives in the last line of the following quatrain exhibit a similar incandescent function.

Rehearsal to ourselves
Of a withdrawn delight
Affords a bliss like murder,
Omnipotent, acute.

It is the adjectives that transform the verbal and mutually irrelevant association of delight and murder into a self-completing metaphor. But, to return to our other quotation, the word *pierce* enlivens not only the first phrase but the whole statement about renunciation; it is the stress or shock of it that is carried forward into and makes specific the general notion—physical but vague—of letting go; and letting go, in its turn, perhaps by its participial form, works back upon the first phrase. The piercing quality of renunciation is precisely, but not altogether, that it is a continuing process, takes time, it may be infinite time, before the renounced presence transpires in expectation in the "Not now." It is—if we may provisionally risk saying so —the physical elements in the word *pierce* and the participial phrase *letting go* that, by acting upon them, make the other words available to feeling, and it is the word *renunciation* that, so enlightened, focuses the feeling as actuality. That operation is almost enough to make the statement poetry; we have only pseudo-names for whatever else it is that it takes. There is no advantage here of meter or rhyme. There is instead the speech-tone of authority, a directness in the manner of the words which has nothing to do with their meaning, and the speech-quality of speed, an inner speed of the syllables like the inner velocity of an atom, which has nothing directly to do with the outward relations of the words. These qualities are characteristic of verse that is felt as actual; at least we say that these qualities exist in verse that exacts the sense of precise feeling in the reader. Perhaps it is simpler to say that there is an excitement in the language beyond the excitement of any meaning we can communicate through any medium different from that of the poem itself: the excitement of being. It is gained, that excitement, by the exercise of the fundamental technique of language as a mode of finding objective form for even the most abstract feelings. A further, and I hope not absurd, simplification is to say that the poet whose work showed these qualities had an aptitude for language; and if that is so, then all we have been saying merely illustrates how much that is complicated and beyond conscious control the word *aptitude* may sometimes simplify.

So be it. Emily Dickinson had an aptitude for language, and in the passage we have examined she needed nothing else to induce her verses to reach their appropriate objective level; for the aptitude included every necessary mechanical relation both to her age and to the general craft of verse. Although the same aptitude persists superficially through the rest of the poem, the persistence is only superficial and not substantial. The rest of the poem is not transformed, as the quoted stanza was, into something felt as actual in which the parts work upon themselves mutually. We can say either that the aptitude was not carried far enough *per se*—the poet did not pay enough attention to the words; or we can say that the conceiving imagination was not strong enough to carry the material through; or we can say that the poet was not sufficiently master of the compositional devices of external form—form as the organizing agent—to give the work crisis and consistency. The first statement is true anyway; the second is probably true; and the third is true in relation to the other two. Perhaps the three statements are merely different emphases of the same idea: the idea we took up a little while ago of the imagination being insufficiently fed into the words of the poem. Either the machinery of the poem was inadequate to objectify its purpose, or the motive of the poem, as it emerged, was inadequate to activate the machinery. The alternatives are not mutually exclusive; a combined view is possible. It is at least plausible to consider that if there is a state of culture which produces or precipitates a body of poetry, then there may also be a state of language—a general level of poetic habit—which is necessary to give that body of poetry relative perfection, and that, further, if there is failure in one quarter, no matter which, it is a likely sign of failure in the other, if not at the same point then round the nearest corner. The trouble is that the condition of language at a given time is just as hard to determine as the condition of a culture. We guess at something wrong or swear that everything was right, and are not sure which case produced the better poetry.

We can say, amiably enough, that the verse-language of mid-nineteenth century America was relatively nerveless, unsupple, flat in pattern, had very little absorptive power and showed no self-luxuriating power whatever. The mounting vitality that shows itself as formal experiment and the matured vitality that shows itself as the masterly penetration of accepted form (say Kyd followed by the mature Shakespeare) were equally absent. The great estate of poetry as an available condition of language lay flat in a kind of desiccated hibernation, and the clue to resurrection was unknown. It is not for nothing that our poets never mastered form in language. Poe and Longfellow accepted the desiccation, contributing a personal music which perhaps redeemed but never transfigured their talents. Whitman and Emily Dickinson, with more genius, or as we have been saying with more favorable cultural situations, were unable to accept the desiccation and drove forward on the élan of their natural aptitudes for language, resorting regardless to whatever props, scaffolds, obsessive symbols, or intellectual mechanisms came to hand, but neither of them ever finding satisfactory form—and neither, apparently, ever consciously missing it. The great bulk of the verse of each appears to have been written on the sustaining pretense that everything was always possible. To see boundless good on the horizon, to see it without the limiting discipline of the conviction of evil, is in poetry as in politics the great stultifier of action.

Hence the great, repetitious wastes in both poets. With no criterion of achievement without there could be no criterion of completion within. Success was by accident, by the mere momentum of sensibility. Failure was by rule, although the rule was unknown, and often doubtless thought of in the shameless guise of simple self-expression. The practice of craft came to little more than so many exercises in self-expression. Thus something over two-thirds of Emily Dickinson's nine hundred odd printed poems are exercises, and no more, some in the direction of poetry, and some not. The object is usually in view, though some of the poems are but exercises in pursuit of an unknown object, but the means of attainment are variously absent, used in error, or ill-chosen. The only weapon constantly in use is, to repeat once more, the natural aptitude for language; and it is hardly surprising to find that that weapon, used alone and against great odds, should occasionally produce an air of frantic strain instead of strength, of conspicuous oddity instead of indubitable rightness.

Let us take for a first example a reasonably serious poem on one of the dominant Dickinson themes, the obituary theme of the great dead —a theme to which Hawthorne and Henry James were equally addicted —and determine if we can where its failure lies.

More life went out, when He went,
Than ordinary breath,
Lit with a finer phosphor
Requiring in the quench

A power of renownéd cold—
The climate of the grave

A temperature just adequate
So anthracite to live.

For some an ampler zero,
A frost more needle keen
Is necessary to reduce
The Ethiop within.

Others extinguish easier—
A gnat's minutest fan
Sufficient to obliterate
A tract of citizen.

The first thing to notice—a thing characteristic of exercises—is that the order or plot of the elements of the poem is not that of a complete poem; the movement of the parts is downwards and towards a disintegration of the effect wanted. A good poem so constitutes its parts as at once to contain them and to deliver or release by the psychological force of their sequence the full effect only when the poem is done. Here the last quatrain is obviously wrongly placed; it comes like an afterthought, put in to explain why the third stanza was good. It should have preceded the third stanza, and perhaps with the third stanza—both of course in revised form—might have come at the very beginning, or perhaps in suspension between the first and second stanzas. Such suggestions throw the poem into disorder; actually the disorder is already there. It is not the mere arrangement of stanzas that is at fault; the units in disorder are deeper in the material, perhaps in the compositional elements of the conception, perhaps in the executive elements of the image-words used to afford circulation to the poem, perhaps elsewhere in the devices not used but wanted. The point for emphasis is that it is hard to believe that a conscientious poet could have failed to see that no amount of correction and polish could raise this exercise to the condition of a mature poem. The material is all there—the inspiration and the language; what it requires is a thorough revision—a re-seeing calculated to compose in objective form the immediacy and singleness of effect which the poet no doubt herself felt.

Perhaps we may say—though the poem is not nearly so bad an example as many—that the uncomposed disorder is accepted by the poet because the poem was itself written automatically. To the sensitive hand and expectant ear words will arrange themselves, however gotten hold of, and seem to breed by mere contact. The brood is the meaning we catch up to. Is not this really automatic writing *tout court?* Most of the Dickinson poems seem to have been initially as near automatic writing as may be. The bulk remained automatic, subject to correction and multiplication of detail. Others, which reach intrinsic being, have been patterned, inscaped, injected one way or another with the élan or elixir of the poet's dominant attitudes. The poem presently examined remains too much in the automatic choir; the élan is there, which is why we examine it at all, but without the additional advantage of craft it fails to carry everything before it.

The second stanza of the poem is either an example of automatic writing unrelieved, or is an example of bad editing, or both. Its only meaning is in the frantic strain towards meaning—a strain so frantic that all responsibility towards the shapes and primary significance of words was ignored. "A temperature just adequate/So anthracite to live" even if it were intelligible, which it is not, would be beyond bearing awkward to read. It is not bad grammar alone that works ill; words sometimes make their own grammar good on the principle of ineluctable association—when the association forces the words into meaning. Here we have fiat meaning. The word *anthracite* is the crux of the trouble. Anthracite is coal, is hard, is black, gives heat, and has a rushing crisp sound; it has a connection with carbuncle and with a fly-borne disease of which one symptom resembles a carbuncle; it is stratified in the earth, is formed of organic matter as a consequence of enormous pressure through geologic time; etc., etc. One or several of these senses may contribute to the poem; but because the context does not denominate it, it does not appear which. My own guess is that Emily Dickinson wanted the effect of something hard and cold and perhaps black and took *anthracite* off the edge of her vocabulary largely because she liked the sound. This is another way of saying that *anthracite* is an irresponsible product of her aptitude for language.

The word *phosphor* in the third line of the first stanza is a responsible example of the same aptitude. It is moreover a habitual symbol word rather than a sudden flight; it is part of her regular machinery for concentrating meaning in a partly willful, partly natural symbol. Phosphor or phosphorus—in various forms of the word—is used by Emily Dickinson at least twelve times to represent, from the like characteristic of the metal, the self-illumining, and perhaps self-consuming quality of the soul. The "renownéd cold," "ampler zero," and "frost more needle keen," are also habitual images used to represent the coming or transition of death as effected seasonably in nature and, by analogue, in man. Examples of these or associated words so used run to the hundreds. The "gnat" in the fourth stanza with his "minutest fan" (of cold air?) is another example of a portmanteau image always ready to use to turn on the microcosmic view. In the word *Ethiop* in the third stanza we have a mixture of a similar general term—this time drawn from the outside and unknown world—and a special significance released and warranted by the poem. Ethiops live in tropical Africa; and we have here a kind of synecdoche which makes the Ethiop himself so full of heat that it would take great cold to quench it. That the contrary would be the case does not affect the actuality of the image, but makes it more intriguing and gives it an odd, accidental character. The misconception does, however, bring out the flavor of a wrong image along with the shadow of the right one; and it is a question whether the flavor will not last longer in the memory than the shadow. Another nice question is involved in the effect of the *order* of the verbs used to represent the point of death: *quench, reduce, extinguish, obliterate.* The question is, are not these verbs pretty nearly interchangeable? Would not any other verb of destructive action do just as well? In short, is there any word in this poem which either fits or contributes to the association at all exactly? I think not—with the single exception of "phosphor."

The burden of these observations on words will I hope have made itself plain; it is exactly the burden of the observations on the form of the whole poem. The poem is an exercise whichever way you take it: an approach to the organization of its material but by no means a complete organization. It is almost a rehearsal—a doing over of something not done—and a variation of stock intellectual elements in an effort to accomplish an adventure in feeling. The reader can determine for himself—if he can swallow both the anthracite and the gnat—how concrete and actual the adventure was made.

Perhaps determination will be assisted by a few considerations on Emily Dickinson's vocabulary as a whole and how it splits up under inspection into different parts which are employed for different functions, and which operate *from,* as it were, different levels of sensibility. It is not a large vocabulary compared to Whitman's, nor rich like Melville's, nor perspicuous like Henry James', nor robust like Mark Twain's. Nor is it a homogeneous vocabulary; its unity is specious for the instance rather than organic for the whole of her work. Its constant elements are mostly found, like most of the poems, in arrangements, not in compositions. The pattern of association is kaleidoscopic and extraneous far more frequently than it is crystalline and inwardly compelled. What it is, is a small, rigidly compartmented vocabulary of general and conventional groups of terms, plus a moderately capacious vocabulary of homely, acute, directly felt words from which the whole actualizing strength of her verse is drawn. The extraordinary thing is how much of the general and conventional vocabulary got activated by the homely word. In the fragment about renunciation, "piercing" and "letting go" are examples. The depressing thing is how much of the conventional vocabulary was not activated by the homely word but distracted by the homely word strained odd.

Let us list a few of the conventional types that turn up most often and most conspicuously. The most conspicuous of all is the vocabulary of romance royalty, fairy-tale kings, queens, and courts, and the general language of chivalry. Emily Dickinson was as fond as Shakespeare of words like *imperial, sovereign, dominion,* and the whole collection of terms for rank and degree. Probably she got them more from Scott and the Bible and the Hymnal than from Shakespeare. There is none of Shakespeare's specific and motivating sense of kings and princes as the focus of society, and none of his rhetoric of power; there is nothing tragic in Emily Dickinson's royal vocabulary. On the other hand, there is a great deal of vague and general assumption that royalty is a good thing and that escape into the goodness of it is available to everyone: like the colorful escape into romance and fairy tale. Besides this general assumption, and more important, there is continuous resort to the trope of heavenly coronation for the individual and a continuous ascription of imperial titles and a chivalric, almost heraldic, code to God and the angels, to flowers and bees. This vocabulary, taken as a whole, provides a mixed formula which rehearsed like a ritual or just a verbal exercise sometimes discovers a poem and sometimes does not. I extract one stanza as example.

> He put a belt around my life,—
> I heard the buckle snap,
> And turned away, imperial,
> My lifetime folding up
> Deliberate as a duke would do

A kingdom's title-deed,—
Henceforth a dedicated sort,
A member of the cloud.

Other vocabularies include words taken from sewing and the kinds of cloth used in women's clothes—*stitch, seam, needle, dimity, serge, silk, satin, brocade,* etc.; legal words—*tenant, rent, litigant, title,* etc.; the names of jewels—*diamond, ruby, pearl, opal, amethyst, beryl,* and *amber;* words taken from the Civil War—*bayonet,* various images of musket and cannon fire, and of the soldier's heroism; words taken from sea-borne commerce—*port, harbor,* various kinds of ships and the parts of ships; the names of distant places—especially of mountains and volcanoes; and, not to exhaust but merely to stop the list, words taken from the transcendental theology of her time. It should be noted that only the first, second, and possibly the last of these groups named or activated anything she found in her daily life; but they had, like the vocabulary of royalty, everything to do with the stretching of her daily fancy, and they made a constant provision, a constant rough filling and occupation, for what did actually concern her—her prevision of death and her insight into the spiritual life. This is another way of saying that in what is quantitatively the great part of her work Emily Dickinson did not put the life of meaning into her words; she leaned on the formulas of words in the hope that the formulas would fully express what she felt privately—sometimes the emotion of escape and sometimes the conviction of assent—in her own self-centered experience. This is partly the mode of prayer, partly the mode of nonce-popular romance (which must always be repeated) and partly the mode of the pathetic fallacy applied to form—the fiat mode of expression which asserts that the need is equivalent to the object, that if you need words to mean something then they will necessarily mean it. But it is not except by accident the mode of the rational or actualizing imagination. The extraordinary thing in Emily Dickinson is, to repeat, that fragmentary accidents occur so often, and the terrible thing is that they need not have been accidents at all. The net result may be put as a loss of consistent or sustained magnitude equal to the impulse. We have a verse in great body that is part terror, part vision, part insight and observation, which must yet mostly be construed as a kind of *vers de société* of the soul—not in form or finish but in achievement.

This is to say that control was superficial—in the use, not the hearts, of words. We saw an example in the word *anthracite* a little above. Let us present two more examples and stop. We have the word *plush* in different poems as follows. "One would as soon assault a plush or violate a star ... Time's consummate plush ... A dog's belated feet like intermittent plush ... We step like plush, we stand like snow ... Sentences of plush." The word is on the verge of bursting with wrong meaning, and on account of the bursting, the stress with which the poet employed it, we are all prepared to accept it, and indeed do accept it, when suddenly we realize the wrongness, that "plush" was not what was meant at all, but was a substitute for it. The word has been distorted but not transformed on the page; which is to say it is not in substantial control. Yet it is impossible not to believe that to Emily Dickinson's ear it meant what it said and what could not otherwise be said.

The use of the word *purple* is another example of a word's getting out of control through the poet's failure to maintain an objective feeling of responsibility towards language. We have, in different poems, a "purple host" meaning "soldiers"; "purple territories," associated with salvation in terms of "Pizarro's shores"; "purple" meaning "dawn"; a "purple finger" probably meaning "shadow"; a purple raveling of cloud at sunset; ships of purple on seas of daffodil; the sun quenching in purple; a purple brook; purple traffic; a peacock's purple train; purple none can avoid—meaning death; no suitable purple to put on the hills; a purple tar wrecked in peace; the purple well of eternity; the purple or royal state of a corpse; the Purple of Ages; a sowing of purple seed which is inexplicable; the purple of the summer; the purple wheel of faith; day's petticoat of purple; etc., etc. Taken cumulatively, this is neither a distortion nor a transformation of sense; it is very nearly an obliteration of everything but a favorite sound, meaning something desirable, universal, distant, and immediate. I choose the word as an example not because it is particularly bad—it is not; it is relatively harmless—but because it is typical and happens to be easy to follow in unexpanded quotation. It is thoroughly representative of Emily Dickinson's habit of so employing certain favorite words that their discriminated meanings tend to melt into the single sentiment of self-expression. We can feel the sentiment but we have lost the meaning. The willing reader can see for himself the analogous process taking place—with slightly different final flavors—in word after word: for example in the words *dateless, pattern, compass, circumference, ecstasy, immortality, white, ruby, crescent, peninsula,* and *spice.* The meanings become the conventions of meanings, the asserted agreement that meaning is there. That is the end towards which Emily Dickinson worked, willy nilly, in her words. If you can accept the assertion for the sake of the knack—not the craft—with which it is made you will be able to read much more of her work than if you insist on actual work done.

But there were, to repeat and to conclude, three saving accidents at work in the body of Emily Dickinson's work sufficient to redeem in fact a good many poems to the state of their original intention. There was the accident of cultural crisis, the skeptical faith and desperately experimental mood, which both released and drove the poet's sensibility to express the crisis personally. There was the accident that the poet had so great an aptitude for language that it could seldom be completely lost in the conventional formulas towards which her meditating mind ran. And there was the third accident that the merest self-expression, or the merest statement of recognition or discrimination or vision, may sometimes also be, by the rule of unanimity and a common tongue, its best objective expression.

When two or more of the accidents occur simultaneously a poem or a fragment of a poem may be contrived. Sometimes the thing is done directly—with the compactness which Mr. Lewisohn compared to that of Goethe, but which had better be called the compactness of that which is unexpanded and depends for context entirely upon its free implications.

> Presentiment is that long shadow on the lawn
> Indicative that suns go down;
> The notice to the startled grass
> That darkness is about to pass.

If the reader compares this poem with Marvell's "To His Coy Mistress," he will see what can be gotten out of the same theme when fully expanded. The difference is of magnitude; the magnitude depends on craft; the Dickinson poem stops, Marvell's is completed. What happens when the poem does not stop may be shown in the following example of technical and moral confusion.

I got so I could hear his name
Without—
Tremendous gain!
That stop-sensation in my soul,
And thunder in the room.

I got so I could walk across
That angle in the floor
Where he turned—so—and I turned how—
And all our sinew tore.

I got so I could stir the box
In which his letters grew—
Without that forcing in my breath
As staples driven through.

Could dimly recollect a Grace—
I think they called it "God,"
Renowned to ease extremity
When formula had failed—

And shape my hands petition's way—
Tho' ignorant of word
That Ordination utters—
My business with the cloud.

If any Power behind it be
Not subject to despair,
To care in some remoter way
For so minute affair
As misery—
Itself too vast for interrupting more,
Supremer than—
Superior to—

Nothing is more remarkable than the variety of inconsistency this effort displays. The first three stanzas are at one level of sensibility and of language and are as good verse as Emily Dickinson ever wrote. The next two stanzas are on a different and fatigued level of sensibility, are bad verse and flat language, and have only a serial connection with the first three. The last stanza, if it is a stanza, is on a still different level of sensibility and not on a recognizable level of language at all: the level of desperate inarticulateness to which no complete response can be articulated in return. One knows from the strength of the first three stanzas what might have been meant to come after and one feels like writing the poem oneself—the basest of all critical temptations. We feel that Emily Dickinson let herself go. The accidents that provided her ability here made a contrivance which was not a poem but a private mixture of first-rate verse, bad verse, and something that is not verse at all. Yet—and this is the point—this contrivance represents in epitome the whole of her work; and whatever judgment you bring upon the epitome you will, I think, be compelled to bring upon the whole.

No judgment is so persuasive as when it is disguised as a statement of facts. I think it is a fact that the failure and success of Emily Dickinson's poetry were uniformly accidental largely because of the private and eccentric nature of her relation to the business of poetry. She was neither a professional poet nor an amateur; she was a private poet who wrote indefatigably as some women cook or knit. Her gift for words and the cultural predicament of her time drove her to poetry instead of antimicassars. Neither her personal education nor the habit of her society as she knew it ever gave her the least inkling that poetry is a rational and objective art and most so when the theme is self-expression. She came, as Mr. Tate says, at the right time for one kind of poetry: the poetry of sophisticated, eccentric vision. That is what makes her good—in a few poems and many passages representatively great. But she never undertook the great profession of controlling the means of objective expression. That is why the bulk of her verse is not representative but mere fragmentary indicative notation. The pity of it is that the document her whole work makes shows nothing so much as that she had the themes, the insight, the observation, and the capacity for honesty, which had she only known how—or only known why—would have made the major instead of the minor fraction of her verse genuine poetry. But her dying society had no tradition by which to teach her the one lesson she did not know by instinct.

FRANCIS OTTO MATTHIESSEN (1902–50) taught at Harvard from 1929 until his death. His *The Achievement of T.S.Eliot* (1935), *American Renaissance* (1941), and *Henry James: The Major Phase* (1944) made clear Matthiessen's stature as a scholar and critic, especially in his balance of biographical, aesthetic, and social interests. His 1945 essay on Emily Dickinson points up areas of criticism which remained to be dealt with before a really adequate evaluation of Emily Dickinson would be possible.

The Private Poet: Emily Dickinson

F. O. MATTHIESSEN

According to the advance agents, a historic event occurred this spring in the annals of American literature, and we are the richer by over six hundred more poems by 'Emily.' Nearly everyone who writes about her plunges at once to cozy first-name calling with this poet who did not enjoy such liberties when she was alive and could prevent them. Millicent Todd Bingham, the editor of this new collection and the author of a volume explaining why it was not published fifty years ago, is no exception. She also goes on the once fashionable assumption that Miss Dickinson 'has always been shrouded in mystery,' just as though George Whicher had not published seven years ago the biography which places her career so lucidly against its local and intellectual backgrounds. To be sure, Mrs. Bingham no longer engages in that favorite guessing-game of the 'twenties, 'Who was Emily Dickinson's lover?' But the ground of extraneous interest has now shifted to the poet's brother and sister and sister-in-law, and the breathless drama builds around a law-suit brought by Lavinia Dickinson against Mrs. Bingham's mother a decade after the poet's death. This suit involved a strip of land willed by Austin Dickinson to Mrs. Todd, and its one importance to literary history is that it broke off all plans which that first editor of Miss Dickinson's poems had had for carrying that work further.

From the *Kenyon Review*, II (Autumn, 1945), 584–97. A review of *Bolts of Melody: New Poems of Emily Dickinson*, edited by Mabel Loomis Todd and Millicent Todd Bingham (Harper & Bros.); *Ancestors' Brocades: The Literary Debut of Emily Dickinson* by Millicent Todd Bingham (Harper & Bros.).

But Mrs. Bingham could not leave it at that. She apparently had to avenge her mother's memory with a detailed account of Vinnie's virulence (her 'mouth was perfectly hideous and full of false teeth'), and of the violent tensions that existed between this old maid and the Dickinsons in 'the other house.' Mrs. Bingham's narrative has been so successful as to inflame Bernard DeVoto's imagination with the notion that this is 'incomparably the best book ever written about Emily.' And he has pushed the present flurry to its limit by declaiming that 'they were all burning . . . they were all damned . . . Emily Dickinson was the supreme poet of hate.' That climactic statement can, of course, be corrected by comparing it with nearly every line and implication of Miss Dickinson's verse, but not all readers of [Bernard DeVoto's] 'The Easy Chair' will go that far.

Amy Lowell once projected a biography of Emily Dickinson in which the effect upon her of each member of her family would be analyzed. Such a book, doing its best to reconstruct the young and formative period of her life, and probing her strong fixation upon her father, might have been valuable. But Mrs. Bingham has not even attempted to write it, since her story begins only with the arrival of Professor and Mrs. Todd in Amherst, less than five years before Miss Dickinson died. The jealousy-ridden Lavinia whom Mrs. Bingham portrays is not the devoted younger sister whom Emily knew. This biographer's material is the unhealthily closed circle of a New England family at the time of its decline, but, though she insists on modern 'frankness,' her story does not read very convincingly. Why, after some years of collaboration, did Lavinia turn so fiercely upon Mrs. Todd? Why, to Mrs. Todd's consternation, did the lawsuit go against her and for Lavinia? Mrs. Bingham hints at some 'sadness' in her mother's life, and just mentions the Amherst gossip of an attachment between Austin Dickinson and Mrs. Todd. If you set out to withhold no 'pertinent' facts in such a drama, you can't give only a highly colored version of one side, especially if you are bent on proving that 'truth, like ancestors' brocades, can stand alone.'

Mrs. Bingham would much better have confined herself to the circumstances of the first publication of Emily Dickinson's poems, though that was hardly the subject for a whole book. As it is, she has printed every scrap of a note that passed between Mrs. Todd and Higginson and the printers of both the poems and letters, without any perspective or principle of selection. The only portions indispensable to our knowledge of the poet are those chapters which extend the already grim picture of the state of the printed text of her poems. No one now needs further persuading of the hopeless inaccuracy in every function of an editor of Austin and Sue Dickinson's daughter, Martha Dickinson Bianchi; but Mrs. Bingham helps clear up a great number of misreadings. She demonstrates how frequently lines were confused, stanzas omitted, and even two poems run together as one. Her most spectacular though by no means most important correction is that involving the final stanza of one of the *Further Poems* of 1929. Instead of the almost meaningless ending,

> Mine be the ministry
> When thy thirst comes,
> Dews of thyself to fetch
> And holy balms,

Emily Dickinson characteristically wrote,

> Dews of Thessaly to fetch
> And Hybla balms.

Unlike Madame Bianchi, Mrs. Todd was a painstaking and accurate transcriber, and her daughter takes after her in this valuable respect. But the paradoxical result is to destroy the one remaining plank of confidence regarding the text as we have it. Hitherto it has been generally assumed that the Higginson-Todd editions gave their poems as Emily Dickinson wrote them, but it now appears that the case was more complicated. In her chapter called 'Creative Editing,' Mrs. Bingham recounts the dilemma with which the original editors felt themselves confronted. They wanted to present their poet to the world, but they did not want the world of the 'nineties to find her too queer, and there was the problem of her eccentric syntax and grammar, to say nothing of her rhymes. Sometimes the issue was that of conventionally correct versus actually spoken usage, for Emily Dickinson, as the new poems show, was quite capable of writing 'It don't sound so terrible, quite, as it did,' or of revealing our native fondness for 'r' by rhyming 'India' with 'too near.' Mrs. Todd seems to have acted as a brake on Higginson in the matter of changes, for though she accepted his arrangement under the general (if not too illuminating) categories of Life, Nature, Love, [and] Time and Eternity, she doubted the validity of the titles he bestowed upon individual poems, and was quite staunch in the kind of resistance that prevented the dog's feet 'like intermittent plush' from being altered to 'in intermittent plash.'

But there were many stanzas that seemed to go flat for want of a rhyme—for instance,

> or later,
> Parting with a world
> We have understood for better
> Still to be explained.

The now familiar final line, 'Still it be unfurled,' is an example, as Mrs. Bingham says, 'of the kind of thing they felt called upon to do.' Despite conscious resistance to temptation on Higginson's part also, compromises were yielded to, and, in the end, 'a good many changes were made.' Sometimes these involved the editors fairly deeply in the texture of the verse, to the point of four changes in the first two stanzas of one of her best-known poems:

> I heard a fly buzz when I died;
> The stillness in the room
> Was like the stillness in the air
> Between the heaves of storm.
>
> The eyes around had wrung them dry,
> And breaths were gathering firm
> For that last onset, when the king
> Be witnessed in the room.

In order to provide a rhyme, that first 'in the room' became 'round my form.' That led, to avoid repetition, to 'around,' in the opening line of the second stanza, being changed to 'beside.' Then 'firm' became 'sure,' and was made to rhyme by substituting for the second 'in the room,' the wholly new phrase 'in his power.' As a result the rhymes click—or almost—but what has been lost is the peculiar desolate effect provided by the echoing 'in the room,' which does not lift the sufferer to God's power, but reverberates with the loneliness of dying.

Sometimes the creative editors omitted a whole stanza that seemed too odd, and in the view of Mrs. Bingham, though such an omission 'might sometimes improve a poem, it was more often a mistake.' Both editors possessed some literary tact, and some of their interpolated rhymes may very well have served to quicken the energy of a verse; but if what is wanted are the poems of Emily Dickinson, every kind of alteration was a mistake.

In her own editing Mrs. Bingham really proceeds on that latter assumption; but in presenting the further poems and fragments that remained in Mrs. Todd's hands at the time of the rupture—the very large number of which Lavinia seems not to have been aware—Mrs. Bingham hardly lives up to her opportunities as an editor. She realizes that the poems 'should eventually be arranged in the order of composition,' but though she has at her command some of the evidence for dating, particularly that furnished by the three markedly different periods of Miss Dickinson's handwriting, she has put the reader in effectual possession of none of it. She contents herself with such tantalizing withholdings as that 'many of these poems were written comparatively early in life,' or that some of the love poems had 'a very special person in mind.' She recognizes the value that could accrue through seeing the chronological progression of Miss Dickinson's poems dealing with specific themes—for instance, with fame, to which she is popularly supposed to have been indifferent, but to varied meditations about which she kept returning to the end. But having noted such a point, Mrs. Bingham then seems to forget her mother's objections to Higginson's titles, and arranges her volume under a series of allusive headings. These are all borrowed from phrases in the poems, to be sure, but out of its context 'Italic Faces' may seem mannered and obscure for a title covering twenty poems, and 'My Pageantry' and 'Our Little Kinsmen' verge on the sentimental.

The poems themselves possess nearly all the qualities to have been found in Miss Dickinson's work before. There is the same exciting verbal action; the familiar liking for plush and satin and purple; the alternation of themes between tension and escape, with her fondness for battle imagery to express the one and her equal fondness for words of romantic distance—Cordillera, Himmaleh, Venetian—to enhance the other. And to counterpoise her recurrence to isolation and death is the quality that so often forms her special signature, her expectant intimacy with nature, and particularly with its smaller denizens, frog, robin, squirrel, spider, and bee. One revelatory new phrase—under which Mrs. Bingham groups some of the most effective of these poems—is 'an ablative estate.' What Miss Dickinson meant by it she indicated thus:

I'd rather recollect a setting
Than a rising sun.

And she gave this reason for her choice:

Because in going is a drama
Staying cannot confer.

Whether or not she was consciously balancing her ablative case against Emerson's emphasis upon 'the optative mood,' the difference between wishing for a more radiant future and accepting the finality of removal is the difference between these two poets, marking the distance traversed between the beginning and the end of the New England renaissance. It marks also why Miss Dickinson possessed the dramatic, indeed, the tragic sense so lacking from Emerson's radiant eloquence. In celebrating the dawn of a new era, he threw to the winds not merely Calvinism but all traditional belief in the inescapable tension between good and evil. She noted, in the final poem in Mrs. Bingham's collection, some of the unforeseen consequences of his emancipation:

Those, dying then, knew where they went,
They went to God's right hand;
That hand is amputated now
And God cannot be found.

The abdication of belief
Makes the behavior small—
Better an *ignis fatuus*
Than no illume at all.

This poem is one of the most impressive of those now added, and if we reckon with whole poems rather than with flashes of quality, comparatively few here rise very near her first rank. Of course, any judgment of such short lyrics as most of hers is extremely subjective, as Higginson remarked in noting that nearly every reviewer of the first collection picked a different favorite. But to specify some of the types of her greatest successes, I doubt whether there could be found here any quatrain with the epigrammatic terseness of 'Presentiment is that long shadow on the lawn'; any longer poem with the dramatic intensity and wholeness of 'I cannot live with you' or 'The last night that she lived';

or any poem with the kind of union between metrical delicacy and philosophical discovery that makes 'Safe in their alabaster chambers'—to this reviewer's taste—her rarest contribution of all. Nor at her polar moods of loneliness and exuberance is there anything quite to match either the starkness of 'My Wheel is in the dark' or her way of outdistancing the release of Emerson's 'Bacchus' by proclaiming herself 'the little tippler / Leaning against the sun.' And though there are a few affecting additions to her never numerous poems of somber compulsion—particularly a poem of suicide beginning 'He scanned it, staggered, dropped the loop' and another, 'The waters chased him as he fled,' which conveys the terrified sensation of being pursued—these again do not approach the sustained horror of the poem which seems to have risen most obsessively from her subconscious, that drama of agonized repression and flight: 'In winter in my room / I came upon a worm.'

Altogether these new poems, though they increase the body of her previously published work by more than a third, will hardly serve to increase the bounds of her reputation. The final critical estimate of such a poet will always depend upon a winnowing, whereby her inevitably few accomplished poems can be shaken free from many pieces which are hardly more than abandoned beginnings of themes that she managed to develop on another occasion. Her work—and its editing—present all the peculiar problems of the private poet.

She was a private poet in a different sense, say, from Hopkins. In reaction against the current modes of Tennyson and Swinburne, he set himself, in his isolation, deliberately to shape a new style in poems that could not have been more highly wrought. Her process was almost wholly instinctive. No matter what shades of difference between her religious values and Emerson's, her way of writing continued to illustrate his conception of the Poet. That she believed no less than he that poetry could be written only in all-sufficient moments of inspiration is apparent from the state of her manuscripts. She wrote on every conceivable scrap of paper, brown grocery bags and the backs of drug store advertisements, with a partiality for the insides of used envelopes. Her verses were set down to satisfy an immediate need, and variant words were added as fast as they occurred to her. Several such manuscripts are given in facsimile by Mrs. Bingham, and it should be obvious that they simply are not subject to customary editing. The present editor states her principle of choice: 'in most cases I used the word she wrote first'; but even if that word was more surely establishable than the facsimiles indicate, Miss Dickinson would presumably have favored more often the last alternative that struck her. How confusing this question can become may be noted from a single poem, 'A sparrow took a slice of twig,' which Mrs. Bingham prints without variants, even though the facsimile yields readings as far from those chosen as 'epicure of vehicles' is from 'a familiar saddle,' and at least a dozen choices for its final line.

It must be recognized henceforth that such poems were not finished, that they existed for Emily Dickinson's eyes alone, and that we cannot tell what she finally intended or whether she had made up her mind. She seems to have tossed many of these fragments aside as soon as her initial impulse was spent; and if they are printed, they can be given accurately only as work-sheets, with all the variants included. Lest the reader fear that such publication would swamp his interest, it should be added that a leading value of such fragments is to give us an insight into the poet's process of creation, and that our sense of her verbal resources is heightened by watching her alternate from 'the blissful oriole' to 'the reeling oriole,' and remain undecided as to whether to call him also 'confiding prodigal' or 'minute Domingo.'

And fortunately, a great number of Miss Dickinson's poems do not deliquesce in this fashion, for those eight or nine hundred which she had copied out and sewed together in fascicles, and which formed the basis for the Higginson-Todd editions, contained a far higher proportion of her final choices. Yet even several of the best known must be printed ultimately as private poems still, with the variants noted not too distractingly in small type at the foot of the page. For example, in the final line of 'He preached upon "breadth" till it argued him narrow,' she thought of calling this individual, with varying shades of irony, 'so religious (enabled, accomplished, discerning, accoutred, established, conclusive) a man!' We cannot rely on any creative editing, for even though the Higginson-Todd choice of 'enabled' was a sensitive one, still Miss Dickinson underlined 'religious,' apparently to indicate her choice. If we are to enter into the full nature of what it meant to be a poet in her circumstances, we must print each manuscript *in toto* as the special case it is.

Otherwise—and that is the reason for bringing up all these editorial issues here—we will almost certainly misconceive her. Indeed, ever since her rediscovery in the 'twenties, she has been variously misunderstood by those who have failed to reckon with enough of her actual background. Since her revival coincided with our renewed taste for the seventeenth-century metaphysicals, some critics wrote as though she was a conscious follower of Donne. But she had none of his sustained control over rhetoric, though she shared with Emerson and Thoreau their great liking for Browne and Herbert. She copied out, late in life, the second and third stanzas of Herbert's 'Matins,' beginning 'My God, what is a heart?' as though to indicate her kinship with some of his spiritual values and with his way of conveying them through the homeliest words. It was a natural mistake for Mrs. Bingham to regard these stanzas as Miss Dickinson's own, and to print them as the climactic poem of one of her sections.

Yet whatever Emily Dickinson's debts to the seventeenth century, it should never be forgotten that Emerson was the great figure in her foreground, and that her conception of poetic language, of how 'the word becomes one with the thing' in the moment of inspired vision, was basically his. She expresses that conception explicitly in one of these new poems, emphasizing the *inwelling* of a mysterious force beyond conscious control:

'Shall I take thee?' the poet said
To the propounded word.
'Be stationed with the candidates
Till I have further tried.'

The poet probed philology
And when about to ring
For the suspended candidate,
There came unsummoned in

That portion of the vision
The word applied to fill.
Not unto nomination
The cherubim reveal.

In another poem, where the subject is also language—'Your thoughts don't have words every day'—she dwells, as Emerson also had, upon the inevitable intermittence of inspiration. This poem should serve as her own warning to those who are bound to find superlative adjectives for every scrap of verse she left behind her. Criticism in this country still tends to make up for former neglect by erecting exaggerated monuments. It seems doubtful whether we are enabled better to perceive Emily Dickinson's rare distinctions when she is loaded with such a formidable weight as Mark Van Doren's foreword description of her as 'one of the great poets of the world.' Calling her such a thing as that plays directly into the hands of those who are determined to justify her every syllable, even some which, it now appears, she did not write.

Take, as a symptomatic case, the vexed question of her rhymes. Because Aldrich, the most genteel of our Victorians, wrote an essay about her called 'Un Poète Manqué' and had the further fatuity to provide his own better-rhymed version of 'I taste a liquor never brewed,' her anti-Victorian defenders have rushed to declare that her every imperfect or off-rhyme was not merely intentional, but a subtle refinement. Without gainsaying her fondness both for assonance and for the suspended rhyme (in which words ending in different vowel sounds followed by the same consonant are made to serve), it should be palpable now that in many cases she missed, in her constrained haste, finding even approximately the right word. Her great gift was for poetic thought—a very different thing from the customary nineteenth-century reflecting in verse—since it involved a fusion between her thought and the image which embodied it. But these further poems make even clearer than it was before that she possessed no comparable gift for versification. Her almost standard measure was the familiar ballad stanza, which was also the 'common meter' of the hymn books of her heritage. She seems hardly to have been concerned with the possibilities of metrical experiment, and many of her best poems are those wherein the vividness of what she had to say stirred her small stanzas with fresh irregularity. In any such long sequence of her less successful work as is provided by much of this new collection, the cumulative impression cannot escape monotony.

Discrimination, therefore, is imperative if the Emily Dickinson boom is not finally to collapse in deflation. As a check to the widespread notion that the 'twenties were entirely responsible for her discovery, it should be recalled that a not undiscerning popularity greeted the three series of poems as they were issued between 1890 and 1896. The review by Howells (Mr. DeVoto's remotely distant predecessor in 'The Easy Chair') penetrated at once to her originality. And although Howells was taken to task by Andrew Lang and other British reviewers for praising 'this farrago of illiterate and uneducated sentiment,' Alice James, writing near the end of her life in an English sanitarium, may be allowed the last word on this matter: 'It is reassuring to hear the English pronouncement that Emily Dickinson is fifth-rate—they have such a capacity for missing quality; the robust evades them equally with the subtle. Her being sicklied o'er with T. W. Higginson makes one quake lest there be a latent flaw in one's vision . . .'

But whatever Higginson's limitations, he and his friends—whom Mrs. Bingham cites—were at least able to place Emily Dickinson against her background. As William Roscoe Thayer wrote: 'Surely our New England Calvinism never brought forth any other flower so sweet and un-Calvinistic.' Several of her most sensitive first readers kept probing the question of her form, as they responded to her compressed intensity. Noting too her particular flavor of New England isolation, Samuel G. Ward called her 'the articulate inarticulate.' Maurice Thompson tried to express the sensation that many others have felt in her straining effort to give order to her material: her 'verse suggests to me a superb brain that has suffered some obscure lesion which now and then prevents the filling out of a thought—as if a cog slipped in some fine wheel just at the point of consummation.' That may overstate the element of strain, but one often feels an almost desperately maintained poise in her letters as well, and she herself summed up for Higginson her frequently defeated struggles for form: 'When I try to organize, my little force explodes and leaves me bare and charred.'

Detailed criticism of her poems, notwithstanding the work of Genevieve Taggard, Tate, Blackmur, Winters, still has much to do. A systematic study of her diction would bring to light many facets of her mind and sensibility—for instance, no one yet has quite given due attention to the pervasive presence of such terms as 'decree,' 'degree,' 'election,' 'capacity,' 'covenant,' 'confirmed,' 'condemned,' 'espoused.' Miss Taggard believes many of these to be owing chiefly to the legal vocabulary of Emily Dickinson's father, but they are more likely to have risen from the theological residue which must always be considered in reaching the nuances of her thought. A valuable essay also remains to be written about her recurrent symbols. The exacting task of arranging her poems around their leading themes cannot be fully undertaken until the manuscripts are available. So far as these are still in the hands of Madame Bianchi's executor, they do not seem likely to come into the public domain where they belong. But Mrs. Bingham has enough material upon which an important beginning could be made, and her unpossessive tone would augur for her willingness to share it. Only when some approximation of chronological order has been established, will we be able to perceive accurately for the first time how often Emily Dickinson kept writing essentially the same poems again and again. We will then be able to follow her, through tentative beginnings and rejected fragments, to her few delicate yet full-blooded marriages between spirit and form.

GEORGE F. WHICHER is represented by another essay in Section II of this volume, but reprinted here is a later discussion with the special merit of developing a clear historical perspective in which to view Emily Dickinson's poetry against Victorian poetry and poetics, both American and British.

Emily Dickinson among the Victorians

GEORGE F. WHICHER

In attempting to estimate the literary heritage that was available to Emily Dickinson, Mr. R. P. Blackmur, in *The Expense of Greatness,* makes the following characterization of the language of poetry current in her time:

> We can say, amiably enough, that the verse-language of mid-nineteenth century America was relatively nerveless, unsupple, flat in pattern, had very little absorptive power and showed no self-luxuriating power whatever.... The great estate of poetry as an available condition of language lay flat in a kind of desiccated hibernation, and the clue to resurrection was unknown.*

And he proceeds to observe that Whitman and Emily Dickinson, in revulsion from the desiccation, were obliged to rely entirely on their

* See p. 213 in this anthology.—Editors' note.

This lecture, delivered at Johns Hopkins University in 1947, was subsequently published in George F. Whicher, *Poetry and Civilization* (Ithaca: Cornell University Press, 1955), 41–62.

own natural aptitudes for language and hence never found satisfactory form, nor apparently were ever conscious of missing it.

But perhaps the case was not so desperate as Mr. Blackmur would make out. Rather than adopt an artificial and lifeless convention, Emily Dickinson sometimes compressed her notes for poems into a kind of grammatical shorthand of her own devising, or she let the words take the natural rhythms of speech without caring much about the pattern. This last is perhaps what Mr. Blackmur had in mind when he said that she was apparently not conscious of her lack of form. It would be truer to say that she fastidiously avoided perfunctory form. When we fix our attention, not on the confusing mass of poems finished and unfinished that her editors have indiscriminately huddled up together, but on the poems which presumably received her final approval, we are left with a new respect for her mastery of language and the inexhaustible variety and delicacy of her sense of form.

But Mr. Blackmur is right in maintaining that Emily Dickinson revolted from the literary standards to which her age paid deference. Indeed, her opposition is clear in her relations with Thomas Wentworth Higginson. She appealed to him to know if her verse were alive. He was not insensitive to such values, and apparently his reply helped to assure her. She said later in her hyperbolic way that it had saved her life. But he also hinted that her inspiration was wayward and that her rhymes observed no law. She quietly ignored his attempts to teach her, and he considerately desisted. This episode plainly shows that however uncertain she may have felt about the value of what she was writing she had no doubts at all about her literary method.

There is very little evidence to show that Emily Dickinson was aware that she was not alone in seeking more living forms of poetry than Victorian practice supplied. It is not even certain that she was consciously a rebel, since she was gifted with a profound and beautiful humility. But at the same time that she was willfully indulging herself in perfecting a sharp, astringent art of expression, other poets were independently seeking to escape from the confining standards of literary decorum. Mrs. Browning, for one, experimented with imperfect rhymes to see if she could not break down the conventions that she regarded as stifling. Emerson, Thoreau, Melville, and Whitman in this country were in various ways flouting the approved elegancies of poetry written for the drawing room. Thoreau, even more than Emily Dickinson, was disheartened by the abyss between his work and the sort of poetry that was currently successful, with the result that he impulsively burned much manuscript which he later wished he had saved.

Among the poets who reacted less violently against the accepted canons was Sidney Lanier, an interesting example of dissidence because his isolation as a southern writer of the Reconstruction Period gave him a certain perspective on the literary scene. In a letter of November 24, 1876, to Bayard Taylor, Lanier expressed his impatience with the feebleness of contemporary verse:

> In looking around at the publications of the younger American poets, I am struck with the circumstance that none of them even attempt anything great. The morbid fear of doing something wrong or unpolished appears to have influenced their choice of subjects. Hence the endless multiplication of those little feeble magazine-lyrics which we all know; consisting of one minute idea, each, which is put in the last line of the fourth verse, the other three verses and three lines being mere sawdust and surplusage.

Lanier, who hoped himself to become a kind of John Keats with an American fiber, recognized the difficulty of making headway against the established expectation of smoothly finished verse. To his wife he spoke out, referring to his poem "My Two Springs":

> Of course, since I have written it to print, I cannot make it such as *I* desire, in artistic design: for the *forms* of today require a certain trim smugness and clean-shaven propriety in the face and dress of a poem, and I must win a hearing by conforming in some degree to these tyrannies,—with a view to overturning them in the future.

Lanier's awareness of differences between what artistic integrity demanded and what it was possible to get into print throws a revealing light on Emily Dickinson's lifelong refusal to submit her poems to publication. She was not one to conform to "these tyrannies," and if the price to be paid for following her innermost convictions was lack of public recognition, she was willing to pay the price. But for poets in revolt against the stultifying restrictions of convention there was no common rallying point. They did their work in isolation without the support of knowing that others were working with them. Robert Frost could say of the fellow worker whose reverence for beauty he divined:

"Men work together," I told him from the heart,
"Whether they work together or apart."

Nevertheless those who have the courage to work apart must devote a certain amount of energy to overcoming the sense of utter loneliness. Generally they are thrown back upon the past and find support in establishing their kinship with the books and writers of other days.

Emily Dickinson was an eager reader. She formed numerous connections with sources of inspiration that made it unnecessary for her to rely entirely on her own aptitude for language while avoiding the stagnation of poetry in her time. The most obvious and sustaining of these influences was that of the Hebrew Bible, supplemented by Calvinistic theology, pulpit eloquence, and the verse of Dr. Watts and other writers of hymns. In her personal letters she often referred to poems by Tennyson, Lowell, and other secular poets as "hymns," and it would not be claiming too much to say that nine-tenths of her own poetry was written in meters made familiar to her by their use in the village hymnal. Some passages in her early correspondence likewise indicate that during her formative years Emily was not one who kept the Sabbath by staying at home, but that she attended church regularly and sometimes was profoundly stirred by the words spoken from the pulpit. Theological terms like election, grace, sacrament, and others were used in her poems with a nice sense of their technical meaning, while her fondness for religious imagery was constantly apparent. Unorthodox and unsettled she may have been in her religious convictions and affiliations, but she never outgrew the deep impression that her religious training had made upon her in childhood.

Most Victorian poets were men and women of religious nature, and their work is profoundly tinged with devoutness. Among them Emily Dickinson occupies a special place because of her instinctive immediacy. Just as in her nature poems she is constantly aware of human implications, so in her religious lyrics she steadily brings the sacred to the level of the human. There is nothing that she respects more than her own soul. In her opinion God exists for man, not man for God. This is no doubt her central heresy. In its poetic consequences it meant that she could not force her mind to assume a "cosmic" point of view. She could sympathize with Moses or other Biblical characters as human beings, but she could not rouse herself to enthusiasm for the drama of salvation in general. Her first readers unconsciously felt the difference, and some of them resented it.

Browning's "Saul" may not unfairly be regarded as a typical Victorian handling of a large religious theme in terms of Biblical characters. The shepherd boy David, who is the narrator as well as the central actor in the poem, pictures the great warrior king of Israel sunk in irremediable melancholy and brooding. In his yearning to relieve the monarch of the shadow of death that weighs upon his spirit, David recognizes an intimation of God's infinitely greater love for His children and a foreshadowing of the divine willingness to atone by Christ's sacrifice for the sins of man. The poem ends with a splendid restatement of the mystery of Christ's incarnation. Throughout the poem the tone has been tender and reverent. Saul, though not one of the prophets, is notably exalted into a figure of heroic size, like a huge bronze statue moving.

Against the background of expectation indicated by Browning let us project one of Emily Dickinson's evocations of a Biblical personage.

> Belshazzar had a letter,—
> He never had but one;
> Belshazzar's correspondent
> Concluded and begun
> With that immortal copy
> The conscience of us all
> Can read without its glasses
> On revelation's wall.

Somehow the story of the handwriting on the wall, which seemed remote and mysterious in the Old Testament, has become as familiar as the postman. Belshazzar is stripped of his oriental splendors. He is merely a representative human being, standing for "the conscience of us all." He "had a letter," just like you and me. And somehow, too, "Belshazzar's correspondent" has come to seem rather immediate. Many people disliked having the trappings of reverence so ruthlessly plucked away. One could read Browning with a gentle glow of admiration, but this poem administered a jolt. It was shocking, dangerous. It was Emily Dickinson.

Like everyone else, she read her Shakespeare. For her Shakespeare was more than a great poet; the *Works* was a unique book, the only book in the world. When she thought that her eyes were failing, she consoled herself by the reflection that she could still listen to its lines read aloud. She may have shared the romantic Victorian habit of regarding the characters in the plays as real people indefinitely extensible both backward and forward in time. She may have applied moralistic standards in judging them. But evidence on these points is not sufficient to be decisive. What is clearly manifest is that she learned from Shakespeare to treat language with an imperial contempt for rule, exchanging the parts of speech as convenience dictated, and sacrificing everything to the vitality of her thought. Resemblances to other poets may be noted, but there can be no doubt that Shakespeare provided her with the model that she studied most closely and absorbed most completely. There are echoes both of his cadences and of his conceits in her writing, but her main debt to him was not for literal borrowings. His liberal practice gave her the conception of language as a plastic medium to be shaped according to her desires. Moreover, her special fondness for *Othello* and *Antony and Cleopatra* indicates a certain maturity in her affection. These are not the plays that would be chosen by one who liked Shakespeare prettified. Emily Dickinson turned to him as one genuine craftsman to another.

Her relations with Donne, Herbert, Vaughan, and other seventeenth-century religious poets are curiously blank. One would suppose that she would have delighted in them, in spite of the fact that they were at the time out of fashion, except as Herbert was perennially read by pious people. It is disconcerting to find that she never referred to Donne at all or gave any indication that she was aware of his work. Vaughan's name she did know, though somewhat uncertainly since she misspelled it, and the one quotation she made from him toward the end of her life came from a poem frequently included in the anthologies. We would not be sure that she had ever seen Herbert's poems if two stanzas from his "Matins" had not survived in her handwriting. Nothing of Crashaw, nothing of Andrew Marvell. If she had lived a generation later, she would almost certainly have discovered her temperamental affinity with these poets. As it was, she recognized the genius of Sir Thomas Browne and once or twice assimilated to her poetry a phrase that may have been taken from him, but she leaves us in doubt concerning her awareness of his contemporaries. In general it may be said, however, that Emily Dickinson read far more than we can now prove that she read.

Early reviews of Emily Dickinson's poems, perhaps prompted by a remark of Higginson's, saw in her work "a distant echo of Blake," but we have no assurance that she had ever read anything of his. In all probability very few of his poems were available in Amherst until Emily was more than halfway through her span of life. Robert Burns, on the other hand, she certainly knew and in her very early poems sometimes imitated. But except for the few phrases that betray her girlish susceptibility to the sentimental warmth of Scottish song, it is difficult to establish any connection between Emily Dickinson and the British poets of the Romantic Movement. Her nature poems, as we have seen, are cast in a different mold from Wordsworth's, her love poems have nothing in common with Shelley's. Coleridge, Scott, and Byron, though she knew some of their work, inhabit another world from hers. Superficially it might be supposed that Landor, the master of graceful and polished epigram, might resemble her more closely than any other early-nineteenth-century poet. But Landor, as a devoted student of the classics, wrote by the book, whereas Emily Dickinson forged her epigrams in the white heat of her eager heart. The difference between them is the difference between the stately communication of men and women in the drawing room and the soul-to-soul communings that occur upstairs.

At the name of Keats, however, we must pause for a moment's consideration. When Higginson, in 1862, asked her about her reading, she replied surprisingly that for poets she had Keats and the two Brownings. At first glance her mention of Keats would seem to furnish an example of her paradoxical fondness for a writer whose work stands at the opposite pole from hers. The art of Keats was an art of invention and expansion, an effort to "load every rift with ore." Her art was one of ultimate compression, a defining of limits, a refining of the thrice refined. Yet if one looks closely at Emily Dickinson's poems one can imagine that he sees traces of Keatsian influence, though rarely among her most characteristic pieces. It is unusual to find her in an expansive moment, but a few love poems written presumably before her catastrophe of frustration have a certain amplitude and even a sensuous delight in piling detail on detail that is almost Keatslike.

I tend my flowers for thee,
Bright Absentee!
My fuchsia's coral seams
Rip, while the sower dreams.

Geraniums tint and spot,
Low daisies dot,
My cactus splits a beard
To show its throat.

Carnations tip their spice
And bees pick up.
A hyacinth I hid
Puts out a ruffled head,
And odors fall
From flasks so small
You marvel how they held.

Globe roses break
Their satin flake
Upon my garden floor,
Yet Thou not there—
I had as lief they bore
No crimson more....

For what it may be worth, here is a somewhat similar passage in Keats's more sedate measure:

Thou shalt, at one glance, behold
The daisy and the marigold;
White-pluméd lilies, and the first
Hedge-grown primrose that hath burst;
Shaded hyacinth, alway
Sapphire queen of the mid-May;
And every leaf and every flower
Pearléd with the self-same shower.

Recent investigation of Keats in the light of theories about the association of ideas that were current in his time has emphasized the experimental quality of certain of his early poems, in which he seems to be recording chance sequences of images that flowed through his mind in states of revery or daydreaming. Emily Dickinson likewise wrote a few poems in which she appears to be reproducing the motions of a mind either actually dreaming or dominated by waking fancy. The strange poem beginning, "In winter in my room," which describes the transformation of a mysterious small worm into a pursuing serpent of hideous power, concludes with the significant words, "This was a dream." It could easily be given a Freudian interpretation, but not by me. Other poems, such as "I know some lonely houses off the road," and "I started early, took my dog," have elements of unreality about them which suggest that they too belong with such dream-inspired compositions as "Kubla Khan." One wonders whether Emily Dickinson, like Keats, was tempted by the example of Coleridge to

> let wingéd Fancy wander
> Through the thought still spread beyond her:
> Open wide the mind's cage-door
> She'll dart forth, and cloudward soar.
> O sweet Fancy! let her loose....

The effect is in any case very much the same as that of a succession of images, real and imaginary, mingled, combined in a structure reared half automatically by the mind and given little intentional shaping. Mr. Yvor Winters has suggested * that in the following poem the sea should be identified with death, as in Whitman's "Out of the Cradle Endlessly Rocking," where the identification is explicitly stated. Whether his idea is accepted or not, the poem clearly resembles a dream and might be similarly interpreted.

> I started early, took my dog,
> And visited the sea;
> The mermaids in the basement
> Came out to look at me,
>
> And frigates in the upper floor
> Extended hempen hands,
> Presuming me to be a mouse
> Aground, upon the sands.
>
> But no man moved me till the tide
> Went past my simple shoe,
> And past my apron and my belt
> And past my bodice too,
>
> And made as he would eat me up
> As wholly as a dew
> Upon a dandelion's sleeve—
> And then I started too.
>
> And he—he followed close behind;
> I felt his silver heel
> Upon my ankle,—then my shoes
> Would overflow with pearl.

* See pp. 188–89 in this anthology.—Editors' note.

Until we met the solid town,
No man he seemed to know;
Then bowing with a mighty look
At me, the sea withdrew.

With the Keats of "The Eve of St. Agnes" and "Hyperion" Emily Dickinson has nothing in common, but there are tantalizing parallels between her work and some aspects of Keats's odes. His psychological observation of the close relationship of melancholy and ecstatic delight in the "Ode to Melancholy" is akin to the discernment which prompted her to write:

For each ecstatic instant
We must an anguish pay
In keen and quivering ratio
To the ecstasy.

The famous identification of Beauty and Truth at the end of the "Ode on a Grecian Urn" must have been in Emily Dickinson's mind when she wrote a lyrical statement of the same identity. It was characteristic of her passion for immediacy that she translated Keats's abstractions into terms of human figures.

I died for beauty, but was scarce
Adjusted in the tomb,
When one who died for truth was lain
In an adjoining room.

He questioned softly why I failed?
"For beauty," I replied.
"And I for truth,—the two are one;
We brethren are," he said.

And so, as kinsmen met a night,
We talked between the rooms,
Until the moss had reached our lips,
And covered up our names.

Nothing in Keats can quite match the eerie imagination of the last stanza, but in other respects the two poets have something in common. Even the sensuously luxuriating Keats who transcribed the blaze of sunset in the magic lines

While barréd clouds bloom the soft-dying day,
And touch the stubble-plains with rosy hue,

has an ethereal counterpart in the Emily who saw from her window

How the old mountains drip with sunset,
How the hemlocks burn!
How the dun brake is tipped with tinsel
By the wizard sun!

and who could picture the clouds of another sunset as

Blazing in gold and quenching in purple,
Leaping like leopards to the sky.

Even Keats, who loved "lucent syrops tinct with cinnamon," could not cherish the names of gems more caressingly than this puritan spinster.

The leading British poets who were her own contemporaries Emily Dickinson absorbed with passionate admiration. Toward Elizabeth Barrett Browning indeed she became almost an idolater, reading everything she wrote and greeting the final collection of her poems with a lyric eulogy beginning,

Her "Last Poems"—
Poets ended.

From traveled friends Emily eagerly collected all they could tell her about the Brownings' menage in Florence. Robert Browning too she fairly worshiped and Tennyson she could quote largely without book. Yet there is hardly a trace of these poets in her own writing. Her poetry, she realized, was not of the same kind as theirs. She supposed, it would seem, that the advantage lay entirely with them. Were they not authors who had won universal public esteem? For herself she hoped not to be considered "the only kangaroo among the beauty," but she could not be sure of the value of her achievement. With rare persistence, nevertheless, she continued to write according to her own system, resisting all Higginson's well-meant efforts to bring her to conformity with Victorian standards.

As compared with the run of poets of the Victorian era, both British and American, Emily Dickinson lives in an atmosphere charged with ozone. She belongs with the small group of writers whose prose or verse was dictated by an overwhelming need of compensatory exertion. The act of creation for her was a purgative action, an aesthetic response to a psychological compulsion. Emily Brontë, Melville, and Dostoievski were of the same type. Tennyson and Browning, Longfellow and Lowell, were of a different order.

To the sometimes overexalted and overstrained sentiment of Victorian poets Emily Dickinson opposed a cool appraising exactitude of vision. She did not attempt to disguise reality by lapping it in rhetoric. Browning might in a moment of exuberant optimism place a spirited glorification of old age in the mouth of his Rabbi Ben Ezra:

> Grow old along with me!
> The best is yet to be,
> The last of life for which the first was made.

But Emily had no illusions about the old. She tended a bedridden mother for seven years. Moreover she had used her own unsparing eyes.

> That odd old man is dead a year,
> We miss his stated hat;
> 'Twas such an evening bright and stiff
> His faded lamp went out.
>
> Who miss his antiquated wick?
> Are any hoar for him?
> Waits any indurated mate
> His wrinkled coming home?
>
> Oh, life, begun in fluent blood
> And consummated dull!
> Achievement contemplating this
> Feels transitive and cool.

No "festal board, lamp's flash, and trumpet's peal" in the dim decline of old age as far as Emily could see.

Tennyson in the first flush of Victorian enthusiasm for the chivalric symbol of "self-reverence, self-knowledge, self-control" could write the slightly ridiculous lines on Sir Galahad:

> My good blade carves the casques of men,
> My tough lance thrusteth sure.

My strength is as the strength of ten
Because my heart is pure.

Emily Dickinson, on the contrary, was impressed by the dearth of miracles in this earthly life.

I took my power in my hand
And went against the world;
'Twas not as much as David had,
But I was twice as bold.

I aimed my pebble, but myself
Was all the one that fell.
Was it Goliath was too large,
Or only I too small?

Or to bring out the difference still further, compare the poetic strategy that Tennyson employed in *In Memoriam* with Emily Dickinson's dealings with death and bereavement in well over two hundred brief poems. Tennyson finely expresses the shock of personal loss, but turns from man's inner world to seek from God and Nature some answer to the dark riddle of mortality. None is forthcoming, for the simple reason that the questions Tennyson poses are not genuine questions at all, but merely demands for emotional reassurance. In the end he relapses upon the rather lame solution that in the course of time the pang of sorrow is dulled and the scheme of things is somehow to be trusted. Emily Dickinson, with a salutary instinct for what is appropriate, never asks any cosmic questions, but focuses her attention steadily on the meaning of death to the individual soul. It is true that

Parting is all we know of heaven,
And all we need of hell.

But death, considered with the intensity of her microscopic gaze, at length yields its own antidote. In physical extinction she discovers the source of spiritual vitality here and now. Without shifting ground or evading the issue, she has reached through "the admirations and contempts of time" to the stability of "the Finite furnished with the Infinite."

In this respect the quality of Emily Dickinson's vision seems to me remarkably like that of Dostoievski. In a study of his fiction Professor Janko Lavrin has written:

A very intensive kind of realism can be obtained by concentrating on man's inner world. It results in the psychological novel in which a religious-philosophic quest merges with "psychology" to such an extent as to become one with it. A quest of this kind frequently represents the author's own inner travail—exteriorized and projected into human characters whose "philosophy" is not a matter of intellect only, but of what might be called one's total inner experience.

Emily Dickinson, since she was not writing novels, seldom projected her thoughts in terms of characters, but she did exteriorize and personify "ideas-emotions" or "ideas-forces," which people, as in a morality play, the stage of her soul. The drama there enacted is a chaotic and often unresolved clash of opposing principles, as in life itself, but she does not let the play end in ruin and the victory of the Conqueror Worm. For her dramatic insights she found the brief lyric a suitable vehicle. A Melville or a Dostoievski might employ a novel, a Pascal or a Nietzsche an aphorism. It is not without significance that many of Emily's poems are aphoristic.

She has been called, I think not very perceptively, a feminine Walt Whitman. We may appropriately close this series of comparisons, therefore, with a short examination of her likenesses and unlikenesses to her great American contemporary. They are alike, as has already been pointed out, in their revulsion from the deadness of mid-century poetry, but on the positive side they have little in common. Whitman's loose democracy, his easygoing assimilation of the crowd, is as different as possible from Emily Dickinson's prim distaste for humanity in the mass.

The popular Heart is a cannon first,
Subsequent a drum;
Bells for an auxiliary
And an afterward of rum.

Their distinctive attitudes emerge rather sharply if we read in close conjunction a well-known poem by each on the spider. Whitman writes:

A noiseless, patient spider,
I mark'd, where, on a little promontory it stood, isolated;
Mark'd how, to explore the vacant, vast surrounding,
It launch'd forth filament, filament, filament, out of itself;
Ever unreeling them—ever tirelessly speeding them.

And you, O my Soul, where you stand,
Surrounded, surrounded, in measureless oceans of space,

Ceaselessly musing, venturing, throwing,—seeking the
spheres, to connect them;
Till the bridge you will need be form'd—till the ductile
anchor hold;
Till the gossamer thread you fling, catch somewhere, O my
Soul.

By avoiding conventional cadences Whitman has here freshened what is in essence a well-worn device—the coupling of a physical object with a moral or spiritual analogy. His poem is built on the same plan as Bryant's "To a Waterfowl" and Longfellow's "The Village Blacksmith," but the poet's reputation for daring originality and his employment of free verse have disguised the commonplace and outworn mode of thought. Against a background of Whitman's more oratorical chants this piece has the effect of a few words spoken in a quiet conversational tone by a man engaged in making a soapbox speech.

Emily Dickinson wrote several poems on spiders. In the one I am quoting she, like Whitman, was pointing her observations at humanity while seeming to speak of the spider.

The spider as an artist
Has never been employed,
Though his surpassing merit
Is freely certified

By every broom and Bridget
Throughout a Christian land.
Neglected son of genius,
I take thee by the hand.

Do not be misled by the ironic ending into thinking that this poem is a sentimental assertion of sympathy for the least of God's creatures. It is nothing of the sort. Emily Dickinson is making an assertion that James McNeill Whistler would have delighted to underscore, namely that artistic merit is certified by the hostility of the vulgar. And what is the "Christian land" where works of genius are brushed off as any housemaid might treat a spiderweb? Is there a suspicion that it could be none other than New England? It is easy to suggest parallels for Whitman's poem, but where else in American literature can we find the like of Emily Dickinson's lambent intellectual satire?

No one tradition can account for Emily Dickinson. Her language is drawn from the Bible and Shakespeare, but likewise from the *Springfield Republican* and Webster's *American Dictionary*. She translates Calvinistic theology into household metaphor and expresses profound psychological insights in the locutions of daily speech. Her transcendental flights never get so far from the ground that they cannot be punctured by fact. Emerson and Yankee humor are blended in her composition.

She stands as a precursor of the modern mind, whom we have not yet fully overtaken. Born seven years before Queen Victoria came to the throne, and brought up to read Tennyson, Browning, Dickens, the Brontës, and George Eliot with transports of appreciation, Emily nevertheless miraculously freed herself from Victorian trammels when she came to write her tiny lyric notations on life. Her novel aim was to find words for the stark integrity of her inner and outer experiences. At a time when everything from the village blacksmith to the chambered nautilus was tagged with an ethical message, Emily believed that a hummingbird, a snake, a mushroom, or a blade of grass was poem enough if she could only get it on her page. With equal honesty she set down her devastating observations of people, her alternations of doubt and faith, her longing for high companionship, her agony of renunciation, and her constant awareness of the creeping shadow of death. Hers was an essentially modern spirit, learning, as we have not yet fully learned, to make the best of a world that has undergone an intellectual fragmentation bombing.

For many years STANLEY T. WILLIAMS (1888–1956), a professor of English at Yale, achieved his greatest distinction in studies of American literature. His *The Life of Washington Irving* (1935) is a definitive biographical and critical study. He was an associate editor of *Literary History of the United States* (1948) and contributed the essay on Emily Dickinson. In the *Cambridge History of American Literature* (1921) Norman Foerster had cautiously predicted an "inconspicuous but secure" place for Emily Dickinson in American letters. Twenty some

years later in the *Literary History of the United States,* Williams confidently emphasizes "an immortality which is now assuredly hers."

Experiments in Poetry: Emily Dickinson

STANLEY T. WILLIAMS

Meanwhile, in the North, Emily Dickinson was writing, garnering up in secret an immortality which is now assuredly hers. Perhaps undesired and certainly unattained in her lifetime, her fame as a breathless, perceptive poet and as an interpreter of the soul's relations with eternity has passed far beyond the applause of a cult into established acceptance; together, she and Walt Whitman (whom she probably never read) represent the farthest pioneerings of the nineteenth century American mind in the trackless regions of spirit, in so far as they are reflected in poetry. Emily Dickinson, with a terrible, beautiful intensity, expressed the most aspiring experience of the Puritan soul, sharp-reined in her by a new realism, and released in distilled, gnomic verse; her extraordinary seizure in art of the apexes of despair and ecstasy may well endure:

At least to pray is left, is left
Oh Jesus! in the air
I know not which thy chamber is,—
I'm knocking everywhere.

Reminding us of Christina Rossetti, of whom she was, except for five days and eight years, the exact contemporary, and of Elizabeth Barrett, without the fulfillment of love in marriage, she lived for fifty-six years on the quiet Amherst street her thrilling life as an adventuress in eternity—and as eternity's witty critic, too. Outwardly there is little to chronicle. To her austere lawyer-father, Edward Dickinson, the treasurer of Amherst College, she was bound by inviolable ties of duty and inarticulate affection. "You know," she wrote of him, "he never played." In the narrow yet superior society of the New England village, and in the cultivated, orthodox home life with her brother Austin and her sister Lavinia, her character took on its distinctive traits of devotion, self-reliance, and ceaseless scrutiny of her own mind. As in Hawthorne, ordinary New England life was in her marrow, but the beginning of some strange celestial apprenticeship is early hinted in a letter of 1853, written at the age of twenty-three: "I do not," she says simply, "go

From the *Literary History of the United States* (New York: The Macmillan Co., 1948), 907–15.

from home." About 1861–1862 she was definitely committed to her retirement from the world.

Small, like a wren, with eyes whose color was like the sherry left by the guest in the wineglass, so she describes herself; soft of voice, quick in the movement of body or mind; even then, as she tended her flowers or baked bread for her father, she was forging mysterious bonds. Events, still obscure in detail or meaning, accented her isolation and projected abroad clouds of misleading legend. Despite her normal girlhood at Mount Holyoke Female Seminary and Amherst Institute, despite her gaiety and her friendliness, we see her also through the eyes of the puzzled townspeople. The winged stories flew: she refused to address her own letters; she listened to music downstairs from the "polar privacy" of her own room; or she flitted on summer evenings, always in white, through her garden, like a moth. She became indeed, in vulgar speech, a village character. For her own good reasons Emily Dickinson's habits of withdrawal from society increased; thus Thomas Wentworth Higginson, editor and literary critic, who divined her greatness without understanding it or interpreting it to the world, remarked: "I saw her but twice face to face, and brought away the impression of something as unique and remote as Undine or Mignon or Thekla." So lovely, so intensely alive, what secret vows were hers, and why?

The minutiae of her story must remain conjectural; we can only speculate with fluctuating assurance on her spiritual experience, recorded in emotional moments (the "esoteric sips of sacramental wine"), often on the backs of envelopes or brown paper bags or on scraps of newspapers or discarded bills. Though neither nun nor mystic, Emily Dickinson was, in many ways, of their identity. Yet her renunciation of life was reinforced by human love and anguish; hers were authentic sufferings, worthy of one who loved truth:

I like a look of agony
Because I know it's true.

Practically all that we can learn of her deep draught of actual experience, we must deduce from a brief autobiographical parable, written in her second letter to Higginson on April 25, 1862:

I went to school, but in your manner of the phrase had no education. When a little girl, I had a friend who taught me Immortality; but venturing too near, himself, he never returned. Soon after, my tutor died, and for several years my lexicon was my only companion. Then I found one more, but he was not contented I be his scholar, so he left the land.

Several men played influential roles in her life, but two especially strengthened her links with eternity. One, a certain Benjamin F. Newton, a young lawyer who had fed her deep-seated craving for study, died early, and conferred on her the privilege of sorrow. The other, an older, married man, the Reverend Charles Wadsworth, a minister second in power only to Henry Ward Beecher, inspired in her an attachment thwarted by his and her own high standards of conduct. About these centers of reality much of her poetry revolves. Yet a close correlation in her life of persons and events in her passionate lyrics is still dangerous: Emily Dickinson was a poet as well as a woman, and we must reckon both with her artistic detachment and with her dramatization of moods. Surely, her love poetry was not, like Emily Brontë's, without factual basis. Love, frustration, and death she tasted with all the eagerness of a sensitive spirit. She lived on, in her garden, in her chamber, more and more the denizen of a metaphysical domain of her own. This world she suffused until her death in 1886 with the light of a severe exaltation, but darkened it at times by her broodings concerning what she called the "underside of [God's] divinity." Her introspection, her "latter-day transcendentalism," belong to the long story of the gradual liberation from the old Puritan orthodoxy.

So cloistered, so fugitive a life, hints at Emily Dickinson's ignorance of the subversive events of her America, such as the fissure of the Civil War, science, or the amazing emergence of our literary pantheon. On one side of her nature she seems to symbolize New England's cultural isolation, its retreat into itself. Yet her lack of particular allusion is deceptive; in some ways she was a legitimate child of her time. The full enormity of war, like other grossnesses, she did not grasp; to her its baseness seemed, she said, "oblique." Yet she knew, if only from the bullet which struck down gallant young Frazer Stearns (son of the president of Amherst College), the grief of others; and its realities she transmuted into the imagery of her verse. "Sorrow," she wrote, "seems more general than it did, and not the estate of a few persons, since the war began." The claims of science, too, though muted in comparison with Lanier's rhetoric, find echoes in her verse. Among our men of letters she was aware of Poe, and of Hawthorne who, she said, "appals and entices." Puritanism, transcendentalism, and even the burgeoning Yankee humor of the times were fertile strata in which sprang up her strong and delicate flowers of thought.

For reasons still regrettable, perhaps her horror of a "frog-like" publicity, or her fear of commercializing her writing, she would never emulate her only "literary" friends, Helen Hunt Jackson or kind, editorial Higginson; she would not soil her pure, white banner of poetry in the world of publishers. "My barefoot rank," she said, "is better." Probably she realized that her conception of poetry was ahead of her time. Yet she loved those who had written openly for humanity; besides the Bible, Shakespeare, and Sir Thomas Browne, she acknowledged Keats, and she ecstatically compared George Eliot to "glory." On the walls of her room hung portraits of this novelist, of Elizabeth Barrett, and of Carlyle. Among her American contemporaries, though specific references are elusive, she was most in debt to Emerson, for staccato forms and also for the bright courage of her tense speech.

It would be helpful to know how faithfully Emily Dickinson conned Emerson's techniques; or how much of her frugal verse economy she derived from her innate distaste for what he called the "jingling serenader's art." Presumably she owes little to others, even to him. Her earliest rhymes show a robust condensation, and in every poem her mannerisms declare the instinctive independence of her craft, itself a protest against such verbosity as Lanier's. Of some eight hundred poems and of the 650 later published in *Bolts of Melody* (1945), relatively few number in length more than a dozen lines. Her favorite measure is reminiscent of the hymn meters with which she had been familiar since childhood, with beautiful variations of three-stress, two-stress, and even one-stress lines. She does not disdain conventional devices—her alliteration and her assonance are effective—but these tricks are likely to take a characteristically impish turn, as in her blithe use of liquids in the conclusion of her eight-line stanza on evening:

> Lightly stepped a yellow star
> To its lofty place,
> Loosed the Moon her silver hat
> From her lustral face.
> All of evening softly lit
> As an astral hall—
> "Father," I observed to Heaven
> "You are punctual."

For the sake of such conciseness, monosyllabic and dissyllabic words predominate, frequently those of the homespun New England life, of which she was so inseparable a part: broom and bonnet; rut, stile, and overcoat. One fancies a cause and effect between her ever more emphatic solitude, with its consequent silences, and her laconic diction in verse; nothing, *nothing* should be communicated save the kernel of the thought—no rind, no glossy surface. Therefore, like other American writers deprived of the smoothing, standardizing influence of the "circle" or of the stings of critical friends, she preserved the stiff, rude edges of her thought; she developed a technique indisputably her own, however much it has puzzled other writers, such as Higginson, or even the determined semiscientific, modern student of poetry. She omitted conjunctions; used half- and quarter-rhymes; played with the subjunctive mood or with legal phrases; dispensed with agreements of nouns and verbs; cut and clipped her sentences. Thus she was often cryptic—"half-idiotic," says one impatient, obtuse critic—and she was always on the wing. Speed was this Atalanta's joy, nor would she stop for a golden apple. Such fleetness she attained partly by her intense, rapid methods of composition; she strove to capture the telegraphic thought. Moreover, in her half-rhymes, her irregularities of speech and rhythm, her spasmodic quality, she mirrored the incongruities and frustrations of human experience; the awkwardness in her poetry became a metaphor of life itself.

Yet the factor of conscious plan in the poetry of Emily Dickinson is almost negligible. For us a penalty of her solitude is her silence concerning the theories underlying her art. There survive, of course, no prefaces, nor any synthesis of her poetic principles, but only here and there flash illuminating implications, in a letter, in hints within the poetry itself. For to this shy, intellectual, spiritually wayward woman her craftsmanship seems to have been a natural glove for her thought. Yet principles she had; in her reflections on the analogies of poetry to life she grappled with age-old problems. A primary one was the relation of the concrete to the abstract; that is, the connection between her New England world, with its pattern of facts, and its divine prototype. Thus she had the philosopher's passion without his reconciling power for the thing seen and the thing unseen, for the biting contrast of appearance and fact.

Now of this conflict she is sternly conscious; this schism is everywhere in her poetry; the lace and surge of the wave; the mist and the Apennine; the film and the thought. She writes in this basic metaphor. Ever she sought an absolute, but rued the price of its momentary attainment:

> Perception of an
> Object costs
> Precise the Object's loss.

So Emily Dickinson's dualism, repudiating such a monism as animates the poetry of Whitman, permeated her life. She is intensely curious, on the one hand, concerning God, and on the other, concerning the daily newspaper (her character of recluse has been exaggerated). The dualism is evident, too, in her poetry, in such a metaphysical concept as

> I died for beauty,

or in a realistic line on a snake:

> A whip-lash
> Unbraiding in the sun.

Thus, from one point of view, Emily Dickinson is a realist examining, as she says, each splinter in the groove of the brain; a witty piquant preceptress on all the common life about her, and also on its divine origins. She writes of the bee, the bobolink, the spider, the bat, the storm, noon, the sunset, or the preacher with his preposterous sermon on "breadth." In this role of commentator on things visible and invisible she aphorizes on God, human love, death, and also on mermaids and angleworms. In her poetry the sublime and the trivial jostle each other and evoke from her mingled reverence and satire, as in the response to her prayer for "content," that is, for a modest little heaven of her own:

> A smile suffused Jehovah's face;
> The cherubim withdrew;
> Grave saints stole out to look at me,
> And showed their dimples, too.

For the poem conveys her conviction, held momentarily, that a voice does not come out of silence. That God answers our prayers, is the certain "swindle."

This is, perhaps, enough; few readers demand more. To adopt her own metaphor, she does little sums of spiritual arithmetic; and her epigrammatic conclusions, sometimes somber or even Freudian as in her dream of the worm, are as memorable as Hawthorne's elaborate clinics in the moral impulse. His symbols too often wear the solemn splendor of his letter A in the heavens; hers shine with the frosty twinkle of the stars. She is a detached critic of men's hopes and fears; this is especially true of her poems on human problems. Yet, particularly in her poetry on nature, she cherishes a fairylike intimacy with plant and bird. No naturalist, still she knew them all and believed that these mute creatures expressed thoughts surpassing her own. At the same time she is enchantingly literal. The snow falls in the ruts like "alabaster wool"; the dog goes along on "feet of intermittent plush"; the bat wears his "small umbrella, quaintly halved"; the moon has a "chin of gold"; the grass "threads the dews all night, like pearls"; the bobolink is the "rowdy of the meadow." She startles with a phrase: the dead, in their alabaster chambers, rest under "rafter of satin and roof of stone." She personifies sharply, in contrast to Lanier's vague figures, Death who stops for her in his carriage; or she invents adverbs:

> Kingdoms like the orchard
> Flit russetly away.

In brief, poetry is her "playmate" with which she tries a thousand games of color, light, and sound. This Emily Dickinson should indeed suffice.

Yet, though perceptive, though alive with spiritual sustenance, this Emily Dickinson is a fragmentary, occasional poetess. The intensities of her despair and exultation suggest a wholeness of experience concealed by her reticence, by the disorder of undated poems, and by editings under such captions as "Love," "Life," "Nature," "Time and Eternity," "Our Little Kinsmen," "The Mob within the Heart," "The Single Hound." Among her tangential poems on nature, on homely incident, on the specters or fancies of her mind are lyrics which, if rearranged in the proper order, reveal her progress in a deepening spiritual life. The late poems in *Bolts of Melody* reveal the growth in Emily Dickinson of this universalizing tendency. Under the swift-running river of her poetry glides ever this deeper current of her being, rising to the surface in sparkles of light or flashes of brilliant intuition, ever submerged yet ever continuing through the recesses of her mind toward that ocean which she invokes so gaily: "Eternity, I'm coming, sir!" In brief, the real meaning of Emily Dickinson's poetry must reside in its inner record of an elevated human spirit suffering, battling, growing toward a victorious purgation. Such an integration of the poetry lifts it from the rank of brittle epigram into an organic unity. It is a kind of American *Vita Nuova,* a rival of *Sonnets from the Portuguese* or of other great verse sequences. She is more than a pretty aphorist; she is an interpreter of universal experience.

A firm exposition of Emily Dickinson's pilgrim's progress of the soul or of her modern cosmology is sadly hampered in several ways. First, the dating of many poems is dubious, the verses in the *Complete Poems* and *Bolts of Melody* demand regrouping, and, even if a chronological order could be established, we should still not be sure that the time of composition did not postdate materially the moment of emotion. This brings us again to the distressing difficulty, that of correlating specific poems with events and crises in the poet's life. For instance, the following familiar lines may—or may not—refer to the deaths of her friends Leonard Humphrey and Ben Newton:

My life closed twice before its close;
It yet remains to see
If Immortality unveil
A third event to me.

Or does a poem on domestic happiness reflect directly a period of hope prior to the frustration of her love affair? How can we be really assured concerning the identities of the "absentee" or the "dim companion"? Who will censure the poet carried away with the beauty of an idea itself? Certainly she may have magnified the little incident of love for poetry's sake, until the dream became the passionate reality in art. Wise is he who can translate the events in these lyrics into actual farewells, into particular conversations, into, for instance, a lantern held high in the garden by her father over the head of an unfavored suitor, into a parting at noon; who can here discover an individual as real as Robert Browning in the songs of Elizabeth Barrett! Finally, as part of this sublimation, there is her identification of human love with heavenly love:

Given in marriage unto thee
Oh, thou celestial host!

Bride of the Father and the Son,
Bride of the Holy Ghost!

Other betrothal shall dissolve,
Wedlock will decay;
Only the keeper of the seal
Conquers mortality.

Yet after homage has been paid to such cautions, most of us will still subscribe to the verdict of the scholar who says that the poems of Emily Dickinson

record with minute veracity the subtle changes in a woman's nature as she becomes conscious of her heart's unalterable commitment, passes through self-sustained illusion and painful disillusionment to an agony of frustration, and emerges at last, impregnably fortified on a new plane of being.

All these verses, in the end, revolve about one axis, and it is idle to speculate on which stage of Emily Dickinson's "Calvary" (a favorite word) produced particular poems. Each type of poem has its faults, from the too playful joy of her "illusion," through the gnawing neurotic agony of her "disillusionment," to the overintellectualized, somewhat jocose eternity of her "new plane of being." As the crown of her growth we must necessarily be most interested in this last phase. At this final point occurred an intense detachment and a crystallization of her memories and sorrows:

I measure every grief I meet
With analytic eyes.

On this plane of being she attains a kind of peace which, ever-simplifying, we may say atoned for her loss of earthly love. In the end she acquired a vivid sense of God, a being whose tantrums, futilities, and "duplicity" perpetually annoyed her—again her conflict between the abstract and the concrete—yet who remained a compensation for her frustration. Hers was an austere heaven, that in which the later poems center, as cold as Emerson's, less serene, too, but more lighthearted, and jocund with her wit. Here dwelt her Friend, her "burglar, banker, Father."

In this world, after her adjustments to earthly griefs, Emily Dickinson lived, finding in it—except for periods of depression, also recorded in her lyrics—a permanence lacking in her human relationships. Here she enjoyed an almost comfortable existence with the Father, the seraphim, and the stoled angels, that is, with her own high thoughts. Her sense of well-being has inspired an opinion, demanding qualification, that she was a mystic: we note her use of the word "light," and her certainty of God:

> I never saw a moor,
> I never saw the sea: ...
>
> I never spoke with God,
> Nor visited in Heaven;
> Yet certain am I of the spot
> As if the chart were given.

She had read the seventeenth century mystics; she mentions Henry Vaughan. Yet other traits of mysticism, namely the passivity, the transiency of the union with God, and the ineffability of the experience are less distinct, less discernible than the poet's own special quality of mind; in particular, her overwhelming sense of everyday fact, her levity, her resolute retention of her own individuality. The contrasts in her nature are amazing; where, in all the august company of mysticism do we find her like? Her conjunction of the cosmic and the comic? She is a saint in cap and bells. Frail and heroic spirit!

Of the several substantial contributions to Emily Dickinson scholarship in recent years, those of THOMAS H. JOHNSON (1902–) are perhaps most significant, primarily because he has established definitively the texts of the whole Dickinson canon of poetry. *The Poems of Emily Dickinson* appeared in three volumes in 1955; his edition of the letters (with Mrs. Theodora Ward) followed in 1958. Both works are generally regarded as authoritative. Johnson also brought out in 1955 *Emily Dickinson: An Interpretive Biography,* and in 1961 *Final Harvest,* a selection of 575 poems from the total of more than 1700. Johnson is chairman of the English department at The Lawrenceville School in New Jersey, has edited other American writers (Edward Taylor and Jonathan Edwards), was one of the general editors of *Literary History*

of the United States (1948), and is now at work on *The Oxford Companion to American History.*

Emily Dickinson: The Prisms of a Poet

THOMAS H. JOHNSON

The papers of Emily Dickinson, her poetry, letters, and indeed whatever remains as a part of her literary heritage, are now available for final editing. Through a generous gift by Gilbert H. Montague, of New York, Harvard University has acquired the great manuscript collection of her poems that Emily willed at the time of her death in 1886 to her sister Lavinia. It is the collection, numbering some 950 items, which formed the basis for all the editions of her poems issued down through 1937, and was gathered in that year as *The Poems of Emily Dickinson,* edited by Martha D. Bianchi and A. L. Hampson. The terms of the gift give title and custody to Harvard of all that Emily died possessed of, including her books, together with family papers, letters by Emily or written to her, and all that appertains to her life, the background of her family, and her literary reputation since her death. The Houghton Library, which will receive the gift, will furnish a Dickinson room with the books, furniture, and other memorabilia.

Certainly not in this decade, perhaps not in this half-century, has a more fortunate event—one long hoped for—occurred in the history of American belles-lettres. Now at last, three quarters of a century after Emily Dickinson's death, scholars will be able to determine with some accuracy the rank she may take among world poets.

There are two points of reference in the life history of Emily Dickinson's poetry. The first is the period of its composition, culminating with her death at the age of fifty-five. The second is the period of its publication, extending from 1890 to 1945. The world knows a great deal about the second, though certainly not all: it is a period of uncertainties, frustrations, and until the latest edition of poems, editorial confusions. There were the two Amherst houses: Emily in the later years shared one with Lavinia, who after Emily's death fiercely devoted herself to the venture of publishing the poetry. There was the other Dickinson house, that of Emily's brother Austin, and Austin's wife Sue, to whom many of the verses had been inscribed during years of sisterly attachment. The

From the *Saturday Review of Literature,* XXXIII (June 3, 1950), 16–17.

bitter partisanships engendered after Emily's death sprang from a desire, shared in common, to present a new poet and a new kind of poetry written by a beloved sister. That the sisters made a sacrificial victim of the object of their love is not a new phenomenon in the history of human devotion.

But it is the first period, the years of actual composition, which is fully important, and the one which so far has been revealed inconclusively and had remained to this moment conjectural. The poems, letters, and other documents now brought together or made available should tell the story.

Why were but seven poems published during her lifetime, and those anonymously? She initiated correspondence with Thomas Wentworth Higginson in her early thirties, and did so to seek literary advice from a liberal-minded gentleman and man of letters who, she hoped, might encourage her to believe that her talent was authentic. But if kindly Mr. Higginson could only surmise the talent (and years later only surmise the greatness of it), without comprehending what to do, surely one would be rash to venture much further in advice, especially of the great. There were one's old friends, Samuel Bowles for instance, who was establishing the *Springfield Republican* as one of the great liberal papers in the country. But if such trustworthy people as Higginson and Bowles believed the verses too heady, too unconventional, indeed perhaps "odd," as the public would take them, it would be futile and ungracious to impose on busy Mr. Fields, the editor of *The Atlantic Monthly,* or the celebrated Mr. Emerson, whose technique had been studied with loving absorption.

Did Emily Dickinson develop her fear of "froglike" publicity because the responses of such literary personages as she consulted, including almost certainly her friend Helen Hunt Jackson, checked her self-confidence, or was her confidence in her own destiny now sure, bracing her to abide the issue? Singleness of purpose was characteristic of the Dickinsons.

Perhaps the evidence may now become conclusive that her dedication was early, guided by the uncertain advice of friends who could do no more than wonder and marvel, and that she selected thus her course effortlessly because she followed her star.

Even a cursory examination of the manuscripts shows that she worked and reworked her verses. Presumably she preserved everything she wrote and left it all to her sister, Lavinia, who assumed, rightly I think, that Emily intended it for publication.

There is reason to hope that the papers will reveal answers to other major questions touching upon her life and art. She left no formal prefaces setting forth her theories of poetry, but much can be adduced from the verses themselves and from letters and other documents when all these are fitted into a proper relationship. It may be too much to expect to find a clear order among the undated poems or to determine an exact chronology. The revisions had been extensive and rough drafts were usually destroyed. Yet the data for biographical appraisal are extensive and the factual basis for much of the poetry is highly probable.

Since virtually all of the poetry has been published, there principally remains the collating of the published texts with the manuscripts, for the canon is not yet established. Mrs. Millicent Todd Bingham, who in 1945 brought out *Bolts of Melody,* a group of 668 hitherto unpublished poems and fragments, points up the problem by noting in her introduction that in many poems Emily Dickinson "supplied alternative words, phrases, or lines, [with] little crosses indicating where the final choice should be inserted." In several instances she made no final choice. Perhaps some degree of chronological order can be discovered, at least the order in which the revisions were completed. It is these revisions, gathered into small groups, which she evidently considered final, for she numbered them and filed them away. Over the years these groups often have been separated and arranged under arbitrary captions to suggest such topics as "Life," "Nature," and "Love."

The basic need is to determine the Dickinson canon. At the moment there is no certainty that her poems as they now exist in print represent what she intended to write. Of the some eight or nine hundred printed before the editing of *Bolts of Melody* even a preliminary examination of the manuscripts from which they were assembled reveals line changes, omitted lines or stanzas, misreadings and bowdlerizations. There seem to have been gatherings of stanzas published as one poem which were never so intended and, conversely, separation of stanzas intended as a unit. There are the selected items, nosegays of verse, a few lines or a stanza adapted to a special occasion, enclosed with a small gift to a friend and neighbor.

Of greatest importance is the fact that now it will be possible to appraise the development of an artist.

Some of the forthcoming autobiographical evidence should be conclusive in solving questions at the moment merely speculative. How did her reading shape her growth? What books did she really con? What were the human influences beyond her family circle that determined her life and thought? There was, of course, the young lawyer, Benjamin F. Newton, whose friendship before his early death gave direction to her career as artist. But just what and how? There was the remarkable —perhaps determining—influence of the Reverend Charles Wadsworth, one of the leading pulpit orators of his day. Again, in what direction and with what fixedness?

All these questions and more at last are capable of some solution. And they are immensely important questions, for Emily Dickinson was a dedicated artist, shy, cloistered, fugitive perhaps, but one who selected a way of life as deliberately as she chose a metaphor. Intense, cryptic, paradoxical, her life and her writing have a unity of purpose that battled to achieve and reveal a universal experience.

MARK VAN DOREN (1894–), teacher, writer, and critic, was educated at the University of Illinois and Columbia, where he is now an emeritus-professor of English. His *Collected Poems* won the Pulitzer Prize in 1940. *John Dryden* (1920; 1945), *Shakespeare* (1939), *The Private Reader* (1942), and *Nathaniel Hawthorne* (1949) attest the perceptiveness and range of his scholarship, but show him at several removes in his analytic method from the "New Criticism."

A Commentary on "I Had Not Minded Walls"

MARK VAN DOREN

I had not minded walls
Were Universe one rock,
And far I heard his silver call
The other side the block.

From Mark Van Doren, *Introduction to Poetry* (New York: William Sloane Associates, Inc., 1951), 12–16.

I'd tunnel until my groove
Pushed sudden through to his,
Then my face take recompense—
The looking in his eyes.

But 'tis a single hair,
A filament, a law—
A cobweb wove in adamant,
A battlement of straw—

A limit like the veil
Unto the lady's face,
But every mesh a citadel
And dragons in the crease!

—Emily Dickinson

The beloved person of this poem is unattainable for another reason than that operating in Mary Morison's case. [Burns's] Mary Morison was attainable whenever she chose to be; she might never so choose, but she was free to make her lover happy; nothing substantial separated them, no third thing outside themselves. In Emily Dickinson's poem there is a third thing, and it will separate two persons forever. The man who is loved can never be reached. Something that seems slight, that indeed is all but invisible, is there between them as big as a mountain, and more rough and hard. It is bigger of course than any mountain; were the entire universe one solid block of rock, this thing would still be greater. The block of rock could be tunnelled through, but this delicate barrier is impregnable. It is convention, it is morality. Or if it is not that—the poem does not give it a name—it is something equally strong. And the business of the poem is to state its strength.

The poem is difficult perhaps. The idea that something in a human mind—or two human minds, or all human minds—may be harder than granite is itself difficult; or it could be to a reader untrained in paradox. But in addition the subject as it exists here is highly personal to the speaker. It is even a secret subject, which she is shy in divulging—shy because it is important, and shy because she is modest. She does not hesitate to confess her own love, but she will not confess for another. The difficulty, such as it is, comes partly from her instinct to protect him; she leaves him unknown to us, as she leaves the subject unknown to all save those who will work it out.

As for him, the beloved person, the first two stanzas come near to suggesting that he is God. In a sense he *is* God, as those greatly loved seem to be. He is too remote and wonderful to possess; he is on the other side of the universe, waiting to be known; and he can be known only by heroic effort. But the last two stanzas remove the suggestion. There is no law against our loving God; the limits interposed between deity and man are not like these. It is a human situation we have, and indeed it is all the more tortuous for that. Yet Emily Dickinson has managed, in the suggestion itself, to deposit in our minds a feeling that the unattainable person is benign and blameless—is a great person, to her at any rate, and worthy of comparison with the greatest Person she knows.

Still she is concealing as much as she can, consistently with the fact that she speaks at all. She writes so tersely, and wraps her message so tightly, that we shall miss it unless we listen close. Her syntax, for example, tends toward oddity; she seems to leave out necessary words, and she ignores certain rules of grammar. She is daring us to paraphrase her poem. Yet it is her desire that we do so, and consequently we shall. A different and weaker statement will result; but then we shall know what the force of her utterance was.

"I would not have minded walls between me and the man I love. If the universe itself were one great wall, as thick as it was high, and built of solid rock; and if, far around on the other side of this obstruction, I heard his silver voice calling to me (or, simply, heard it and knew it was his), then I would cheerfully tunnel through to where he was. He would have started too; tunnels are built from both ends, and meet in the middle; suddenly, therefore, the last bit of rock between us would be gone, and I would have my reward. My reward, because the effort was chiefly mine. My tunnel reached his. Then the reward—my opportunity to look into his eyes. But this is an idle story. Nothing of the sort ever happened or will happen. No such opportunity exists. There is no wall, no universal block between his eyes and mine. Something worse is there—something as thin as a single hair, a filament; something as unreal (yet how real!) as a human law. It is as if a cobweb had been woven out of adamant, the hardest stone; or as if a fortress, though built only with straw, turned out to be more invincible than stone. Something stands between us that looks like nothing at all—a veil, say, on a lady's face. But every part of it is terrible in its power to resist penetration. Suppose it *is* a veil. Well, every mesh of it is a citadel, and every fold of it contains a dragon."

The paraphrase says less than the poem does—so much less that we may learn from the difference what poetry is. The only merit of the prose is that it calls attention to some of the things Emily Dickinson is doing. It accentuates, for instance, her changes of tense. She begins with "I had not," goes on to "I would," and ends in the strict present: "It is." The present fact, the controlling and only fact, is painful; so she has come to it with delays and diversions, pretending for the while that something else was fact. But nothing else was, whereas this *is.* Then there are the suppressed words, the units of grammar and syntax which she forces us to supply. *If the* universe were one rock, and *if* I heard his silver call *on* the other side *of* the block—she does not use the italicized terms, any more than she says in the next stanza: Then my face *would* take recompense. Meanwhile she has written "sudden" for "suddenly," as later on she writes "unto" for "to"—for once a longer word, but this is because it has a more formidable sound than the one we would use in prose, as befits the fact that the situation itself is now absolutely formidable.

What the paraphrase does not do, however, is more significant than what it does. It gives us no sense of the nervous quickness with which Emily Dickinson moves toward the conclusion of her tragic statement. It is not in verse, and it is not in stanzas; nor does it rhyme. Emily Dickinson uses line, stanza, and rhyme to give what she is saying velocity and terror; or, at the end of the second stanza, softness and joy.

> Then my face take recompense—
> The looking in his eyes.

The absence of rhyme between "groove" and "recompense," and the consonance rather than rhyme between "his" and "eyes"—these are bold surprises, even if in the service of an imaginary moment which is not bold at all: two lovers, long separated, are quietly together at last. The failure of perfect rhyme between "walls" and "call" in the first stanza is of another order. The silver call is singular, as it must be, and therefore clear and slender, as the walls are not. So, in the third stanza, the refusal of "adamant" to rhyme with "hair" expresses its implacable hardness. So, in the fourth stanza, "citadel" and "crease" rebel against the law that they repeat the civil music of "veil" and "face." The sound of the long *a* drops suddenly to the sound of short *e* in "every" and "mesh" as well as in "citadel"; and the last line converts it altogether, in the harsh word "dragons" and in the "crease" through which their malevolence can be imagined to hiss. The gentle alliteration in "limit," "like," and "lady" is also gone out of our ears, along with any sense of proportion we might have had permitting us to inquire whether a mesh could ever be a citadel, or dragons inhabit creases.

The stanza looks like a ballad stanza, and yet is not. The first line is short, like the second and fourth; only the third has four feet. The third line in every case is long and full; and each time this has a different function. The drawn-out, lucid silver call; the leisurely taking recompense; the cobweb announcing that it is not silk but adamant, and saying so with special emphasis on the last syllable of that mighty word; the hoarse voice issuing from each mesh of the veil, proclaiming itself, astonishingly and yet convincingly, to be a medieval stronghold —each of these third lines works its own magic, assisting the poem of which it is a part to become one of the most potent in any tongue.

AUSTIN WARREN (1899–) as scholar and critic has a range of interests both rich and diverse. Educated at Wesleyan, Harvard, and Princeton, since 1949 he has been professor of English at the University of Michigan. Among his many books and essays, *Richard Crashaw* (1939), *Theory of Literature* (with René Wellek, 1948), *Rage for Order* (1948), and *New England Saints* (1956) are outstanding. His 1957 essay-review of Thomas H. Johnson's *The Poems of Emily Dickinson* (1955) surveys clearly the major Dickinsonian interests as they had emerged by mid-twentieth century: the critical relevance of her biography, the achievement of definitive texts, the character and range of her themes, and her general significance in American literature and culture.

Emily Dickinson *

AUSTIN WARREN

I

Thomas Johnson has produced what has long been desired—a carefully edited and annotated *complete* text of Emily Dickinson's poems.

It fills three large volumes. The format seems, and is, incongruous

From *Sewanee Review*, LXV (Autumn, 1957), 565–86

with the nature of Emily's poems, so characteristically and richly short —and, as Johnson remarks, always in revision shortened, not lengthened.

This is not the edition in which to enjoy Emily. I recall the pleasure of reading her in the slender gray volumes of the 1890's. For pleasure, as for edification, Emily should not be read in big tomes, or much of her at a time. Johnson prints 1775 poems. I felt the immediate need to reduce them to three hundred or less. Many of her poems are exercises, or autobiographical notes, or letters in verse, or occasional verses. There are poems which are coy or cute; others which are romantically melodramatic.

But the business of the scholar is to publish all the "literary remains," to establish a correct text, to elucidate obscure words or references,—whenever possible, by the citation of apposite passages from his writer's other poems or prose (in Emily's case, there are her own brilliant letters); to make possible the study of a poet's development by fixing, with what precision may be possible, the dates of composition.

These tasks of an editor Johnson has carefully and satisfactorily fulfilled. To do them, it was necessary to have access to Emily Dickinson's original manuscripts,—her penciled jottings, her worksheets and the little stitched books or "packets" into which at intervals she collected her final or semi-final versions. These "packet" versions provide—when, as for the vast majority of the poems, they are available—the authoritative text, that of the author's most considered judgment.

In the past, Emily Dickinson suffered from two sets of editors. Mrs. Todd could decipher Emily's handwriting; but she and Colonel Higginson, the minor poet and man of letters who became Emily's half-reluctant mentor, felt the need to amend so far as they could Emily's deviations from normal educated usage—her provincial words, her use of the subjunctive in subordinate clauses, her "inaccurate" rhymes. Emily's niece, Mme. Bianchi, less skilled at the handwriting, latterly difficult, was given to exploiting her aunt's strangeness. It used to be thought that Mme. Bianchi, who so shrewdly "discovered" further poems at marketable season, perhaps constructed some of the weaker ones; but this conjecture is tacitly refuted by a study of the originals.

In "Notes on the Present Text," Johnson exhibits his fidelity to

---

* *The Poems of Emily Dickinson. Including variant readings critically compared with all known manuscripts.* Edited by Thomas H. Johnson. The Belknap Press of Harvard University Press, 1955. 3 vols.

Emily's spelling (some of it, like "Febuary," is notation of rural New England speech habits), her capitalization, and her punctuation. The latter are capricious. She inclines to capitalize nouns (after the fashion of Carlyle and the German language); her capitalization of adjectives cannot be reduced to principle. The dash is almost her exclusive mark of punctuation, exceeding much the latitude allowed to nineteenth century women. It sometimes stands for the comma, sometimes indicates the pause of anticipation or suspense, sometimes might be described as equivalent to the phrasing marks of music. But categories do not suffice. Take No. 344, for example:

'Twas the old—road—through pain—
That unfrequented—one—
With many a turn—and thorn—
That stops—at Heaven—

This—was the Town—she passed—
There—where she—rested—last—
Then—stepped more fast—
The little tracks—close prest—

The dashes before "through pain," "and thorn," "at heaven," and "last" mark the pauses of suspense and anticipation. Those separating off "That unfrequented one," an appositive, might, in current use, be commas or dashes. Those at the ends of lines 5 and 6 stand for commas or semicolons. But what of the dashes separating "old" and "road," or "unfrequented" and "one," or "This" and "was," "There" and "where"? These seem designed to phrase: in the first two instances, indicating stress on both the adjective and the noun, in the last two, giving the stress of italics to "This" and "There"; probably the enclosure of "rested" is also to ensure its being stressed. The dash in the eighth line seems intended to emphasize the seeming contradiction between "little" and "close prest."

I analyze this specimen to show both the oddity of Emily's pointing and also the difficulty of repunctuating it in any fashion which does not constitute an interpretation. Johnson says, "Quite properly such 'punctuation' can be omitted in later editions, and the spelling and capitalization regularized, as surely she would have expected had the poems been published in her lifetime." Editions for general reading should undoubtedly "regularize"; but how to treat Emily's punctuation is the difficult point. Apart from her periods, the overall effect of the dashes is either to reproduce pauses in her own reading of the poems or to render the clauses and phrases a fluidity of transition lost by a rigid system. The best method I can propose is to omit—after the fashion of some contemporary poetry—all punctuation, or all save that of the period: a method which would not, in any case I can summon up, obscure the comprehension of her poetry.

The poems, through no. 1648, are now presented in a chronological arrangement—the dating based partly on allusions to contemporary events, partly on the dates of letters in which they were enclosed, partly on the changes in Emily's handwriting (on which an "expert" contributes a special essay), partly on the order of the "packets" in which the final versions were placed, from the earliest packet, assembled in 1858, to the latest in 1872.

The packet poems constitute two-thirds of her poetry. Nos. 1649–1775 Johnson does not attempt to date. These poems, for which no autograph copies exist, are printed from transcripts, chiefly those made by Emily's sister-in-law. Though properly put together, at the end of Vol. III, their authenticity can scarcely be doubted. They include a few of Emily Dickinson's snake poems and "Elysium is as far as to/The very nearest Room."

Long ago I worked out my own chart of Emily's poetic development, setting off as "early" the conventional and sentimental pieces, and using as my tests for the mature poems the increasing substitution for rhyme of assonance and consonance and the increasing freshness and precision of language. I postulated a consistency of method: expected the poems systematically to grow more Dickinsonian. Having achieved her manner, her best style, she could not, I supposed, have turned back to styles not so definitely hers.

This theory was too neat. Emily did, to the end, "look back." Unlike Mozart and Beethoven and Hopkins and James, she had no "late manner" so integrally held that she could not, in conscience, deviate therefrom.

This inconsistency was certainly helped by her ambiguous character of being a poet yet not a publishing poet. She never sharply differentiated between poetry and occasional verse and prose. The prose of her letters is so metonymic and metaphoric and cryptic as to be always the prose of a poet and thus to admit the intercalation of verse written as prose.

In 1860, Emily wrote "If I shouldn't be alive/When the Robins come" with its admirable "trying/With my granite Lip" and "How many times these low feet staggered/Only the soldered mouth can tell"; but in the same year she wrote the sentimental piece with its bit of Scots—probably represented for her by Burns—"Poor little Heart!/Did they forget thee?/Then dinna care!" and the balladic repetition of "That scalds me now—that scalds me now" of no. 193. In 1861, she wrote "There's a certain slant of light" but also "Why—do they shut me out of heaven"—one of her "little girl" pieces. And in "about 1865" she wrote the quatrain, of which I italicize some words:

> To help our *Bleaker* Parts
> *Salubrious* Hours are given
> Which if they do not fit for Earth
> *Drill silently* for Heaven—

She had written "Arrange the heart" and rejected it for "Drill silently"—an improvement both in sparing the "heart" and in giving the double-sensed *drill* (the martial discipline; the carpenter's tool if not then the dentist's also). Yet at the same time she wrote "Let down the Bars, Oh Death," a tritely sentimental sheep-and-shepherd poem.

Emily added to her styles without subtracting; and in maturity she wrote a new kind of poetry without relinquishing the liberty of slipping back into her earlier modes.

II

It used to be said of Emerson that his "bad" rhymes were due to a deficient ear—a theory once and for all disproved by the publication, in the first volume of Rusk's *Letters,* of the earliest poems of Emerson, written in perfectly accurate heroic couplets. Even the early Whitman could rhyme and meter acceptably. And Emily's first known verses, written in the early 1850's, demonstrate likewise that her subsequent deviation was purposed. Her "Valentine" poem faithfully rhymes "swain" and "twain," "air" and "fair." But, having said that, I have to add that none of them would have become known as poets for these "correct" productions. By intuition, and by relatively conscious theorizing, they had to create new kinds of poetry.

Like Whitman, Emily took off from Emerson, whose *Poems* and *Essays* she owned and knew; but Whitman took off from Emerson's theory of the poet and his poetic and rhetorical essays; Emily, from Emerson's own practice as a poet: his short-lined rhyming; his gnomic quatrains and gnomic short poems like "Brahma"; his "Hamatreya."

This lineage from Emerson was blended with another lineage—that of the hymnal. Several times she quotes Isaac Watts' hymn beginning, "There is a land of pure delight":

> Could we but climb where Moses stood
> And view the landscape o'er,
> Nor Jordan's stream, nor death's cold flood
> Should fright us from the shore;

and the stanza, with its alternating 4 and 3, remains one of her metrical favorites. She creates a counterpoint or descant on Watts, relaxing the rhyming of lines 1 and 3 and the personalizing of Watts' congregational pieces:

> 'Tis not that Dying hurts us so—
> 'Tis Living—hurts us more—
> But Dying—is a different way—
> A Kind behind the Door—

Short meter, long meter, common meter—the standard hymn stanzas—are her mold, not to break but to render pliant.

Emily's language is her own mixture of provincialisms, standard speech of her time, the concrete and the abstract, the words of young people and the theological words of orthodox preachers (e.g., infinite). Her use of language is almost unfailingly meditated and precise. Worksheet drafts for a few of her poems provide the list of alternatives from which she chose. In the poem on the Bible (no. 1545), the epithet finally elected—"warbling"—was chosen out of these possible dissyllables: "typic, hearty, bonnie, breathless, spacious, tropic, warbling, winning, mellow." None of these dissyllables seems inevitable; but warbling—the unpremeditated singing of a bird or a rustic—seems the best candidate. Of a clergyman ("He preached upon 'Breadth' till it argued him narrow") she asserts satirically that Jesus would not know how to "meet so *enabled* a man," choosing her epithet from "learned, religious, accomplished, discerning, accoutred, established, conclusive." Emily needs a trisyllabic word: but she certainly also distinguished it from "able": to "enable" is legally, as by authority, to make one what, by nature, he is *not:* it suggests the pretentiousness of borrowed righteousness or of learning extraneous to the personality.

Previous editions have printed the last stanza of "I never saw a Moor" as

> I never spoke with God,
> Nor visited in heaven;
> Yet certain am I of the spot
> As if the chart were given.

Johnson reads, for the conventional "chart," the word "checks," in the colloquial sense of railroad tickets, quoting in adequate support Emily's prose, "My assurance of existence of Heaven is as great as though, having surrendered my checks to the conductor, I knew that I had arrived there." In no. 391, "A Visitor in Marl," Mme. Bianchi's *Unpublished Poems* reads "March" for "Marl." Neither here nor when, in a note, he cites Emily's writing of her dead father as "lying in Marl," does Johnson gloss this unusual but accurate word. The "Visitor" is Death; and the word "Marl" means an earthy, crumbling deposit chiefly of clay, mixed with calcium carbonate, or earth (in the sense of clay): it means the cadaver. These two examples will illustrate that Emily used the words she meant, and the gain of their restoration.

III

As Allen Tate long ago remarked, Emily stands, among New Englanders, between Emerson and Hawthorne,—of whom she wrote that he "entices—appalls." Her rearing was in Trinitarian Congregationalism—often in New England villages referred to as—in contrast to Unitarian heresy—the Orthodox Church. Unlike the rest of her family (some of whom capitulated early, some later), Emily never "joined the church," never would fix the content of her belief; but she knew what her neighbors and her pastor believed, and—like Emerson in his attacks on Harvard College—had the personal comfort and poetic license of cherishing favorite scepticisms without supposing that they would undermine, and hence render impossible of attack, the solid faith of others, the solid force of institutions. She lacks Hawthorne's sense of sin, and isolation for privacy is hardly an evil to her; the analogy to Hawthorne lies rather in her obsession with death and futurity,—still more the sense of mystery: as in the remark (put on the lips of Holgrave), "I begin to suspect that a man's bewilderment is the measure of his wisdom." Her deepest poems are metaphysical or tragic; her mode of vision symbolist—thinking in analogies. Emerson (whose *Essays* an early "tutor" gave her) may have flexed her mind, encouraged her speculations and her questionings of orthodoxy; but her mythology remains—what Hawthorne's was and Emerson's never—Biblical and Trinitarian. She is a rebel—but not, like Emerson, a schismatic.

A third ancestor comes often to my mind,—Sir Thomas Browne, a writer dear to the 19th century New Englanders, especially to the Concord men, and known and cited by Emily. "For prose," she wrote Colonel Higginson, she had "Mr. Ruskin, Sir Thomas Browne, and the *Revelations*." These are very special kinds of prose certainly; and I don't hesitate to say that Emily's poetic style is not only that of some Emerson poems ("The Humble Bee," "Hamatreya," "Mithridates," "Days") but that of Browne's *Religio* and *Christian Morals*. Her world view is the Brunonian sense of the natural world, so full of curious objects in the eyes of most men—though, as Browne remarks, he doesn't know how we can call the toad ugly when it was made by the express design of God to assume that shape. Nor is Emily going to simplify the complexity of a God who made the bat. Of the bat, Emily writes (1575):

> Deputed from what Firmament—
> Of what Astute Abode—
> Empowered with what Malignity
> Auspiciously withheld—
>
> To his adroit Creator
> Ascribe no less the praise—
> Beneficent, believe me,
> His Eccentricities—

Browne heaps up technical difficulties which beset the acceptance of the Bible and orthodox theology: he delights to list such difficulties as occasioned Bishop Colenso (of Arnoldian memory) the loss of his faith—the statistics of an Ark capable of holding all the creatures said to have entered.

Emily's most characteristic difficulties are with the morals of the Bible, especially of the Old Testament—which in her time and place had not been subjected to the "Higher Criticism." She "knew her Bible" well, the total Bible: it was her prime mythology. She neither rejects nor accepts it without question and reservation. Its histories are rich and plausible human documents; its doctrinal books, like St. Paul's epistles, are testimonials for consideration, propose questions and speculations for her theological sensibility to ponder. She would have been shocked equally by having the Bible treated as negligible, or even as "literature," or by accepting it as an infallible silencer of speculation.

Her famous "The Bible is an antique volume" was originally written for her nephew Ned and given the title, "Diagnosis of the Bible, by a Boy"; but the boy was not alien to the woman who understood his boredom and his bafflement: the final version is hers.

The Bible is an antique Volume—
Written by faded Men
At the suggestion of Holy Spectres—
Subjects—Bethlehem—
Eden—the ancient Homestead—
Satan—the Brigadier—
Judas—the Great Defaulter—
David—the Troubadour—
Sin—a distinguished Precipice
Others must resist—
Boys that "believe" are very lonesome—
Other Boys are "lost"—
Had but the Tale a warbling Teller—
All the Boys would come—
Orpheus' Sermon captivated—
It did not condemn—

The sympathy with Satan and Judas is for rebels against laws they don't understand, or it comes from a feeling that, since sin must needs come into the world, and since the Crucifixion was foretold and necessary, we should not be too hard on the unhappy perpetrators. The mushroom is a "Judas Iscariot" to the rest of Nature. Elsewhere (no. 120) she remarks that there are shocking instances of God's injustice: "Moses wasn't fairly used; Ananias wasn't." But it's temerarious to make such protestations. The same God who made the Lamb made the Lion: He who provided good and suffers the little ones to come unto Him also permits sin and evil—that "where Sin abounded, Grace may much more abound."

There have been times in which the pious felt the need to defend God, to prop Him up—as though it were our business to support the Rock and Word and Comforter. Emily is too orthodox—i.e., too inclusive—to forget that behind God the Son, Himself sturdy, is God the Father, the Creator of all things and the Abyss of Godhead, unexhausted by what His creatures understand of His ways: moving in a mysterious way His wonders to perform, and best known not defining Him.

Yet in allowing for God's ways not being our ways we mustn't use language equivocally but apply our humanly highest standards. Writing on Abraham, Isaac, and God (no. 1317), Emily doesn't hesitate to identify God with "tyranny" and to find the moral of the averted human sacrifice in the reflection that, even with a "Mastiff," "Manners may prevail." The existence of a God Emily never doubts. The "fop, the Carp, the Atheist" value the present moment, yet "their commuted feet The Torrents of Eternity/Do all but inundate."

The problem of Belief is ever with her.

> The abdication of Belief
> Makes the Behavior small—
> Better an ignis fatuus
> Than no illume at all—

"Belief, it does not fit so/When altered frequently." There must be a Heaven because there certainly are saints on earth; and sanctity argues its survival. But how prove a sky to a mole? *"Too much of proof affronts Belief."* The turtle won't try to demonstrate to us that he can move—but, when we have turned our backs, he does. "That oblique Belief which we call conjecture"—is the attempt to guess what Heaven is like—to picture "What eye hath not seen"—what the "mansions" of Heaven look like. Emily speculates on the state of the dead: whether they know what is happening to us or are too removed; or whether, on the contrary, they are nearer to us for the absence of their bodies. But these are conjectures unanswered by Scriptures. Straight belief is uncircumstantial; content to affirm what it cannot map or delineate. And, for Emily, belief is straight.

IV

I heartily wish that conjecture about Emily's lovers might cease as unprofitable. Of course her poems are all "fragments of a great confession": of course she wrote out of her life, her life on various levels.

But books on who her "lover" was turn attention from the poems to the poet, and substitute detective work for criticism. Her readers of the 1890's did not require to know what "who" or "whos" gave her insight into love and renunciation, nor need we.

It is when the best of philosophers make blunders not inherent in their systems but extraneous to it—when Berkeley, in his neo-Platonic *Siris,* advocates the panacea of tar water,—that we legitimately seek a biographical explanation. And when a good poet writes inferior poems we are concerned with the reason for the badness, in order to leave, inviolate, the goodness of the other poems. But the "goodness" is not so to be explained.

One must distinguish biography from literary biography, distinguish between the study of the empirical person who wrote poems and that undeniable "personality" present in poems which makes them recognizable as written by the same person. What is biographically peculiar to the empirical person is not relevant to the "good poems," those intelligible to and valued by competent readers, which are elucidatory of our own experiences. To be sure, literary criticism can scarcely avoid a psychology of types—as it cannot dispense with a knowledge of the culture in which a poet was reared,—and, certainly, cannot lack a close intimacy with the state of the language from which the poet makes artfully expressive deviations. But biographical studies and culture-history—for those who practice them, ends in themselves—are to be used by a critic with caution and delicacy. Scholarship as such restricts a great poet to her own time, place, and empirical self. Criticism must delicately "clear" the poems for present use and evaluation—show what is for our time, or, more grandiosely, what is for all times.

I make these commonplaces of neoclassical and contemporary criticism, conscious that, in what immediately follows, I may seem to diverge from them. There is a "lion in the way" of contemporary readers of Emily—the lion of biography. It has proved impossible not to pursue, to an extent, the facts gathered and the speculations offered by those who have sought to attach Emily's power as a poet of love and death to some single love and renunciation.

A widely informed and sensible work is Mrs. Bingham's *Emily Dickinson's Home: Letters of Edward Dickinson and His Family, with Documentation and Comment* (1955), which, as commentary, combines social history with family biography: I would commend specifically the chapters, "The New England Way," "Recreation," "Funerals and Fears," "Dickinson 'Difference.'" The daughter of Mrs. Todd, Emily's first editor, takes in her stride the loves, real or imaginary; and she cites the testimony of Emily's brother, William Austin. A year his sister's senior, Austin was a collector of paintings and enamoured of shrubs, the honorable assumptor of his father's responsibilities to college, town, and family, yet a more flexible and troubled character. Austin, to whom, while he was away from Amherst, Emily wrote copious letters, who, in manhood, lived in the house next door in troubled marriage with "Sister Sue," who was the affectionate brother, seems to me the most competent judge of his sister's personality. What was his judgment of the "lovers"? Asked, after Emily's death, the direct question, "Did she fall in love with the Rev. Mr. Wadsworth?" he thought not. He said that "at different times" Emily "had been devoted to several men." He even went so far as to maintain that she had been several times in love, in her own way. But he denied that because of her devotion to any one man she forsook all others. Emily "reached out eagerly, fervently even, toward anybody who lighted the spark ..."

Wadsworth certainly mattered to Emily; and the time of his removal from Philadelphia to San Francisco, a distance prohibitive of prompt access to him by letter, coincides with significant alterations in her life and poetry. Yet this was a fantasy of love, constructed about a man whom she scarcely knew and who was doubtless never aware of her idealization. Her sense for what is real always won out over whatever presented attractive fantasy.

There were, I think, many loves in Emily's life, loves of varying kinds and durations. There were infatuations with Sister Sue and Kate Anthon, perhaps with Helen Hunt Jackson—loves "natural" enough and permitted by 19th century standards. There was a succession of males to whom she attached her devotion: some of them, like Gould, Humphrey, and Newton, and Colonel Higginson, her "teachers"; some more awesome characters.

Her father, Edward Dickinson, was a kind of version of God the Father: stern and implacable, yet a tower and rock of strength; mysterious in his ways, but doubtless always acting for the best; the man of moral rigidity who was none the less capable of ringing the church bell as for a fire so that his neighbors emerge from their houses to share a magnificent display of northern lights. Her feeling for her father was, I should guess, dominant. Her "poems about God," the "Papa in Heaven," are little girl compounds of pertness and humility addressed to a powerful and puzzling big man, to Admirable Omnipotence. Her figures psychically distant and impressive—Father, the Rev. Mr. Wadsworth, Mr. Bowles, the Editor of the *Springfield Republican,* were all "Fathers"; and God she made in their image and likeness.

It seems archetypally true of Emily to say that God was her Lover. The God whom she reverenced was not the Son, the "Paragon of Chivalry," like her brother Austin and indeed herself, but God the Father, the Lover at once infinitely attractive and infinitely awesome, one partly revealed by the Son and His nature, but only partly revealed; finally, the unattainable God. "He who loves God must not expect to be loved in return."

All of Emily's lovers were unattainable: either members of her family or women or married men; and they were doubtless loved, in her way, precisely because they were unattainable,—did not, could not, expose, even to herself, the nature of her dedication.

Emily's life is no riddle. New England had—and has—many maiden ladies like her, and many widows who are like maiden ladies. There are many who have loved unsuccessfully or insuitably—whom fear or pride have kept from the married state; many who have loved "above them," could love in no other way, and who prefer singleness to some democratic union. The father who prefers his daughters not to marry, who needs them at home with him, is matched by the daughter so filial as to prefer the tried arrangement. There is nothing monstrous—or even necessarily thwarted or blighted—about such women. They have their friends and their duties; they can nurture their own sensibilities and spiritualities—grow sharper in consciousness for their economy.

Many gradually withdraw from the world as Emily did. The circumference shrinks as friends die or depart; the pattern of life becomes more rigid. But the withdrawal can be gain if there is something to withdraw to. Most spinsters have, like Emily, their brand of humor, their mode of ritual—perhaps even their habitual way of dressing; but what differentiates Emily is that she had her poetry. She need not avert or circumvent woe save by the strategem of poetry. She need not keep her grief to herself; she could give it to consciousness and to paper—could face it by naming it.

Many richnesses sustained Emily—among them her sense of "degree," of status, of family. Of "degree" she was positively and negatively aware. When she wasn't a little girl, to be fed a crumb, she was a Queen or an Empress, jewelled and triumphant on a throne. At once no man was "good enough" for her to marry, and those higher than she were so much higher as to seem out of reach or, in fantasy, grandly, by their election, to lift her to equality.

She was a Dickinson, the daughter of a "Squire," whose father had been one of the founders of Amherst College, whose brother was, if epigone, the honorable successor to greatness. The bonds between her and her family were such as to sustain her pride.

She was not, however she might seem to Boston, a rural poetess or spinster, but a princess. When Colonel Higginson proposed visits to Boston, access to her intellectual and literary "peers" (Julia Ward Howe, for example, or Mrs. Sargent and her monthly convenings of paper-readers and polite disputants), Emily could not be moved from Amherst. She never came to Higginson: he, and other professed admirers, had to come to her, to her home, where she could set the tone and dictate the ritual. Emerson might leave Concord for the Saturday Club; like Thoreau, Emily stayed at home.

It has often been regretted that she did not, like Whitman, tender her poems to Emerson's sympathetic inspection rather than to Higginson's mixture of admiration and critical gentility; but Emerson, despite his elegant courtesy, his mode of listening to others, could not at once be heeded—and dismissed. Emerson was polished "granite"—a master, like Emily herself, and (unlike her chosen mentors) a master in a domain too closely impinging on her own. In reputation "above" her, she was a poet-in-verse such as he but adumbrated. He could not serve in the convenient capacity of Higginson nor incite the terror of forbidden presences.

How perceptive, how shrewd to estimate those who would serve, was this New England spinster. She seized upon what she needed, but seizure sufficed: she had no taste for neighbors.

V

After the fashion of nineteenth century anthologies like Bryant's *Family Library of Poetry and Song* and Emerson's *Parnassus,* Emily's poems were first published under the headings, "Life," "Nature," "Love," and "Time and Eternity." But these categories are far from being mutually exclusive; indeed, they cannot be separated in any good poet or verse, and are not in Emily and Emily's,—for a poet thinks analogically, thinks in terms of the interaction and interpenetration of these or any other spheres of being.

Nature, to Emily, is "Animated." She anthropomorphizes: bobolink, butterfly, rat, and the snake—no stranger to us, doubtless, than our fellows, whom, in turn, we metamorphose from the creatures. Inanimate Nature is also animate, like animal or person or ghostly presence.

An awful Tempest mashed the air—
The clouds were gaunt, and few—
A Black—as of a Spectre's Cloak
Hid Heaven and Earth from view.

Even the machine—the railroad train—is Animated Nature in the poem, one of a brilliant series in which, as in the Old English Riddle Poems, the object is characterized but never named, conceptualized. Her train is a mythological beast which first, catlike, *laps* the miles and *licks* the valleys up and which ends, horselike, by *neighing* and *stopping,* "docile and omnipotent/At its own stable door."

What moves is living; but death is immobile, and so are its approximations—loss, departures, removals.

Superficially, to be sure, Emily is in the line of those village versifiers whose function was to elegize the dead in broadside or for incision on slate or marble gravestones; and many of her poems were either composed, or later made to serve, as tributes to her deceased relatives, friends, Amherst acquaintances, the distant admired (Charlotte Brontë and George Eliot). Then, too, she was reared in a period in which poets like Poe, Bryant (who celebrated death from "Thanatopsis" till his own), anthologies like Cheever's *Poets of America,* and newspaper poems, often cut out and preserved in scrapbooks, made the "topic" appear particularly suited to verse. The frequency with which mortuary accounts appeared in her newspaper, the Springfield *Republican,* prompted Emily to ask a friend in 1853: "Who writes those funny accidents, where railroads meet each other unexpectedly, and gentlemen in factories get their heads cut off quite informally?" It was Amherst custom, as it was elsewhere in New England, to visit cemeteries on Sunday afternoons. The local graveyard adjoined the Dickinson orchard on Pleasant Street; and, during her youth, funeral processions passed by the Dickinson house.

These circumstances supply a tradition and mollify, if not remove, suspicion of Emily's morbidity. But, if they elucidate, they do not explain Emily's death poems, which are unlike Poe's and unlike Bryant's.

To the most cursory scanner, Emily was "much obsessed by Death." "Goings away," departures, whether to geographic distances or by felt disloyalties, spacial and psychic separations, absences from us, all disjunctions, can be felt, and were, by Emily, as deaths. In a rather usual pattern of reaction, she wrote her Death poems with a quality of magnitude almost proportioned to, for her, the unimportance of the intimated "person in mind,"—the *occasion* for a poem, not its motive or momentum.

Emily's "white election," we know, began around the year 1862. This "white election": could it not have been Emily's acceptance of Death, her suicide without suicide? What "facts" are supposed to explain the "problem of Emily" point to some one, a Person unacknowledgeable to her consciousness. Her poems suggest compelled flights from impending, threatening consciousness of that person or persons.

How angry we feel when one towards whom we had felt, or protested we did, dies on us. He or she has up and left us. Ashamed of anger towards the "loved dead"—or those loved who have separated from us, one denies the feeling. Emily's "white election" is not wholly devoid of moral blackmail, consequent guilts—rich pasture for poetry.

The poems about death are ranging in kind and tone. One says that Emily's poems about death are sometimes written from the point of view of the observer; in others, she is witnessing her own death by anticipation ("You'll be sorry when I'm dead" or "I want to die"); in others she is contemplating present destitution by loss ("My life closed twice before its close"). The poems don't have to be in the first person to be self-regarding.

> On such a night, or such a night,
> Would anybody care
> If such a little figure
> Slipped quiet from its chair—

and " 'Twas the old—road—through pain" and the other poems about the death of a little girl seem, unavoidably, Emily in such postures, quite as much as "If I shouldn't be alive . . ."

Of all the poems about death one is temerarious in distinguishing the observed from the imagined or fictive. "Looking at Death, is Dying" (281) is a maxim to be attended—even though it occurs in a poem not about death but about loss. How can one write about death without having experienced it? For whom the bell tolls, it tolls for the onlooker and is his *memento mori.*

The dead are variously conceived of,—sometimes as in their graves, quiet despite the bustle of the day and of history ("How many times these low feet staggered," "Safe in their alabaster chambers"). "I'm sorry for the dead today," light in tone, lightly pities the sleeping farmers and their wives who "rest" while the festival of haying goes on in the village about them. In another poem, the grave is a cottage where a girl plays at "Keeping house" and prepares "marble tea." And the gravestone is a kind of death-mask for the dead beneath it: it tries to thank those who gave the robin a "memorial crumb," and tries with "granite lip."

Perhaps the most brilliant of the death-in-death poems is "A clock stopped—/Not the Mantel's," a masterpiece in the employment of a conceit coterminous with the poem—a definition once proposed for Donne's poem but more accurately applied to such of Emily's as this. Most of what is said fits approximately both sides of the equation; and that intellectual work which is the conceit serves, as we know, to distance the poem.

Like a train, a clock may be felt near to animate. In fable, a clock stops when its owner dies; at any event, it measures the clock-time by which men live. The Doctor is a "Shopman," a clock-repairer; but he cannot set the heart's pendulum to swinging again. To the dead, hours, and minutes and "Seconds," are alike now meaningless. They are meaningless compared with the "Decades"—more than the meter can justify this understatement for "centuries"—the "decades of Arrogance" which separate "Dial life" from the "Degreeless Noon" of Eternity. The "Trinket," the diminutively precious object, has gained the accrual of "awe"; and the onlooker feels the "arrogance" of the dead—their unconcern for us.

This poem appears to take the stance of the onlooker; but does it? It can well be argued that the poet imagines herself at the lofty distance of death, envisages how those others will feel as they watch and witness. In a poem like this the distinction between the imagined and the imaginer becomes impossible to fix. In Emily's poems, the referent and its metaphoric referend are often difficult to distinguish.

"There's a certain slant of light" is a poem ostensibly about winter afternoons with their "Heavenly Hurt" and their "Seal Despair"; when that winter light goes, " 'tis like the Distance/On the look of Death." In this poem "Death" is a metaphor for winter light and at the same time winter light is a metaphor for death: one inclines to say, preponderantly the latter. "I like a look of Agony/Because I know it's true" invokes the glazing of the eyes in death; but "Beads upon the Forehead" are invoked by "Anguish"; and the death is not the death of the dead but of the living. "A *wounded* Deer—leaps highest" in the "Ecstasy of *death";* yet the next metaphors, the *"smitten* rock" and the "trampled steel" are not death but, by anthropomorphic transfer, versions of that present anguish of which mirth is the cautious "Mail."

"It can't be Dying! It's too Rouge—/The Dead shall go in White" (no. 221) is a poem ostensibly about a sunset, a traditional symbol for death; but, by the familiar figure of suggesting by denying, she has occasion to speak of a kind of death. The reference to white suggests Emily's own habitual garb from this time on. In the Orient, as she may have known, white is the color of lovers who have come through great tribulation and washed their robes (cf. no. 325; Revelation 7:14) and as the color of her "blameless mystery"—perhaps in contrast to the blame-suspect black veil of Hawthorne's clergyman. White is the color for her kind of death-in-life; and the poem seems dynamized by it, with the sunset metaphor.

Suggestion by negation is most powerfully used in "It was not Death, for I stood up," a poem about death-in-life. The state deanimizes the self.

> The Figures I have seen
> Set orderly, for Burial
> Reminded me, of mine—
>
> As if my life were shaven,
> And fitted to a frame,
> And could not breathe without a key . . .

It felt like the stopping of a clock, like frost-frozen ground (deanimizing images); but most like chaos—chaos without "even a Report of Land/To justify—Despair."

These poems about despair are probably the best poems Emily ever wrote; but they cannot be taken as her total "message to the world." Reading her work does not induce despair. For herself first, and then for her readers, the very articulation of despair is effectual movement towards its dispelling. The autonomy of Nature and the "creatures" constantly arouses her fascinated apprehension of the variety and flexibility of nature. If anger and fear paralyze, "self-reliance" has its resources unessayed without the felt need:

> If your Nerve, deny you—
> Go above your Nerve—
> He can lean against the Grave,
> If he fear to swerve—

> 'Tis so appalling—it exhilarates—
> So over Horror, it half Captivates—
> The Soul stares after it, secure—
> A Sepulchre, fears frost, no more—

Then there are Emily's poems about immortality, which she both doubted and affirmed—affirmed not only on Bible testimony but from the argument that as there are saints there must be a Heaven—as there is grandeur, it cannot finally perish. These poems are variously mythic: there is no Biblical warrant for "fleshless lovers" meeting in Heaven. Whatever Emily's personal belief—centrally, a belief in belief—her after-death poems are readily translatable into other terms. As God is the resource, within or without, which transcends the resources we thought were our limits, so eternity is a name for ultimate definitions of the total personality:

> Of all the Souls that stand create—
> I have elected—One—
> When Sense from Spirit—files away—
> And Subterfuge—is done—

The final sense of Emily's total achievement is the power of poetry to register and master experience.

CHARLES R. ANDERSON (1902–), Carolyn Donovan Professor of American Literature at Johns Hopkins University since 1957, has taught at Georgia and Duke universities, and from 1950 to 1957 was chairman of the English department at Johns Hopkins. He has published studies of Melville, and was general editor of the centennial edition of Sidney Lanier's works (1945). "Center," taken from his *Emily Dickinson's Poetry: Stairway of Surprise* (1960), like most recent criticism of the poet, assumes the fact of her greatness and concerns itself with some aspect of her genius—in this case the essential method of her poetry.

Center

CHARLES R. ANDERSON

Emily Dickinson was reasonably clear in her conception of the artist's proper goals and explicit about the integrity of her vision. Instead of trying to leap into the divine 'circumference' he must explore outward from the center of experience, content if his meanings reach their full expansion only with posterity. But how does he create, what goes on at the 'center'? This is the unanswerable question, yet one that neither poet nor critic can let alone. The ultimate mystery of poetic creation she confessed was beyond her grasp:

This is a Blossom of the Brain—
A small—italic Seed
Lodged by Design or Happening
The Spirit fructified—

Shy as the Wind of his Lodgings
Swift as a Freshet's Tongue
So of the Flower of the Soul
Its process is unknown....

The subject of her poem is the fully formed work of art, but the process of its flowering can only be expressed metaphorically. Its germ was a 'Seed,' so different from the garden variety she describes it as 'italic,' the

From Charles R. Anderson, *Emily Dickinson's Poetry: Stairway of Surprise* (New York: Holt, Rinehart and Winston, 1960), 63–76.

type used for foreign borrowings. The novelty of this adjective redeems the triteness of the seed-flower metaphor. Whether it was dropped according to some inspired design or by accident can never be known, nor whether it grew in the mind or the spirit, for what is first called a 'Blossom of the Brain' becomes in the end a 'Flower of the Soul.' So the old dilemma of the respective roles played by the intuition and the shaping power of reason is left unsolved. Its motions upward into final form are elusive as the wind and swift as floods in spring, and 'Its process is unknown.'

On one aspect of the mystery of composition she is confidently articulate, however: the psychic pressures that compelled her to expression. Through an apt metaphor she rendered her conviction in remarkably compact form:

> Essential Oils are wrung—
> The Attar from the Rose
> Is not expressed by Suns—alone—
> It is the gift of Screws—
> The General Rose decay—
> While this—in Lady's Drawer
> Make Summer, when the Lady lie
> In Spiceless Sepulchre.

The flower image buried at the heart of this poem was valuable to her because of the tradition she could count on to enrich her meaning without employing it derivatively. The rose as symbol for the transiency of life, a favorite of poets because of its obvious beauty and fragility, had filled the preceding century with popular lyrics like Richard Henry Wilde's 'My life is like the summer rose.' She was skillful in evading the hackneyed, even while exploiting it as part of her poetic strategy. The whole convention of mutability is brought into play with a single line, 'The General Rose decay,' but this is not her theme. Instead, what can be salvaged from death's decay and how it is transmuted into a new life.

Flowers are everywhere in her poetry and letters, representing life at its fullest glory. For her the perfection of flowers was the damask rose, but in spite of several attempts she could not embody her favorite in a successful poem as the direct theme. Yet the essence of this perfection furnished her a striking metaphor of the perfume of life, so adequately sustained throughout the present poem that she did not need to violate the unity of her conceit by explicit reference to her real subject, how poetry is extracted from experience. The modern Webster defines 'essence,' in its philosophical sense, as the inward nature of anything, underlying its manifestations. The edition of a century ago carried this one step further by citing Locke's distinction between nominal and real essence, the latter being 'that which makes anything to be what it is' though unknowable to the senses. And as applied to perfumes, those qualities or virtues refined from grosser matter, her Lexicon was even more helpful by calling them 'essential oils.' This provided the opening words of her poem, a sensuous image embodying the Platonic idea of essence in the rich condensation suggested by oil—superimposed on the common meaning of 'essential' as indispensable.

The second line goes on to specify this as attar of roses, one of the most costly ingredients of perfume, described in her Webster in terms of its exotic origin: 'A highly fragrant concrete obtained in India from the petals of roses.' India was a loaded word for her, typifying opulence in awesome degree, and this is certainly included in her meaning here. To a young friend getting married she sent her congratulations 'that the shortest route to India has been supremely found,' and in a poem on her own moment of love she defines it in the concluding line as 'My drop of India.' These refer to the ecstasy of love, but since she frequently equates love with poetry it becomes clear that for her India, brought into this poem by 'Attar from the Rose,' is symbolic of the heaven-on-earth that includes them both.

That perfume is merely her metaphor for poetry, rather than her real subject, seems corroborated by her apostrophe to an unnamed genius written the year before:

> This was a Poet—It is That
> Distills amazing sense
> From ordinary Meanings—
> And Attar so immense
>
> From the familiar species
> That perished by the Door—
> We wonder it was not Ourselves
> Arrested it—before— . . .

The rude accents of the first line make emphatic her equation of poetry with perfume. There are some interesting points in this poem, chiefly that although the poet's materials are 'ordinary' and 'familiar,' what he distills from them is 'amazing' and 'immense.' But this is a less effective use of the perfume metaphor, since it is limited to a statement of resemblances with only a vague suggestion of the process in the word 'distills.' The importance of the poem under consideration is that the conceit is expanded there to include her theory of how poetry comes into being. Like all essential oils, it is hard to come by. Just as attar of roses is a fragrant concrete extracted from the petals of the flower, so poetry is condensed from experience, hers being notably compact.

It takes so much of the one to make so little of the other and there is only one way, it must be 'wrung.' The process of making perfume is rendered with precision in twenty words, several of which work equally well both ways, illustrating the process of creating poetry by subtle indirection:

Essentials Oils are wrung—
The Attar from the Rose
Is not expressed by Suns alone—
It is the gift of Screws—

Poetry and perfume are not natural products 'expressed by Suns alone.' They are manufactured by man's cunning artifice. This is at the opposite pole from the theory of composition of the Transcendentalists. Emerson epitomized this concept of organicism by declaring that poems should grow like corn or melons in the sun, and Whitman boasted that he put the theory into practice. Dickinson was nearer to Poe in her emphasis on craftsmanship, but nearer to the moderns in her theory of language as the instrument by which the essential oils of poetry are 'ex-pressed.'

This word fits perfume-making exactly in its root meaning and poetry in its derived sense, to represent in words or symbolize in art. Just as the presses used on flower petals are operated by 'screws,' so the powerful forces that produce the extract called poetry are those that operate on the poet to turn the stuff of life into enduring art. There is a fine irony in her use of the word 'gift.' It functions not only in its simple sense of a present, but in its figurative meaning of 'an endowment conferred by the Author of our nature,' according to her Lexicon. Taken straight this would support the loose romanticism of her predecessors in applying the term 'gifted' to poets, but she gives it an unexpected turn. By the shock of juxtaposition, 'It is the *gift* of *Screws,*' she adds to the requirement of innate genius the felt pressures of experience and the technical disciplines self-imposed by the artist.

The second half of the poem seems to veer off on a new theme, the re-creative power possessed by the thing thus created, the life of art that goes on beyond the death of the artist. But with her the immortality of poetry is frequently a complementary idea to the process of creation, and in this poem the two parts are firmly knit by the perfume metaphor which is dominant to the end:

> The General Rose decay—
> While this—in Lady's Drawer
> Make Summer, when the Lady lie
> In Spiceless Sepulchre.

Perhaps it was her desire to emphasize the absolute truth of what she was saying that led her to the puzzling verb forms employed here, 'decay,' 'make,' 'lie.' Her usage is certainly idiosyncratic, but one may conjecture a purpose that fits with the general intention of this poem. By omitting the final *s* she was trying to get down to the basic stem of the verbs, their pure uninflected verbal quality, paring away number, mood, and even the partial limitation in time implied by the present tense. By this ruse she was seeking to escape from all particularity—of quantity, quality, even calendar—into the Absolute: rose decay, just as poet die, but perfume make summer.

One other personal reference need not remain conjectural. The attar of roses, appropriately laid away in the lady's drawer, refers to the manuscripts of this private poet preserved in a similar way. Taken out by her, both perfume and poems, their fragrance can recall the life that has been compressed into them, odor being the psychological key to remembrance. Even when poet and rose are long dead this fragrance remains with power to 'make summer' again, and summer for her is emblematic of life. 'It is art that *makes* life.' This was the passionate statement of belief by Henry James at the height of his career, and she shared with him this belief in its creative power. Once, thanking a friend for a painting of flowers, she wrote: 'Your Hollyhocks endow the House, making Art's inner Summer, never Treason to Nature's.'

The perfume of poetry recreates the calendar summer, which itself has created the rose of life, out of which perfume and poetry were first expressed. By contrast the rose-life, now decayed, lies in 'Spiceless Sepulchre,' not being an essential oil. The final line is especially felicitous and saves the poem from the near-disaster of a variant conclusion, 'In Ceaseless Rosemary,' which would have introduced a sentimental note and an alien theme, distracting attention from the immortality of poetry to that of the poet. Much more appropriately, the fragrance has left the body to be transmuted into spirit, and the process has been brought full circle. By implication one more unifying structure can be adduced. As mortality is enclosed in the tomb and perfume in its phial, so the poet's meaning is contained in the form of the poem. Because of the particular perfume chosen, this can be pushed one step further. Attar of roses, as a 'fragrant concrete,' needs no outside container. Content and form are one and the same, inseparable as in the perfect poem.

The dual theme so successfully fused here makes a link backward to all those poems concerned with the recreative power of art and forward to those concerned with the particular pressures that compelled her to create. These rather than specific events of her life were the wellsprings of her poetry, as she herself testified many times. 'You told me Mrs. Lowell was Mr. Lowell's "inspiration,"' she once wrote Higginson, for example, adding: 'What is inspiration?' The main categories of her subject matter, tallying the main divisions of this book, illustrate clearly enough what were the 'screws' that ex-pressed her poetry: an almost unbearable sensitiveness to natural beauty, the ecstasy and despair of earthly and heavenly love, a compulsion to break through appearances to ultimate realities on both sides of the grave. Fortunately there are also explicit comments on how they operate, which will be helpful in formulating her theory of the creative process.

The kind of poetry she aspired to write was the lyric of passionate intensity and intellectual power. This even led her to be attracted to inferior models at times. In the decade before her active career began, for example, she found herself much pleased with a volume of poems by Alexander Smith sent by her brother. 'They are not very coherent,' she commented, 'but there's a good deal of exquisite frensy, and some wonderful figures, as ever I met in my life.' Smith was one of the 'Spasmodic School' of poets, who created a small sensation in the 1850's but were quickly satirized for their extravagance, overwrought metaphors, lavish emotion and disjointed thought. She outgrew this taste, just as she escaped any serious influence from Elizabeth Barrett, whose passionate utterance she once admired as the very type of 'Divine Insanity,' the witchcraft that can make days step to 'Mighty Metres' and turn noon into heaven through 'very Lunacy of Light.'

Her mature aspiration was towards controlled power, violence surprised by the mind and snared in a net of words, such as she could have learned from the religious poets of the seventeenth century. Their special qualities as defined by Eliot, who rediscovered them for twentieth-century readers, sound like the qualities of her poetry as emphasized in these pages. In spite of striking parallels between her work and theirs, however, there is only slight evidence of any acquaintance with Donne, Herbert, and Vaughan, her only known favorite among the 'metaphysicals' being Sir Thomas Browne. Yet, with some possible suggestions from them she managed to recapture a similar mode largely by her own efforts. Emerson was a kindred spirit in some ways, as in his description of the ideal poet. 'Merlin's blows are strokes of fate,' he said; freeing himself from conventions, such a bard can mount to paradise by the 'stairway of surprise.' But the search for influences yields little in the case of such a burry original. A native intensity of mind and heart gave her all the power she could manage. Her chief problem was control, and what she learned of it she learned mostly in her own way.

Her awareness of the problem is revealed in the correspondence with Higginson. Even when the relation of pupil to preceptor becomes a game, one must give due weight to her reiterated concern over lack of control. There is some seriousness beneath the surface wit when she writes, 'You think my gait "spasmodic—" I am in danger— Sir— You think me "uncontrolled—" I have no Tribunal.' She is obviously spoofing when, with a new batch of poems, she asks in mock humility: 'Are these more orderly? ... I think you called me "Wayward." Will you help me improve?' But the statement tucked in between these petitions reveals clear-sighted self-criticism: 'I had no Monarch in my life, and cannot rule myself, and when I try to organize—my little Force explodes—and leaves me bare and charred.' This important pronouncement the critic would do well to bear in mind as he surveys the shelf of her writings.

One can evaluate more justly her real successes if he faces candidly the possibility that on the whole hers was a poetry of fragments. This holds not merely for the five hundred poems abandoned before reaching the stage of final drafts, but for many of the presumably finished ones. The flash of inspiration almost always ignited her poetic materials but all too frequently burned itself out before she could temper and mold them into form. A remarkable experience is afforded by merely scanning the Index of First Lines in the complete edition of her 1775 poems. A sample, with very little selection, will illustrate:

Back from the cordial grave I drag thee...
Baffled for just a day or two...
Banish air from air...
Be mine the doom...
Beauty be not caused—it is...
Beauty crowds me till I die...
Because I could not stop for death...
Before I got my eye put out...
Behind me dips eternity...
Belshazzar had a letter...

Almost without exception the reader is drawn to seek out the texts referred to by these provocative first lines, but not one in ten fulfills the brilliant promise of the opening words. It would be a mistake to discard the rest as failures. Some of the purest art has been caught in fragments, it could be argued by those who admire the notebooks of Leonardo and the sketches of Goya over their finished paintings. The student of poetry can find much that is rewarding in these notations recorded by the sensitive pencil of Emily Dickinson, even when her craft failed to match her powerful perceptions. But the critic concerned with close readings may properly adhere to the fiat placing a higher value on poems that have achieved final form.

One reason so many of her thoughts exploded before they found words lies in the very intensities she was bold enough to try to capture. The extravagance of the metaphors she used in describing her preference for the poetry of power is meaningful. 'If I read a book [and] it makes my whole body so cold no fire can ever warm me I know *that* is poetry,' she told Higginson at the time of his first visit. 'If I feel physically as if the top of my head were taken off, I know *that* is poetry. These are the only ways I know it. Is there any other way.' She knew the other ways, but the kinds of poetry they defined did not interest her. Her conventional literary friend was clearly shocked to find what an eruptive force lay beneath the quiet surface of this secluded life. It was with such as him in mind that she wrote: 'On my volcano grows the Grass,' but if one could see the fire below, it would fill him with awe.

Equally baffled her young cousins must have been to receive this account of a concert by Rubinstein: 'He makes me think of polar nights Captain Hall could tell! Going from ice to ice! What an exchange of awe!' If ordinary life and discourse could be represented by the temperate zone, only fire and ice could symbolize the higher reaches of artistic expression. 'My own Words chill and burn me,' she confessed.

This concept of violence as the only mode for giving utterance to the poet's experience of awe is rendered with some effectiveness in a poem that illuminates the problem of controlling power with form:

To pile like Thunder to its close
Then crumble grand away
While Everything created hid
This—would be Poetry—...

This is certainly the kind of poetry she tried to write. This is close to Emerson's ideal of the 'artful thunder' that 'makes the wild blood start.' There is even some hint of his theory of imitating natural forms in the thunder-clap simile. But she knew it took the control of art to keep such powerful perceptions from crumbling into fragments in the act of expression. The vast endowments needed by the artist led her, according to an earlier poem, to despair of ever being one. She could not be a painter, she says, but merely wonder how it would feel to have fingers whose celestial skill evokes 'Such sumptuous— Despair.' Not a musician, for marveling at the power of the cornet to float her off to the horizons, upborne as a balloon 'By but a lip of Metal.' Even more unattainable seemed the awful privilege of being a poet, at least the kind she aspired to in the concluding lines:

Had I the Art to stun myself
With Bolts of Melody!

All too frequently her force does explode, as in the poem under consideration. To express oneself like a thunderbolt, 'This— would be Poetry' she had begun. But in the end this powerful figure is replaced by that of fire, the burning bush; such a poet would 'consume' himself, 'For None see God and live.' Elsewhere, in reworking the Biblical account of God's apparition on Mount Sinai, she scouts Moses' boast as an improbable fable, declaring 'No man saw awe.' Out of the fragments of these poems some interesting links can be made. The poetic experience is equated with religious awe, so that ultimate perception would be like seeing God. But this is impossible, and the poet can only hope to catch a glimpse and record it in earthly forms before he is consumed. Fire and ice, volcanoes, thunder and lightning—only the most violent images drawn from nature seemed adequate for the intensities that compelled her to expression. She had moved a long way in both theory and practice from the ideal of emotion recollected in tranquility.

The central lines of the thunderbolt poem veer off on a tangential theme, equating poetry with love. As with other lyric poets, the impulse to creation came to her 'coeval' with the experience of love, she says. In a letter of 1862 she had joined them in close sequence: '*My* business is to love.... *My* business is to *sing*.' Sometimes it was the surge of ecstasy, though usually with the implication of fulfillment denied. More often it was the pain of love that wrung the poem from her, if she could find adequate controls. Once she explicitly relates the inadequacy of her form to the overmastering power of such emotions:

> Sang from the Heart, Sire,
> Dipped my Beak in it,
> If the Tune drip too much...
> Bear with the Ballad—
> Awkward—faltering—
> Death twists the strings—

She found encouragement from identifying herself with the 'Martyr Poets' who 'wrought their Pang in syllable.' And she knew that suffering and despair were the mainsprings of her art. There must be a loss or woe 'To bend the eye/Best Beauty's way.' This is also the only path to the house of awe. The contentment of a happy life is like a 'quiet Suburb,' she says; it is only through affliction that she can 'range Boundlessness,' through agony achieve 'A nearness to Tremendousness.'

Two passages in the letters, convincingly related by her biographers to the experience of love and loss, specifically name these as psychic pressures responsible for her poetry. During her first great creative outburst in the spring of 1862, she described in stricken terms what is now generally accepted as the departure out of her life of one whom she had chosen as her muse and the object of an intense spiritual adoration: 'I had a terror—since September—I could tell to none—and so I sing, as the Boy does by the Burying Ground—because I am afraid.' And referring to a much earlier friend, who had died in 1853 just after expressing belief in her poetic genius, she said: 'Death was much of Mob as I could master—then.' This seems to explain the lapse of her creativity during the next five or six years, just as the sentence following suggests in its poignant nature referents that a dawning new love was what brought her back to poetic life: 'And when far afterward—a sudden light on Orchards, or a new fashion in the wind troubled my attention—I felt a palsy, here—the Verses just relieve.' What counts for the student of her poetry is not the identification of the autobiographical experiences but the language in which these powerful emotions found expression.

The conjoining of love and death held a particular fascination for her. Despite her wavering attitude towards immortality, she was teased with the hope that fulfillment denied here might be achieved in heaven. Then there was the dark obsession with the grave itself, situated at the center and looking both ways: 'That *Bareheaded life*—under the grass,' she wrote, 'worries one like a Wasp.' This is no exploitation of horror in the manner of the Graveyard School, but a concern with death as the extinguisher of vitality. For pain and loss were not the only springs of her poetry. The intensity of her response to life was another of the compulsions that made creation necessary for her. 'I find ecstasy in living,' she told Higginson, 'the mere sense of living is joy enough.' Lest this be taken as mere sensuous rapture, she adds in a poem that this is what enables finite man to be a creator like 'The Maker of Ourselves':

> To be alive—is Power— . . .
> To be alive—and Will!
> 'Tis able as a God—

So the sequence runs from awe to love and pain, from loss to despair and death, and back again to love and the ecstasy inspired by natural beauty.

In an early poem, drunk with the joy of living, she expresses her transport in terms of a cosmic spree. Borrowing from the humorous tall tale its hyperbolic fantasy and other extravagant techniques, she writes:

> I taste a liquor never brewed—
> From tankards scooped in Pearl—

Not all the Vats upon the Rhine
Yield such an Alcohol!

The temptation can hardly be resisted to read this as a parody of Emerson's transcendental rendering of poetic inspiration in 'Bacchus,' which begins:

Bring me wine, but wine which never grew
In the belly of the grape...

It adds to the burlesque that hers is a malty brew instead of the traditional Dionysiac wine. Having repudiated the false, she proceeds to extol the true in soaring imagery:

Inebriate of Air—am I—
And Debauchee of Dew—
Reeling—thro endless summer days—
From inns of Molten Blue—

Even so Emerson describes as nourished by the 'dews of heaven' the true vines which produce the archetypal

Wine that is shed
Like the torrents of the sun
Up the horizon walls...

All nature participates in her bacchanal:

When 'Landlords' turn the drunken Bee
Out of the Foxglove's door—
When Butterflies—renounce their 'drams'—
I shall but drink the more!

At this point the poems diverge widely. Nature is brought into Emerson's revel too but in a very different way:

That I intoxicated,
And by the draught assimilated,
May float at pleasure through all natures;
The bird-language rightly spell,
And that which roses say so well.

His wine is the Plotinian 'flowing' of divine spirit. Drunk with it, the poet merges with nature, breaks through convention, annihilates time and space, and recovers his lost heaven. The 'remembering wine,' by analogy with the Platonic doctrine of 'reminiscence,' enables him once again to draw on the blue tablets 'The dancing Pleiads and eternal men,' as on the first day of creation. Dickinson declines to participate in any such inebriate visions. Her beery spree lands her in heaven too, but in a different condition. She continues to drink

Till Seraphs swing their snowy Hats—
And Saints—to windows run—
To see the little Tippler
Leaning against the—Sun—

This unorthodox scene of hurrahing in heaven, with its bold metaphor converting the sun into a celestial lamp-post, may well be a comic version of spiritual intoxication as set forth in the Book of Revelation, as has been noted. But the parallels with 'Bacchus' are even more striking. The close echoes of its language up to a climactic point and the sudden turn to an opposite conclusion seem to suggest a conscious parody of its doctrines. At any rate, neither here nor elsewhere is there any evidence that she accepted the mystical bases of Emerson's transcendental esthetic: that the poet can absorb the spirit that energizes nature and so achieve merger with the Oversoul. Parody or not, this is simply a humorous fable of the poet's inspiration, drunk with the joy of life and elevated into a very sensuous heaven.

Yet there is significant meaning to be drawn from it too. Cosmic inebriation is another deliberately extravagant metaphor to go along with thunder, fires, and volcanoes. For hypersensitivity to natural beauty was another of the pressures that produced her poetry. In a late poem she wrote:

So gay a Flower
Bereaves the Mind
As if it were a Woe—
Is Beauty an Affliction—then?
Tradition ought to know—

And in two letters near the end of her life she said, first that she lived 'In a World too full of Beauty for Peace,' and again: 'How vast is the chastisement of Beauty, given us by our Maker!' At times her reaction to beauty in nature sounds like the lyric cry of pain that had become a convention since the early nineteenth century:

> Beauty crowds me till I die
> Beauty mercy have on me
> But if I expire today
> Let it be in sight of thee—

But this has less kinship with her romantic predecessors than with Jonathan Edwards, who held that the visible universe is 'an emanation of God for the pure joy of creation, in which the creatures find their justification by yielding consent to the beauty of the whole even though it slay them.' She rejected the theological dogma implied in this thesis, for she kept God and nature sharply differentiated, even while she seized for her own purposes its esthetic doctrine.

Beauty is her name for the ecstasy with which we perceive that nature is the process of dying into immortality. She also kept man and nature separate, but as a sensitive and perceptive poet she was constantly drawn to speculate on its possible meanings for her, a subject that must be explored further in order to define how the poet makes use of nature. She herself has left a subtle aphorism defining its relation to her poetry: 'Nature is a Haunted House—but Art—a House that tries to be haunted.' This is her cryptic explanation. It can only be solved after a thorough analysis of her theory of perception, the last step in a complete formulation of her esthetics and the necessary prelude to an understanding of her nature poetry.

One of America's most distinguished men of letters, ARCHIBALD MACLEISH (1892–) has achieved many honors, among them appointment as Rede Lecturer at Cambridge University (1942), Librarian of Congress (1939–44), and Boylston Professor of Poetry at Harvard (1949–62). He was awarded the Bollingen Prize in poetry (1953), and has three times been given the Pulitzer Prize, most recently in 1958 for *J.B.*, a verse drama. His essay on Emily Dickinson is both a

personal tribute to a great poet and a summary of the firm recognition she enjoys as a poet in the 1960's.

The Private World

ARCHIBALD MACLEISH

Criticism, according to H.D.F.Kitto in the Preface to his *Greek Tragedy,* is of two kinds: "the critic may tell the reader what he so beautifully thinks about it all, or he may try to explain the form in which the literature is written." It is a pithy saying but it disposes neither of all the literature nor, unhappily, of all the critics. In addition to critics who explain the form and critics who expose the beauty of their thoughts, there are also, in our television age, critics who merely exhibit themselves. And in addition to literature which can be explained by explaining the forms, there is literature which seems to exist outside its forms or in spite of them. Emily Dickinson's poetry is an example. She is one of the most important of modern poets but her importance is not defined by the forms in which she wrote.

Prosodically considered, her forms are among the simplest of which the English language is capable—usually a three- or four-beat line handled much as similar lines are handled in the hymnals:

> A solemn thing—it was—I said—
> A Woman—white—to be—
> And wear—if God should count me fit—
> Her blameless mystery—
>
> A timid thing—to crop a life
> Into the mystic well—
> Too plummetless—that it came back—
> Eternity—until—(271) *

The pattern is varied even in the early poems:

> Our share of night to bear—
> Our share of morning—

* In the poems printed here Mr. MacLeish follows the numbers and punctuation of Thomas H. Johnson's 1955 edition of *The Poems of Emily Dickinson.* A few minor changes in the text have been made with Mr. MacLeish's permission.

From Archibald MacLeish, Louise Bogan, and Richard Wilbur, *Emily Dickinson: Three Views* (Amherst: Amherst College Press, 1960).

Our blank in bliss to fill
Our blank in scorning—

Here a star, and there a star,
Some lose their way!
Here a mist, and there a mist,
Afterwards—Day! (113)

But a protracted reading of Emily's poems leaves most of us with a metronome ticking in the ear. And even when a single poem is read alone one is apt to end with the puzzled feeling one has in Blake, that the simplicity of the prosodic form has nothing to do with the density of the sense—unless, perhaps, it has everything to do... but for a different reason.

What is true of prosodic form is true also of form otherwise considered. Poems may have visual structure as paintings have and in much the same way. The images of a poem are no less visible because they are presented directly to the imagination by the suggestion of words. We all have our own pictures of Yeats's *Byzantium,* no two of them the same, but they are pictures notwithstanding and they give the poem a sensuous shape which is at least the skeleton of its form if it is not the form itself. In Emily's poems, however, things are otherwise arranged. There are images but they are not always visible images nor are they images brought into focus by the muscles of the eye. "Polar expiation" is sensuously intelligible to a degree equalled only by the most vivid images but its print is not upon the retina. And the same thing is true in one way or another of many of her most unexpected and most effective figures—"... that white sustenance/despair," for obvious example. Like the brush strokes of a beautifully inked Chinese character, they are, but are not, pictures of the reality expressed. So the "blue and gold mistake" of Indian Summer (130). So "the Distance/On the look of Death" (258), "My Splendors are Menagerie" (290), "But dying is a different way/A kind behind the door" (335), "Amethyst remembrance" (245). She can, of course, make visible pictures when she wants to. The "Fairy Gig," which says hummingbird in the poem which begins "Within my garden rides a Bird/Upon a single wheel" (500), is as vivid as the famous little poem which makes the portrait whole:

A Route of Evanescence
With a revolving Wheel—

A Resonance of Emerald—
A Rush of Cochineal—
And every Blossom on the Bush
Adjusts its tumbled Head—
The mail from Tunis, probably,
An easy Morning's Ride—(1463)

But this marvelous image which expresses the almost invisible bird by the stir of the flowers he has touched is less characteristic of her method than that earlier poem in which men and Pleiads are revealed to the eye by their disappearance:

Members of the Invisible,
Existing, while we stare,
In Leagueless Opportunity,
O'ertakeless, as the Air—(282)

Imagery and rhythm are not, of course, the only bricks of poetic structure. Mallarmé was of the opinion that poems are made of neither but of words. But an explanation of Emily's use of words will not explain her poetry any better than an account of her metrics or her figures. That she had a passion for words we know both from her poems and from her own confession: her years of life with the lexicon. That she could master them, line after line testifies:

A Gnat's minutest Fan
Sufficient to obliterate
A *Tract* of Citizen—(422) (Author's italics)

and the marvelous duplicity of the word "interview" in the poem:

A Charm invests a face
Imperfectly beheld—
The Lady dare not lift her Veil
For fear it be dispelled—

But peers beyond her mesh—
And wishes—and denies—
Lest Interview—annul a want
That Image—satisfies—(421)

Moreover she offers again and again, as unostentatiously as though she herself set little value on it, that most arduous of all the proofs of verbal mastery in verse, the ability to survive without adjectives. She uses them so rarely to plump out a rhythm that when we come on one so used—

> But no man moved me—till the tide
> Went past my *simple* shoe— (Author's italics)

we are convinced that the meaningless word must have mysterious meaning.

But for all the instances which prove her passion for words and her skill in prompting and deploying them it is still not her words which make her poems. By modern standards—and I should say by right standards—her vocabulary is often as abstract and generalized and inert as her poems are precise and vivid. She has a little harbor full of frequently voyaging words any one of which would now be regarded as leaky enough to sink an ordinary lyric: Grace, Bliss, Balm, Eden, Calvary, Crown, Morn, Noon, Bee, Bird, Earl, Pod, Plush, Peninsula, Circumference and so on. Her poems somehow support them: she is able to persuade us to read them not as wornout generalizations, borrowed, many of them, from the hymnals from which she borrowed her metrics, but as symbols whose very banality makes them, in the innocence of her context, new. But in spite of this paradoxical triumph no one, I think, would contend that Emily's words explain Emily.

I would not undertake to deny that there *are* formal elements in her work which have more than formal significance. One of the most obvious is the freedom which embarrassed her first editors and has delighted and instructed her scholars ever since. The use of assonance, both of vowels and consonants, which liberated her from one of the more awkward inadequacies of our language, turned out, in the end, to be something more important than a means of escape. Consider what the assonance of *cool* and *still* does to the sense of the first stanza of the following poem and what the flat rhyme of *gay* and *away* does to the second:

> To make one's Toilette—after Death
> Has made the Toilette cool
> To only Taste we care to please
> Is difficult, and still—
>
> That's easier—than Braid the Hair—
> And make the Bodice gay—

When eyes that fondled it are wrenched
By Decalogues—away—(485)

But the truth is that with Emily Dickinson as with all great lyric poets the explanation of the form is a less reliable key to an understanding of the work than some of our contemporaries among the critics would like us to believe. The work of poetry, like every other work, is shaped by the living creature and no school of criticism can successfully shrug off that fundamental fact if it hopes to survive. The reading of biography is, of course, no substitute for the reading of the texts of the poems themselves, and the reading of the texts of the poems as peep holes into love affairs of one kind or another is as reprehensible as any contemptuous professor has ever called it, but nevertheless and notwithstanding, the poet is there within the poem and must be reckoned with. A poem by Donne is not a poem by Landor precisely because Landor is not Donne. And the fact that Landor is not Donne is a fact of some importance. Indeed, it is more than an important fact: it is the crucial fact in the reading of both poems.

Coleridge's great definition of poetry, it will be remembered, is cast in terms not of poetry but of the poet. And Emily Dickinson is one of the most cogent demonstrations of the reason why. The "unusual order" and the "more than usual emotion" which makes the poet in Coleridge's definition and in Emily Dickinson's work are Emily's order and Emily's emotion and could never be anyone else's. Universal in their meaning though many of her greatest poems are, they are nevertheless hers as the universality of Keats's poems is his. Her words, like the words of every true poet, have a voice—a particular voice. It is by reason of the particularity that the universality signifies. Universal truths enunciated by a universal voice would not be poetry. They would not even be interesting. (Or perhaps I should not say "even": "En Art," as LaForgue observed, "il s'agit d'être intéressant.") But perceptions of the universality of particular aspects of the human experience, when spoken truly by the particular voice that comprehends them, can be poetry. And when that particular voice is Emily Dickinson's at her most particular best they can be very great poetry indeed.

To me, therefore, it is the voice rather than the form which supplies the key to her work, or rather to what Mark Van Doren once called "the *quality* of her genius"—a quality which, he thought, might well remain a mystery forever. That quality, I think, is the quality of the voice in which she speaks—the particularity of the voice. Which means, of course, that the mystery is the mystery of the woman—but not in the ordinary sense in which those words are used together. It is not, that is to say, the mystery of the woman recluse of the house on Main Street. It is not the mystery of the girl who may or may not have met the Reverend Charles Wadsworth in Philadelphia when she was twenty-four and loved him all her life though seeing him only twice again. It is the mystery of the poet who is speaker and actor in her own poems, the poet who says:

I'm ceded—I've stopped being Theirs—
The name They dropped upon my face
With water, in the country church
Is finished using, now,
And They can put it with my Dolls,
My childhood, and the string of spools,
I've finished threading—too—

Baptized, before, without the choice,
But this time, consciously, of Grace—
Unto supremest name—
Called to my Full—The Crescent dropped—
Existence's whole Arc, filled up,
With one small Diadem.

My second Rank—too small the first—
Crowned—Crowing—on my Father's breast—
A half unconscious Queen—
But this time—Adequate—Erect,
With Will to choose, or to reject,
And I choose, just a Crown—(508)

who says:

I like a look of Agony,
Because I know it's true—
Men do not sham Convulsion,
Nor simulate, a Throe—(241)

who says:

My Triumph lasted till the Drums
Had left the Dead alone

And then I dropped my Victory
And chastened stole along
To where the finished Faces
Conclusion turned on me
And then I hated Glory
And wished myself were They.

What is to be is best descried
When it has also been—
Could Prospect taste of Retrospect
The tyrannies of Men
Were Tenderer—diviner
The Transitive toward.
A Bayonet's contrition
Is nothing to the Dead. (1227)

No one can read these poems or any of the tens of others like them without perceiving that he is not so much reading as being spoken to. There is a curious energy in the words and a tone like no other most of us have ever heard. Indeed, it is the tone rather than the words that one remembers afterwards. Which is why one comes to a poem of Emily's one has never read before as to an old friend.

But what then is the tone? How does this unforgettable voice speak to us? For one thing, and most obviously, it is a wholly spontaneous tone. There is no literary assumption of posture or pose in advance. There is no sense that a subject has been chosen—that a theme is about to be developed. Occasionally, in the nature pieces, the sunset scenes, which are so numerous in the early poems, one feels the presence of the pad of water-color paper and the mixing of the tints, but when she began to write as poet, which she did, miraculously, within a few months of her beginnings as a writer, all that awkwardness disappears. Breath is drawn and there are words that will not leave you time to watch her coming toward you. Poem after poem—more than a hundred and fifty of them—begins with the word "I," the talker's word. She is already in the poem before she begins it, as a child is already in the adventure before he finds a word to speak of it. To put it in other terms, few poets and they among the most valued—Donne comes again to mind—have written more *dramatically* than Emily Dickinson, more in the live locutions of dramatic speech, words born living on the tongue, written as though spoken. It is almost impossible to begin one of her successful poems without finishing it. The punctuation may bewilder you. The density of the thing said may defeat your understanding. But you will read on nevertheless because you will not be able to stop. Something is being *said* to *you* and you have no choice but hear.

And this is a second characteristic of the voice—that it not only speaks but speaks to *you*. We are accustomed in our time—unhappily accustomed, I think—to the poetry of the overheard soliloquy, the poetry written by the poet to himself or to a little group of the like-minded who can be counted on in advance to "understand." Poetry of this kind can create universes when the poet is Rilke but even in Rilke there is something sealed and unventilated about the creation which sooner or later stifles the birds. The subject of poetry is the human experience and its object must therefore be humanity even in a time like ours when humanity seems to prefer to limit its knowledge of the experience of life to the life the advertisers offer it. It is no excuse to a poet that humanity will not listen. It never has listened unless it was made to—and least of all, perhaps, in those two decades of the Civil War and after in which Emily Dickinson wrote.

The materialism and vulgarity of those years were not as flagrant as the materialism and vulgarity in which we live but the indifference was greater. America was immeasurably farther from Paris, and Amherst was incomparably farther from the rest of America, and in and near Amherst there were less than a dozen people to whom Emily felt she could show her poems—and only certain poems at that. But her poems, notwithstanding, were never written to herself. The voice is never a voice over-heard. It is a voice that speaks to us almost a hundred years later with such an urgency, such an immediacy, that most of us are half in love with this girl we all call by her first name, and read with scorn Colonel Higginson's description of her as a "plain, shy little person . . . without a single good feature." We prefer to remember her own voice describing her eyes—"like the sherry the guest leaves in the glass."

There is nothing more paradoxical in the whole history of poetry, to my way of thinking, than Emily Dickinson's commitment of that live voice to a private box full of pages and snippets tied together with little loops of thread. Other poets have published to the general world poems capable of speaking only to themselves or to one or two beside. Emily locked away in a chest a voice which cries to all of us of our common life and love and death and fear and wonder.

Or rather, does *not* cry. For that is a third characteristic of this unforgettable tone: that it does not clamor at us even when its words are the words of passion or of agony. This is a New England voice—it belongs to a woman who "sees New Englandly"—and it has that New England restraint which is really a self-respect which also respects others. There is a poem of Emily's which none of us can read unmoved—which moves me, I confess, so deeply that I cannot always read it. It is a poem which, in another voice, might indeed have cried aloud, but in hers is quiet. I think it is the quietness which moves me most. It begins with these six lines:

I can wade Grief—
Whole Pools of it—
I'm used to that—
But the least push of Joy
Breaks up my feet—
And I tip—drunken—(252)

One has only to consider what this might have been, written otherwise by another hand—for it would have had to be another hand. Why is it not maudlin with self-pity here? Why does it truly touch the heart and the more the more it is read? Because it is impersonal? It could scarcely be more personal. Because it is oblique?—Ironic? It is as candid as agony itself. No, because there *IS* no self-pity. Because the tone which can contain "But the least push of Joy/Breaks up my feet" is incapable of self-pity. Emily is not only the actor in this poem, she is the removed observer of the action also. When we drown in self-pity we throw ourselves into ourselves and go down. But the writer of this poem is both in it and out of it: both suffers it and sees. Which is to say that she is poet.

There is another famous poem which makes the same point:

She bore it till the simple veins
Traced azure on her hand—
Till pleading, round her quiet eyes
The purple Crayons stand.

Till Daffodils had come and gone
I cannot tell the sum,
And then she ceased to bear it—
And with the Saints sat down. (144)

Here again, as so often in her poems of death—and death is, of course, her constant theme—the margin between mawkishness and emotion is thin, so thin that another woman, living, as she lived, in constant contemplation of herself, might easily have stumbled through. But here again what saves her, and saves the poem, is the tone: "She bore it till . . ." "And then she ceased to bear it—/And with the Saints sat down." If you have shaped your mouth to say "And with the Saints sat down" you cannot very well weep for yourself or for anyone else, veins purple on the hand or not.

Anyone who will read Emily's poems straight through in their chronological order in Thomas H. Johnson's magnificent Harvard edition will feel, I think, as I do, that without her extraordinary mastery of tone her achievement would have been impossible. To write constantly of death, of grief, of despair, of agony, of fear is almost to insure the failure of art, for these emotions overwhelm the mind and art must surmount experience to master it. A morbid art is an imperfect art. Poets must learn Yeats's lesson that life is tragedy but if the tragedy turns tragic for them they will be crippled poets. Like the ancient Chinese in *Lapis Lazuli,* like our own beloved Robert Frost who has looked as long and deeply into the darkness of the world as a man well can, "their eyes, their ancient glittering eyes" must be *gay*. Emily's eyes, color of the sherry the guests leave in the glass, had that light in them:

Dust is the only Secret—
Death, the only One
You cannot find out all about
In his "native town."

Nobody knew "his Father"—
Never was a Boy—
Hadn't any playmates,
Or "Early history"—

Industrious! Laconic!
Punctual! Sedate!
Bold as a Brigand!
Stiller than a Fleet!

Builds, like a Bird, too!
Christ robs the Nest—
Robin after Robin
Smuggled to Rest! (153)

Ezra Pound, in his translation of *The Women of Trachis,* has used a curiously compounded colloquialism which depends on just such locutions to make the long agony of Herakles supportable. Emily had learned the secret almost a century before.

But it is not only agony she is able to put in a supportable light by her mastery of tone. She can do the same thing with those two opposing subjects which betray so many poets: herself and God. She sees herself as small and lost and doubtless doomed—but sees herself always, or almost always, with a saving smile which is not entirely tender:

Two full Autumns for the Squirrel
Bounteous prepared—
Nature, Hads't thou not a Berry
For thy wandering Bird? (846)

and

I was a Phoebe—nothing more—
A Phoebe—nothing less—
The little note that others dropt
I fitted into place—

I dwelt too low that any seek—
Too shy, that any blame—
A Phoebe makes a little print
Upon the Floors of Fame—(1009)

and

A Drunkard cannot meet a Cork
Without a Revery—
And so encountering a Fly
This January Day
Jamaicas of Remembrance stir
That send me reeling in—
The moderate drinker of Delight
Does not deserve the spring—...(1628)

I suppose there was never a more delicate dancing on the crumbling edge of the abyss of self-pity—that suicidal temptation of the lonely—than Emily's, but she rarely tumbles in. She sees herself in the awkward stumbling attitude and laughs.

As she laughs too, but with a child's air of innocence, at her father's Puritan God, that Neighbor over the fence of the next life in the hymnal:

> Abraham to kill him
> Was distinctly told—
> Isaac was an Urchin—
> Abraham was old—
>
> Not a hesitation—
> Abraham complied—
> Flattered by Obeisance
> Tyranny demurred—
>
> Isaac—to his children
> Lived to tell the tale—
> Moral—with a Mastiff
> Manners may prevail. (1317)

It is a little mocking sermon which would undoubtedly have shocked Edward Dickinson with his "pure and terrible" heart, but it brings the God of Abraham closer to New England than he had been for the two centuries preceding—brings him, indeed, as close as that growling watch-dog in the next yard: so close that he can be addressed politely by that child who always walked with Emily hand in hand:

> Lightly stepped a yellow star
> To its lofty place—
> Loosed the Moon her silver hat
> From her lustral Face—
> All of the Evening softly lit
> As an Astral Hall—
> Father, I observed to Heaven,
> You are punctual—(1672)

But more important than the confiding smile which makes it possible to speak familiarly to the God of Elder Brewster is the hot and fearless and wholly human anger with which she is able to face him at the end. Other poets have confronted God in anger but few have been able to manage it without rhetoric and posture. There is something about that ultimate face to face which excites an embarrassing self-consciousness in which the smaller of the two opponents seems to strut and "bear it out even to the edge of doom." Not so with Emily. She speaks with the laconic restraint appropriate to her country, which is New England, and herself, which is a small, shy gentlewoman who has suffered much:

> Of God we ask one favor,
> That we may be forgiven—
> For what, he is presumed to know—
> The Crime, from us, is hidden—
> Immured the whole of Life
> Within a magic Prison . . . (1601)

It is a remarkable poem and its power, indeed its possibility, lies almost altogether in its voice, its tone. The figure of the magic prison is beautiful in itself, but it is effective in the poem because of the level at which the poem is spoken—the level established by that "he is presumed to know." At another level even the magic prison might well become pretentious.

But it is not my contention here that Emily Dickinson's mastery of tone is merely a negative accomplishment, a kind of lime which prepares the loam for clover. On the contrary I should like to submit that her tone is the root itself of her greatness: The source of poetry, as Emily knew more positively than most, is a particular awareness of the world. "It is that," she says, meaning by "that" a poet, which "Distills amazing sense /From ordinary Meanings," and the distillation is accomplished not by necromancy but by perception—by the particularity of the perception—which makes what is "ordinary meaning" to the ordinary, "amazing sense" to the poet. The key to the poetry of any poem, therefore, is its particularity—the uniqueness of its vision of the world it sees. In some poems the particularity can be found in the images into which the vision is translated. In others it seems to exist in the rhythm which carries the vision "alive into the heart." In still others it is found in a play of mind which breaks the light of the perception like a prism. The particularity has as many forms almost as there are poets capable of the loneliness in which uniqueness is obliged to live. With Emily Dickinson it is the tone and timbre of the speaking voice. When she first wrote Colonel Higginson to send him copies of her verses she asked him to tell her if they "breathed" and the word, like all her words, was deliberately chosen. She knew, I think, what her verses were, for she knew everything that concerned her.

I should like to rest my case, if I can call it that, on a short poem of four lines written probably on the third anniversary of her father's death. It is one of her greatest poems and perhaps the only poem she ever wrote which carries the curious and solemn weight of perfection. I should like you to consider wherein this perfection lies:

> Lay this Laurel on the One
> Too intrinsic for Renown—
> Laurel—vail your deathless tree—
> Him you chasten, that is He! (1393)